Breaking the Mould

British Art of the 1980s and 1990s

The Weltkunst Collection

Breaking the Mould

British Art of the 1980s and 1990s

The Weltkunst Collection

Edited by Catherine Marshall
Essays by Richard Cork and Penelope Curtis
Foreword by Declan McGonagle

Lund Humphries Publishers, London
Irish Museum of Modern Art, Dublin

First published in 1997 by
Lund Humphries Publishers Ltd
Park House
1 Russell Gardens
London
NW11 9NN
in association with
Irish Museum of Modern Art
Royal Hospital
Military Road
Kilmainham
Dublin 8

British Library Cataloguing in Publication Data
A catalogue record for this book is available from the British Library

ISBN 0 85331 744 5

Designed by Ray Carpenter
Made and printed in Great Britain by
BAS Printers Limited, Over Wallop, Hampshire

Distributed in the USA by
Antique Collectors' Club
Market Street Industrial Park
Wappingers Falls
NY 12590
USA

Acknowledgements

The Irish Museum of Modern Art is deeply indebted to the Weltkunst
Foundation and in particular to Nicholas Ward-Jackson for lending this
important collection and to Nicholas Serota for allowing us to print from
the text of his oration at the funeral of Adrian Ward-Jackson.

We would like to thank the artists and their galleries including Elizabeth
McCrae and the staff at the Lisson Gallery, Charles Booth-Clibborn and
the Paragon Press, Clisenhale Gallery, Douglas Hyde Gallery, Matts
Gallery, Karsten Schubert, Jay Jopling/White Cube Gallery.

We are grateful to Richard Cork and Penelope Curtis for their thoughtful
and illuminating essays, to Ronan McCrea for researching and compiling
the bulk of the essays about individual artworks and Brenda Moore-
McCann for her careful cataloguing of works on paper and the artists'
biographies.

Anjali Raval at Lund Humphries deserves a special word of thanks for her
patience, tact and good humour. The Museum would also like to thank
copy editor John Gilbert and designer Ray Carpenter and all who gave
generously of their time, knowledge and support.

Catherine Marshall
Curator of the Collection

Illustration on page 6:
Michael Leonard,
*Portrait of Adrian Ward-Jackson in
the manner of Ingres*, 1985

Contents

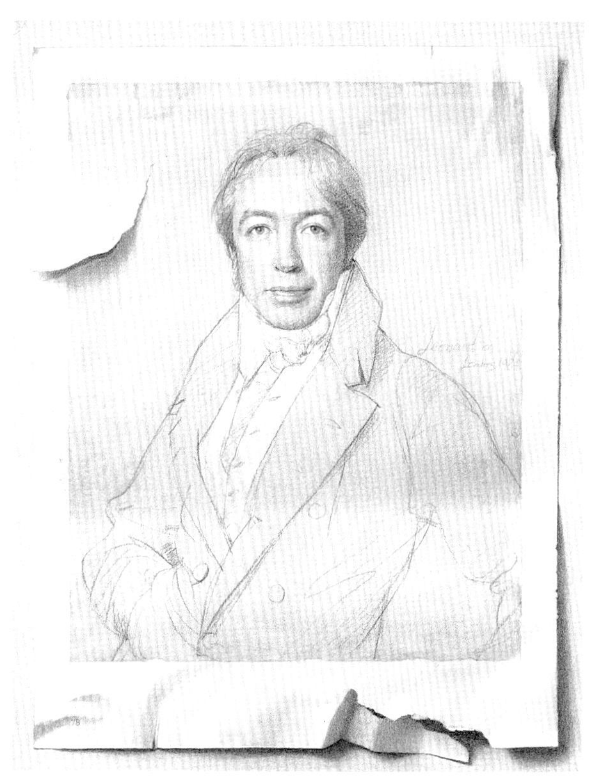

. . . At the still point of the turning world. Neither flesh nor
    fleshless;
Neither from nor towards; at the still point, there the dance
    is,
But neither arrest nor movement. And do not call it fixity,
Whether past and future are gathered. Neither movement
    from nor towards,
Neither ascent nor decline. Except for the point, the still
    point,
There would be no dance, and there is only the dance.
. . .

T. S. Eliot
Burnt Norton

Adrian Ward-Jackson

A Tribute

ADRIAN WARD-JACKSON was a collector for whom each object in the collection which he formed for the Weltkunst Foundation involved a personal commitment to the vision and the artist. The Weltkunst Collection began during a decade in which he formed a close association with a then emerging generation of British sculptors that included Deacon, Kapoor, Houshiary and Wilding. It was a commitment, however, informed by a deep feeling for nature and for the art of earlier times. That feeling can perhaps best be understood by knowing a little about Adrian's formative influences and passions; and the following observations are taken from the address which I gave at Adrian's memorial service on 15 October 1991.

Adrian's life was centred on the eye, and especially on the eye which searches for real quality in what it surveys. His interest in painting was kindled at Westminster, but nurtured by his parents, through annual visits to Venice during his adolescence. Here Adrian gained a feeling for colour, shape and light which never left him. And he gained a special feeling for the rich reds, the velvets and the shimmer that we associate with Venetian rather than Florentine painting; in other words for a suffusion of colour rather than line.

Leaving school and bypassing the academic route that might have dulled a brightening eye, he was encouraged by his father to travel to Vienna where he worked for a year as an assistant to the distinguished Raphael scholar, Konrad Oberhüber. It was Oberhüber, perhaps surprisingly, who encouraged him to look at contemporary art, as well as at the Old Masters. But his real contribution to Adrian's education was to nourish the eye and to teach the value of dogged research – a devastating combination which was to be the basis for Adrian's professional success.

Adrian had a particular talent, not so much for discovering lost masters in country houses or sales, but rather for recognising that a doubted or tarnished work was indeed a great masterpiece. Led by his natural eye for quality, he would meticulously put together the provenance, re-establishing credibility which he knew by instinct to be there. Two great masterpieces, Lorenzo Lotto's *Venus and Cupid*, now at the Metropolitan Museum, and Andrea Mantegna's *Christ's descent into limbo*, now in Mrs Johnson's collection, pay testament to this approach. By coincidence they neatly reflect the two sides of his character; the first secular, flamboyant, even profane; the second, deeply spiritual and a meditation on the inner world.

Adrian had always been attracted to the vitality and beauty of dance, making regular visits from school to Covent Garden, often alone. From the mid-1980s he threw himself into the world of classical ballet, joining the Board of the Royal Ballet, advising the Weltkunst Foundation and encouraging the commissioning of new ballets, a practice which he further stimulated when he became involved in the Rambert Dance Company. There his natural authority quickly led to his election as Chairman and the success of the Company in recent years owes much to his leadership. The energy and commitment that he brought to these appointments led naturally to others, including a place on the Arts Council.

And slowly the wheel turned, to a renewed acquaintance with contemporary art, beginning with the formation of a collection for Weltkunst, then assisting the Tate in the collection of drawings by young sculptors and ultimately to the Chairmanship of the Contemporary Art Society. Adrian had a special regard for the artists of today. He believed in strong relationships between artist and collector, between creator and patron. Perhaps this was because he was also a creator himself, returning in the mid-1980s to the experiments with watercolour and gouache which he had begun at Westminster.

Adrian's courage during these last years was quite humbling in its depth. Even though he worked so hard for Aids Crisis Trust, few of his friends and colleagues knew of his illness until the final months. He continued to share his joy, but he would not share his pain. Now, in the watercolours one can see the deepening and the serenity which precede death for those who have led a full and rich life. One of his last watercolours is entitled *Looking at snow*. Three sheets record, against a white ground, the blurs and dots which were a constant presence in his field of vision during the final months. They show a rare spirit whose inner eye was not dimmed by the illness which took him from us and whose friendship, inspiration and sheer *brio* gave so much to all who knew him.

Nicholas Serota
Director, Tate Gallery, London

Breaking the Mould

Declan McGonagle

THE WELTKUNST COLLECTION of British contemporary art began in 1986 on the advice of Adrian Ward-Jackson, who died in 1991. The Weltkunst Foundation was founded in 1981 and was responsible for a series of imaginative donations to the Royal Opera House, Covent Garden, Glyndebourne, Ballet Rambert and many other British institutions. In 1992 the directors of the Weltkunst Foundation decided to complete the Collection and lend it to major institutions in Adrian's memory. They asked Adrian's brother, Nicholas, to co-ordinate its acquisition and loans policy. Since 1994, when the Collection was offered on loan to the Irish Museum of Modern Art, he has worked closely with the Museum's curators, initially to realise a large-scale exhibition of the Collection in the summer of 1995, and secondly to acquire new works in consultation with the Museum staff. The Museum, as a new institution, has a standing policy of negotiating long-term loans of coherent bodies of contemporary artworks. The Weltkunst Collection has energised this process and individual works are regularly shown in the context of the Museum's own collection displays.

The early 1980s was a remarkable period, when sculpture established a new critical position for British art in the world. In fact, many of the artists at the core of the Weltkunst Collection who were involved directly with this surge of activity established their reputations outside Britain first. These artists, who came to widespread attention in the early 1980s, developed startling new visual vocabularies which electrified the environment for making and showing art in Britain at the time. But these artists also owe a debt to a previous generation who had established the 'New Art' of the early 1970s. Artists such as Barry Flanagan, Art & Language, Richard Long and Gilbert & George, among others, brought into 'play' performance, photography, text and installation – alternatives to established processes and associations. I believe this debt is also carried by those younger artists in Britain who emerged in the 1990s and are now included in the Collection. Although there is a concern here with deconstructing the art object and breaking the mould of tradition, there is still a connection with what has gone before – a traceable line of descent from Henry Moore and Anthony Caro and from a particular tradition of object-making in Britain concerned with its status, its worth and its value.

The artists of the 1980s added play and process to product and this may well be the reason they were initially celebrated outside Britain. Their practice in general counterpointed and in many cases breached the parameters which were established by Moore and then investigated and extended by Caro. If Henry Moore provided the sculptural object in British art for a period, then Caro dismantled it. It may be that the narrative for significant sculpture in Britain has ever since been concerned with the process of dismantling the autonomous object.

If play means to transcend what is given through lateral rather than linear experimentation, where available resources are used inventively, then the play of artists who are represented in the Weltkunst Collection amounts to a seismic shift in sculptural practice in Britain. As a result we are now in a different place operating with different content and *not* merely different forms.

It is also worth remembering that by 1980 painting had re-emerged as a central force in art under a variety of headings in the international context. The critical momentum of the previous decade had stalled in the late 1970s and the market had also become frustrated. The impulse to figure the world crystallised around a number of large-scale exhibitions from the 1980s onwards but particularly following the *New Spirit in Painting* exhibition at the Royal Academy in London in 1980. This new figuration became widespread to the degree it did because it answered the needs of both the critical and commercial markets. This is not a criticism of a process which is always with us but an acceptance that the commercial market follows the critical market and the involvement of both is needed to establish development or a sustainable shift in practice at any given time. The man-made urban, industrial and cultural environments, rather than the natural world, provided a material motor for this shift. It supplied accessible materials and procedures for making art in this first flush of new activity. It was only later that, braced with self-confidence, some artists could turn to more traditional means, using metal and casting, for example, without limiting or defining their practice by those traditions. New possibilities for form and content were tested. Metaphor, allegory and humour were redeployed in sculpture in ways that echoed what was happening in contemporary international painting.

What is interesting is how ideas which were articulated in painting elsewhere, even temporarily, were, in Britain, articulated in sculptural practice. Yet this emerged without a collapse into simply descriptive sculpture. It did not involve observation and description of the world from a position outside the subject but an acceptance by British artists like Cragg and Deacon that they were living *in* the subject – literally in the case of Antony Gormley.

That these artists were in a position to take on these possibilities was a result of the expansionist precedent set for sculptural practice, as mentioned earlier, by the British artists of the 1970s.

The definition of sculpture had been expanded to the point where it could now be anything and do anything. Unusually, the artists responsible for this were not dependent on teaching at Art College. In fact some seminal artists of the 1970s did no teaching at all, yet their expanded practices had a huge effect within the British art school system which produced the 1980s generation who form the core of the Weltkunst Collection. This expanded definition of sculpture has been taken even further by the current generation of British artists, the most interesting of whom are also represented in this Collection.

The key strength in the Weltkunst Collection is the way it measures this shift and provides a prism through which relationships with earlier developments can be examined. The Collection is a map of the distinctions as well as the connections between generations. This new generation is attempting to make something that has not been made before. It could be said that they work outside 'art' but in 'life', rejecting the idea of art as a discrete enterprise. Many address the banality of everyday life and its associations, some include and in a few cases manipulate the transactional processes which underpin the art world. They address the real world but do so without theatricalising it. The work of these artists links directly to lens-based work by northern European artists, mostly using photography, who present a world which at first looks dispassionate, even banal, but in which the artist and viewer are complicit. Perhaps it was the sense of complicity that made it easy for the mass media to pick up some of the younger artists in the 1990s and bracket them with contemporary pop music and a nostalgic reading of the 1960s. I would argue that the boundaries between generations are porous and no defensible line should be drawn around particular periods or groups of artists. It is always more interesting and more fruitful to look at the tides that give the art buoyancy across periods and generations, rather than accepting a calendar frame which is risky in the short term, misleading and untrustworthy in the long term.

It could be useful, however, to take this trajectory and look not only at art historical shifts from Caro to the artists around which the Weltkunst Collection is centred, but also to consider the potential for the context where the Collection is now housed, in the Irish Museum of Modern Art, to add new readings and wider meaning.

The 1960s/1990s shift has important resonances in Ireland because it was in the former decade that Ireland started to embrace rather than resist Modernism. From then until now, an accelerating negotiation has been going on throughout Irish society in economics, in politics, in culture, which has led to an acknowledgement of a post-industrial, post-colonial and now post-modern condition. This condition is part of the subject of the Irish Museum of Modern Art as well as part of its identity. It allows for juxtapositions between works in this Collection and this context.

The term 'British', for instance, used to carry certain predetermined and problematic voltage in the Irish context. It is no longer an automatic negative because this process of renegotiation – a renegotiation of pre-determined positions and identity, is going on in the Irish and increasingly also in the British context. The literary critic Terry Eagleton has argued that British culture has not always acknowledged but has always benefited from the presence and input of non-white, non-European cultures – by-products perhaps of an imperial past and still problematic but clearly reflected in the weave of the literary landscape. But it is also present in the visual arts and in the Weltkunst Collection in particular. The inclusion of works by artists such as Houshiary, Kapoor, Doherty and Phaophanit represent and celebrate that dimension of diversity in contemporary identity. For these artists, identity is a negotiation not a given, and for many the negotiation is with ideas of Britishness.

The Irish Museum of Modern Art has a degree of critical distance from the home ground of British art. In the context of this Collection, it is possible for the term 'British' to be seen as a term of expansion and inclusion rather than closure and exclusion.

The Weltkunst Collection, therefore, like the best in art, represents a state of becoming rather than being, a process not a terminus for art. The art historical intersects with the sociological in the Collection, and, in my opinion, the Irish Museum of Modern Art seems an enabling context in which to test and explore its meaning and its implications as well as to celebrate it as a collection of individual achievements.

The Museum of Modern Art in Ireland, like some others, has to operate in a binary of construction and deconstruction. It is concerned with unfixing and testing meaning while simultaneously working within given definitions of a museum. This involves exhibition making, mediation between artist and the public, and wider cultural meanings. Just as the Weltkunst Collection has challenged the pattern of traditional collecting, so too has the Museum set out to break the mould of traditional institutional practice.

The strength of the Weltkunst Collection lies in the fact that it embodies the very questions that have to be addressed at the end of the twentieth century and helps to lay the ghost of the nineteenth-century concept in art and society of the autonomous object and the integrated self.

British Sculpture in the
Late Twentieth Century

Richard Cork

THE PRODIGIOUS RENAISSANCE enjoyed by British sculpture over the last ninety years shows no sign of faltering. Ever since Jacob Epstein, Henri Gaudier-Brzeska and Eric Gill transformed the possibilities for sculptors in Britain before the First World War, a remarkable momentum has been maintained. Owing debts to their seniors, and yet continually questioning accepted ideas about what sculpture can be, successive generations pushed their work centre-stage. Having in previous centuries occupied a position subservient to painters, modern British sculptors shook off their inferior status. Indeed, they have often taken the lead in challenging and extending the supposed limits of visual art in general. Over the decades since Barbara Hepworth and Henry Moore came to formidable maturity during the inter-war period, men and women alike have proved that outstanding British sculptors can gain high international reputations.

Yet there was a period when the radical broadening of sculpture's potential scope threatened to make the word itself redundant. Writing on *The Art of Sculpture* in 1956, Herbert Read still felt confident enough to assert that 'since Rodin's time there has arisen what is virtually a new art – a concept of a piece of sculpture as a three-dimensional mass occupying space and only to be apprehended by senses that are alive to its volume and ponderability, as well as to its visual appearance'. By 1964, however, Read had decided that 'one must ask a devastating question: to what extent does the art remain in any traditional (or semantic) sense sculpture? . . . . Virtually everything, one must say, has been lost that has characterised the art of sculpture in the past'. Having once supported the most innovative sculptors of his own generation, he convinced himself late in life that sculpture as an art of solid form seemed to be disappearing. After Read's death in 1968, the movement away from sculptural mass was accelerated by the widespread interest in dematerialisation. As so many of the works in the Weltkunst Collection demonstrate, the word 'sculpture' rapidly came to be applied to anything that sculptors themselves wished to do.

Dissolution or Redefinition?

At St Martin's School of Art, where Anthony Caro and Phillip King had revolutionised British sculpture in the early 1960s, alternative developments began to flourish later in the decade. Under the enlightened atmosphere created by Frank Martin, this singular art school became a crucible both for Caro's allies and a restless younger generation, who took issue with what they regarded as an unnecessarily narrow idea of sculpture's multifarious potential. Barry Flanagan, who had arrived at St Martin's in 1964, moved away from the machine-like simplification in metal and fibreglass favoured by the Caro school. He poured and scooped sand, stuffing sacks with polystyrene, laying lengths of rope over an entire gallery floor and using light as a medium by letting it fall across an installation of objects.

Richard Long, who came to St Martin's two years after Flanagan, was even more

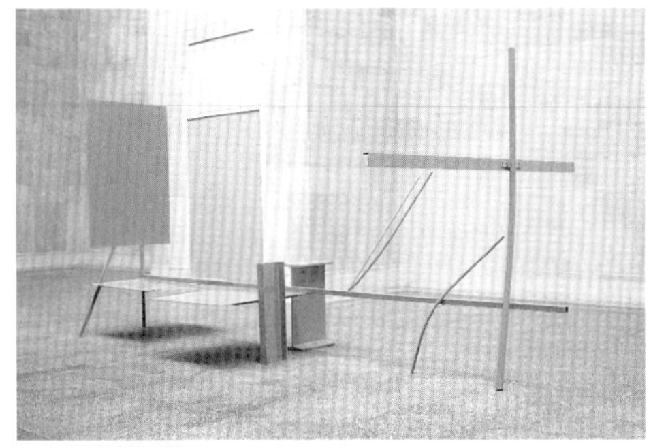

Anthony Caro
Early one morning
1962
Painted steel
290 × 620 × 335 cm

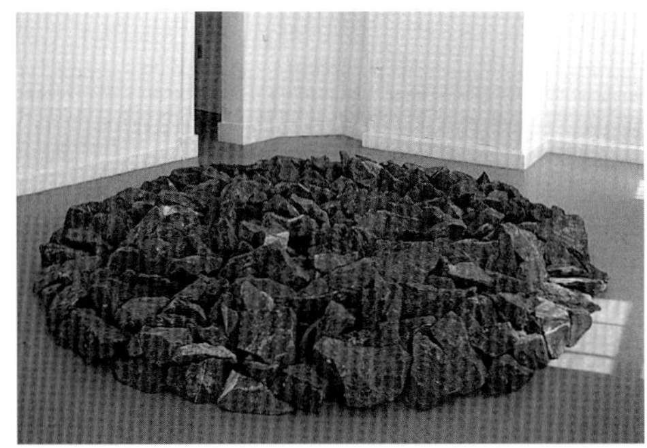

Richard Long
Kilkenny limestone circle
1991
Kilkenny limestone
400 cm (diameter)

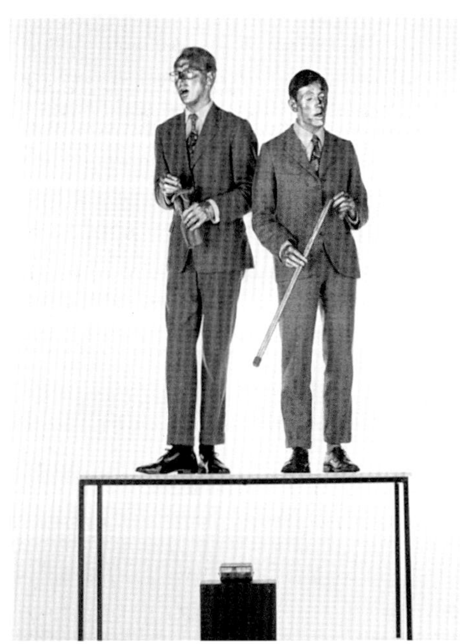

Gilbert & George
The singing sculpture
1970

opposed to Caro's essentially urban art with its industrial materials and indoor locations. Single-minded and original from an unusually early stage in his career, Long preferred to deal with the natural world in the most direct way possible, moving outdoors and taking his inspiration and materials from the countryside itself. Maps, words and photographs charting the central act of walking were as important to him as sticks and stones. The fusion between his outdoor sculpture and its location is often so complete that his work honours the natural world with a profoundly satisfying sense of inevitability. One fellow-student, Hamish Fulton, came to concentrate on the camera's resources alone in his exploration of time, distance and the essential sanctity of nature. Fulton subsequently decided to refine the experience by dispensing with any alterations to the landscape. The photograph, with attendant caption, thereby came to stand for Fulton's journeys in the remote regions he favours, and he felt no need to follow Long's example by making floor sculptures in galleries as well.

Two of their contemporaries at St Martin's, Gilbert & George, went even further. They called themselves 'Living Sculptures', and blurred the distinction between art and life so successfully that everything – even staring at a fall of snow from their Fournier Street window – could be regarded as legitimate sculptural material. Meeting sculptures, singing sculptures, meal sculptures, lecture sculptures, standing sculptures, magazine sculptures, posing sculptures and postcard sculptures: all these inventive variations on the sculptural theme were conducted by this paradoxically polite yet subversive duo between 1969 and 1972. No one, however, subjected the role of the art object to a more sustained examination than Art & Language, who initially addressed themselves to an assessment of 'those fraudulent conceptualisations by means of which normal art was supported and entrenched'. Caustic, irreverent and determined to ask each other 'what sort of concept is art?', the members of Art & Language used analytical philosophy to help them scrutinise and expose the discourse underlying cultural production. Soon after the group formed in 1968, they decided to emphasise that contemporary art objects function according to their designation. They have continued to be concerned with the context surrounding the artwork. While continuing to make material objects, Art & Language force us to realise the indissoluble relationship between object and context.

With hindsight, we can now see that the broadening of sculpture's scope to encompass activities as diverse as land art, performance and photographic experimentation had reached its zenith by the mid-1970s. After that, artists either pursued these and other developments without necessarily nominating them as 'sculpture' at all, or discovered new ways of returning to the three-dimensional object armed with the freedoms claimed during the previous decade. In 1974 Bernard Meadows invited me to deliver the Lethaby Lectures on sculpture at the Royal College of Art, where he taught with admirable open-mindedness in a department that produced a succession of notably independent young sculptors. I called the lectures 'Sculpture Now: Dissolution or Redefinition?', and accompanied them with an international exhibition that included Flanagan, Fulton, Gilbert & George and Long among the British contributors. The final lecture came to the conclusion that 'true dissolution could never be a conceivable reality', since we had so much to gain from a 'redefining process' which would 'further a growing comprehension of sculpture's potential within art and society'.

It seemed a large hope to harbour at the time, but since those lectures were delivered sculpture has indeed undergone a 'redefinition' more gratifying and sustained than anything I dared to expect in 1974. Most of the animosities between different kinds of sculptural practitioners have mellowed over the last two decades, and from the threatened 'dissolution' an impressive new range of work has been produced by sculptors who emerged in the late 1970s and beyond. Many of them are represented by important work in the Weltkunst Collection. While often affirming the three-dimensional object once again, they have clearly benefited from the liberating example of their forerunners. Indeed, sculpture during the 1980s and 1990s has displayed such questioning rigour and imaginative resourcefulness, in its strategies and materials alike, that it remains at the forefront of British art as a whole.

The 'New British Sculpture'

By the beginning of the 1980s, a fertile redefinition of the sculptural object had begun to occur. It coincided with the emergence of a fresh generation in the *Objects and Sculpture* exhibition, held at the ICA, London and the Arnolfini Gallery, Bristol in 1981. Several of the show's participants, who included Richard Deacon, Anish Kapoor and Bill Woodrow, went on to exhibit regularly at the Lisson Gallery, where Tony Cragg also displays his work. So they became known as exponents of the 'New British Sculpture' – even though, as Lynne Cooke rightly pointed out, the sobriquet was so bland that it 'attests to the diversity of the group, to their eluding reduction to a common denominator'. When Tony Cragg initially established himself as a pioneer of the so-called New British Sculpture in the late 1970s, attention concentrated on his preference for plastic detritus. The novelty of this material as a sculptural ingredient, combined with its references to proliferating obsolescence, dominated most of the discussion about his work. But the sharp, inventive and witty deployment of these 'debased' elements implied a complex attitude on his part. Even as he appeared to be proposing that our culture had become irrevocably defiled, Cragg jolted the viewer into an awareness of the true character of materials too often dismissed as rubbish. His formal finesse and eye for seductive colour persuaded us to reconsider objects from which we usually feel estranged.

Cragg shared this sense of alienation, and behind everything he produced during the 1980s lies a fierce commitment to understanding more about the industrial transformation of our contemporary environment. He equates this quest with survival. Confronted by the prospect of living in a permanent state of disaffection, removed from the escalating artifice around him, he attempts to establish encounters with the man-made world just as enriching and profound as those provided by the organic, natural order. Later in the decade, he discovered the fascination of investing utensils as banal as a laboratory test-tube with the 'primitive' dignity of an imposing vessel in cast steel. Even here, however, the metamorphosis ultimately makes us return to Cragg's starting point and reconsider the test-tube as an object in its own right.

Although Bill Woodrow was once the sculptor most commonly associated with Cragg, the differences between them are as marked as their areas of shared concern. With satirical high spirits, dexterity, mordant imagination and an acute eye for the unexpected, Woodrow in the 1980s transformed the battered remnants of our throwaway society into sculpture with an independent identity of its own. His fundamental method, in this Lazarus-like enterprise, was deceptively straightforward. The detritus he salvaged from inner-city skips, dumps and waste-lots was sliced up, so that a new image emerged from the material he cut free. The directness with which Woodrow tore into the junk objects was nakedly exposed: they

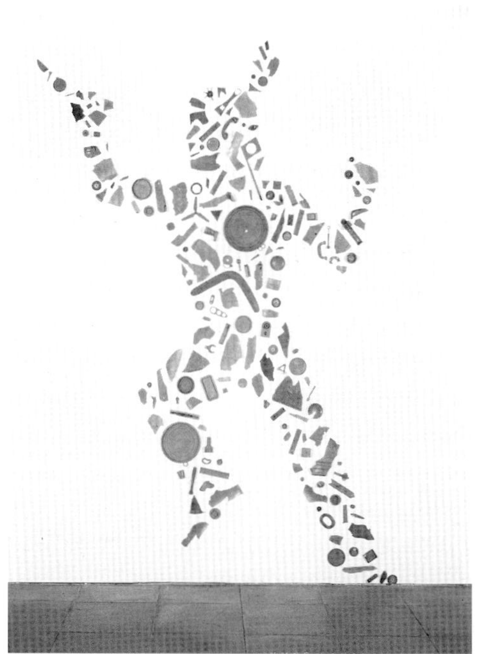

Tony Cragg
Red skin
1982
Plastic
320 × 210 cm

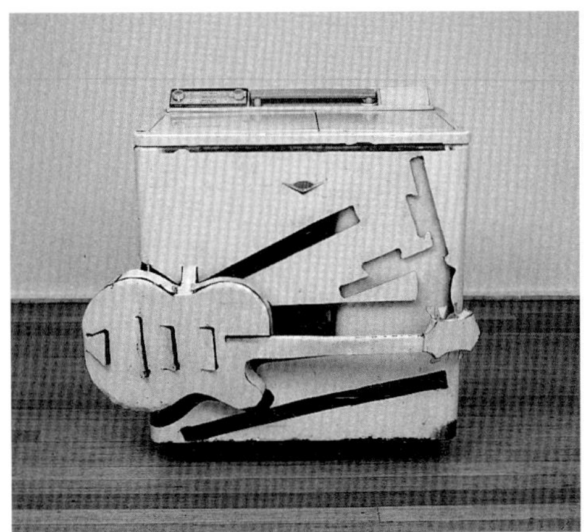

Bill Woodrow
Twin tub with guitar
1981
Washing machine
76 × 89 × 66 cm

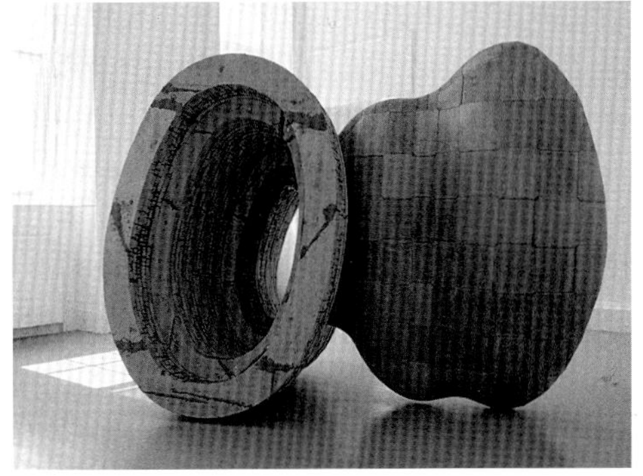

Richard Deacon
Kiss and tell
1989
Plywood, epoxy, timber
80 × 155 × 93 cm

remained there, jagged and gaping, as testaments to the surgical efficiency of the sculptor who conducted the operations on their frayed bodies.

But just as a surgeon makes incisions in order to generate renewed life, so Woodrow's cutting energies were dedicated to an almost ecological belief in the importance of recycling the unwanted and supposedly 'useless' cast-offs he selected. Although he made no attempt to stitch up the wounded objects, umbilical cords often attached them to the images created from their shattered frames. The worn-through and the new, the familiar and the bizarre, were displayed together so that we could witness the passage from one to another and wonder at the extra-ordinary change Woodrow engendered.

In this more recent work, images of exploitation and violation go hand in hand, proving that Woodrow's vision is darker and more bitter than before. Everywhere he looks, civilisation and human existence appear either threatened or utterly defiled. Like Boyd Webb, whose wittily apocalyptic vision he shares to a certain extent, Woodrow regards late twentieth-century life with consistent foreboding. Whether he looks inwards or outwards, ominous conclusions are reached about the body personal and the body politic alike.

The gravity underlying his work contrasted favourably with the febrile gimmicks and puerility which marred, here and there, the otherwise exhilarating upsurge of vitality enjoyed by British sculpture in the 1980s. High spirits can easily deteriorate into silliness, and some young sculptors were unable to distinguish between novelty-seeking and authentic invention. That is why Richard Deacon will be endured long after some of his contemporaries have become irretrievably tiresome. Avoiding callowness and sensationalism, he stays close to a set of steady concerns that yield results as memorable as they are eloquent.

Unlike Cragg and Woodrow, Deacon does not employ the detritus of urban society. Although he has used corrugated iron, linoleum and concrete, which belong clearly enough to the modern world, they seem more neutral than the battered utensils and plastic refuse scavenged by Woodrow and Cragg. Deacon refers to his material as 'stuff', and he is equally happy working with traditional substances like wood and brass. For his imagination is fired by the oblique yet haunting relationship between mythology and contemporary life.

During a visit to the USA a year after leaving the Royal College of Art in 1978, Deacon became preoccupied with Rilke's *Sonnets to Orpheus*. Lacking the facilities to make sculpture there, he embarked instead on a series of drawings which became instrumental in defining his singularity as an artist. His earlier involvement with rectilinear forms gave way to a more organic language, and the image of Orpheus as a singing or listening head assumed a special potency. Openness and enclosure, lyricism and plain statement, the mechanical and the sexual, functionalism and poetic licence – these are the oppositions which his sculpture manages to conjoin in surprising and resonant new amalgams. Unlike so many artists, who become trapped inside an arid formula, Deacon abhors the idea of repeating himself. Each new sculpture has a sense of fresh adventure, with a continually unpredictable use of materials. The best of them are as difficult to resist as Orpheus' music must once have been, reverberating in the mind long after the last of his lyre's strings was stilled.

Dislocation, Insecurity and Architectural Initiatives

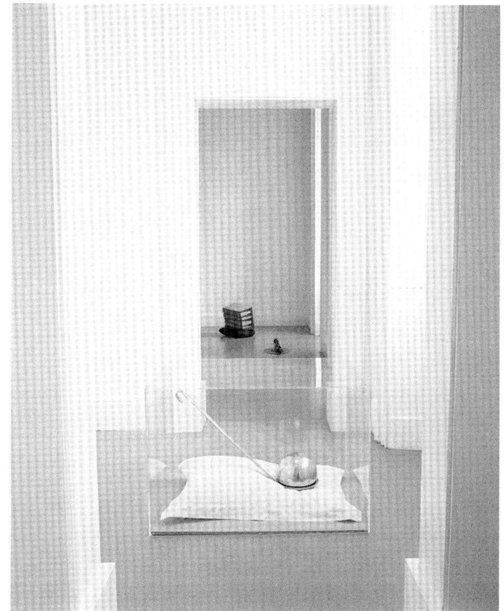

Richard Wentworth
Preserve
1987-8
Steel, concrete, dud light bulbs
35 × 44 cm (diameter)

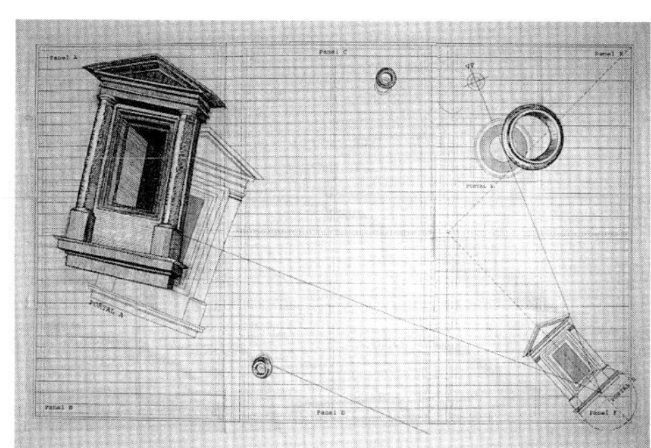

Edward Allington
Quadratura
1995
Mixed media
Infinite dimensions (conceptual piece)

Deacon's lack of interest in cast-off objects marks him out from the majority of the sculptors with whom he is usually associated. One, Richard Wentworth, often takes everyday utensils as his springboard. But Wentworth's acute eye for bizarre juxtapositions and quirky, disquieting images makes him a singular artist. At its simplest and most arresting, his interest in vertiginous propositions sometimes takes the form of plates, bowls and saucers ranged in profusion on a precarious surface; even when we have noticed that the crockery has been securely lodged, the ensemble still appears doomed to plummet and smash. Bent on looking at ordinary things as if he had no idea of their conventional use, Wentworth invites us to discover poetry even in the most banal material. Nothing could be more quotidian than the steel office desk in a work called *Balcone*. Yet the garden tools installed in the far edge of the desk, with a neatness that belies the provocative mystery of their presence, have a transforming effect. These hoes, rakes, brooms and shovels seem to insist that the 'real' labour, tough and manual, makes the office work appear anaemic. The implements, however, all look trapped by the drill holes keeping them in place. And they eventually become subservient to the priorities symbolised by the bureaucratic desk.

The theme of confinement dominated his major exhibition at the Serpentine Gallery in 1993. Steel cages occupied most of the space, ranged across the floor in apparently random profusion. Most of them contained an object – a bell, mirror or ball of twine – but the mesh prevented us from seeing them clearly. The cages generated frustration, and appeared after a while to be drifting like jettisoned cargo on an open sea.

If Wentworth is wrily preoccupied with images of bewilderment and futility, Edward Allington uses the language of classical form to explore dislocation, uncertainty and cultural fragmentation. Fascinated in particular by architectural motifs, he deploys traditional symbolism only in order to emphasise the unknowability of the elements in his art. The relationship between architecture and sculpture is a constant concern, and in the 1980s Allington worked with buildings as hallowed as James Gibbs's St Martin's-in-the-Fields and as uncompromisingly industrial as the power station at Saarbrücken in Germany. Although he was prepared to erect on the power station's cooling towers a large steel-clad structure with a classical portico, Allington has always been conscious of the uncertainty bedevilling any attempt sculptors may make to co-operate with architects.

Even so, that did not stop him working in 1995 with Catrina Beevor and Robert Mull, of Beevor Mull Associates, on an intriguing project called *Quadratura*. The title refers to the name for illusionistic ceilings, the creation of which in the sixteenth and seventeenth centuries often occasioned an alliance between art and architecture. Allington and his collaborators took St Peter's Church in Cambridge as their focus, planning their own aspirational ceiling and thereby advocating the desirability of a quadratura for today.

Eric Bainbridge would understand why Allington has been fascinated by architecture for so long. His work focuses on enlarging and camouflaging the kind of everyday objects we might expect to find in a contemporary interior. During the 1980s his attitude was playful, often irreverent. *Occurrence on an endless column* contains within its title a reference to Brancusi's magisterial sculpture at Tirgu-Jiu in Romania. But judging by the displaced forms at the base of Bainbridge's work, the column is about to collapse; and two animals, probably blown up from modest toy-like origins, tumble precariously on top. Their coats are made from the same fake fur fabric that Bainbridge used in much of his subsequent sculpture.

By 1990, however, the fabric had been reversed – a move that stresses the material's synthetic quality while still preserving the powerful, surprisingly sensuous impact of its colour. Alongside this new emphasis on artificiality, Bainbridge moved towards a greater severity in his choice of forms. Gambolling animals dropped away, and in their place he concentrated on single images such as a mirror or an air freshener. The enlarging and coating of these mundane domestic objects, which Bainbridge has described as 'unacceptable according to educated, middle-ground taste', lend them a sense of mystery. It makes us realise how strange they are even in their original contexts. And as if to remind the viewer of the buildings where they are likely to reside, he based one of his most monumental sculptures on the concrete stairwell of a block of flats. The result is enigmatic and utterly unclassifiable, reinforcing the sculptor's own belief that all attempts to systematise reality are bound to end in frustration.

The more the work of certain British sculptors is examined, the more it turns out to be impelled by architectural concerns. In the case of Richard Wilson, the galleries which invite him to show often provide a stimulus to explore their spaces. Nothing he has made since is as breathtaking as his early masterpiece *20:50*, that oceanic expanse of sump oil flooding its room with an ominous, eerily reflective and yet astonishingly seductive blackness. Nor is anything else in his output as hallucinatory as *She came in through the bathroom window*, where Wilson removed an entire wall-wide expanse of windows from Matt's Gallery and suspended it, at a disorientating angle, within the space.

All the same, the desire to be an agent of uncanny disruption runs through everything he produces. Over the last decade, as an ingenious mini-retrospective of his drawings and models at Gimpel Fils revealed in 1996, Wilson has thrived on confounding the expectations we bring to particular spaces. He wants to shake us free from a lazy acceptance of the gallery's seemingly unarguable authority. At Gimpel Fils, the impeccable white purity of its 1970s interior was challenged by a diagonally positioned 25-metre-long wall where Wilson's exhibits were lodged in irregular niches. And in 1996, at the Serpentine Gallery, a Grade II listed former tearoom occupying a fiercely protected landscape in Kensington Gardens, he staged a heretical series of spatial invasions.

Responding with relish to the imminent renovation of the gallery, he gouged holes out of floors, walls and ceilings and placed builders' cabins in three of the rooms. Similar sheds would soon be erected outside the Serpentine, when the real work of alteration began. By bringing them inside, Wilson invited us to realise that the gallery would shortly find itself completely overtaken by forces from another world. Nobody knew, until the renovation was finished in the autumn of 1997, just how successful it had been. In that respect, Wilson's installation mirrored the uncertainty and risk accompanying any such venture.

Growth and Containment

Before Barbara Hepworth proved otherwise, the mere notion of a woman gaining international prominence as a sculptor seemed almost heretical in a profession traditionally peopled by men. Working in Rome around the middle of the nineteenth century, the American sculptor Harriet Hosmer warned a female art student: 'Learn to be laughed at, and learn it as quickly as you can.' Hepworth's success helped younger generations of women to gain reputations more easily, but only during the 1980s did a significant number win prominence in Britain as sculptors.

One of the earliest to secure widespread attention at that time was Alison Wilding. But she did so without the aid of controversial strategies. At first, set beside other, more flamboyant contemporaries, her work may appear withdrawn, reticent and lacking in a sense of danger. Seen on her own, however, and aided by the chance to display a large range of sculpture, Wilding's tension and complexity soon became evident. At the Tate Gallery, Liverpool, which staged a retrospective survey of Wilding's work in 1991, her fascination with duality led to the exploration of two contrasted elements meeting in unpredictable ways. Sometimes, the outcome promoted a feeling of stability and protection. Elsewhere, though, the results were more disconcerting. In the monumental *Receiver*, a tower of galvanised steel rears upwards with seeming impregnability; but its skin is pierced at intervals, as if the tower has at some stage been assailed. The frank declaration of screws near the joins – a strategy that allies Wilding's work with Deacon's – does little to alleviate the sense of a citadel under siege. Moreover, the steel cylinder is joined near its base to a pod-like form in dark oak. Is it a malignant growth, or a beneficent organism swelling in the shade of the tower's bulk? The question is left open, by an artist unafraid of exploring ambiguity and avoiding facile resolutions of the conflicts she discovers within her sculpture.

Fascinated by the opposition between industrialised materials and their more primordial counterparts, Wilding often brings them into unlikely conjunctions. In the smallest work on view, a wall piece called *Fruit*, wriggling lines of brass swarm all over a dark lump of tektite – a glassy substance of uncertain origin. At first, the brass appears to play a reassuring role, grasping the tektite and preventing it from falling to the floor. But then another interpretation suggests itself. The brass takes on the character of tentacles, threatening to crush the substance in its grip.

As Wilding's work continues to demonstrate, women sculptors are today working with enormous assurance in an area once considered even more of a male preserve than painting. Take Avis Newman, whose reputation was initially established with canvas and brush. At her 1996 Camden Arts Centre exhibition, where Newman held her first show in Britain for five years, large paintings and small objects were both displayed. In most of the canvases, the mark-making proved elusive. It hovered on the edge of invisibility, and broke up into particles so small that they resembled flocks of birds wheeling far above the ground. In her latest paintings indistinctness prevails. The particles have been completely absorbed in dense fields of subdued colour, and absence becomes an unavoidable reality.

Only in her boxes does Newman retain a hold over the solidity of objects. Supported by white plinths and encased in perspex containers, these wood rectangles await our examination. Some contain shells, arranged neatly on ledges like prized items in a collection. Others are hard to fathom, such as the box opening on one side to reveal a dour, stained surface within. The more enigmatic their contents become, the more reminiscent they are of Newman's paintings. But two containers hang on walls and they frame strongly contrasted clusters of identifiable objects: a heap of dark stones in one and, in the other, five white feathers fanning out gracefully against a painted gesso backdrop. Aspiring to the condition of light, they seem to link up with the birds hinted at in some of her paintings.

Containment is also a fundamental preoccupation in Veronica Ryan's work. During the 1980s she began to explore the conflict between fruitfulness and decay. Forms evocative of pods and seeds appeared with growing frequency, but they were countered by an inescapable threat of disintegration. Fascinated by the interplay between present and past, Ryan drew partially on memories of her early years in the Caribbean. Born in Montserrat, she has spent her adult life in both London

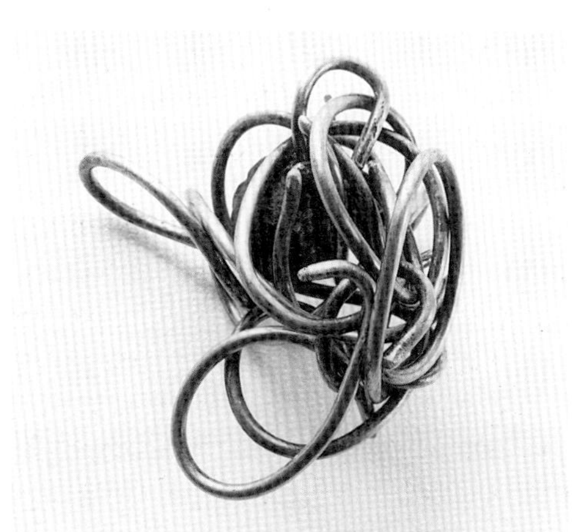

Alison Wilding
Fruit
1990
Brass and tektite
10 × 10 × 9 cm

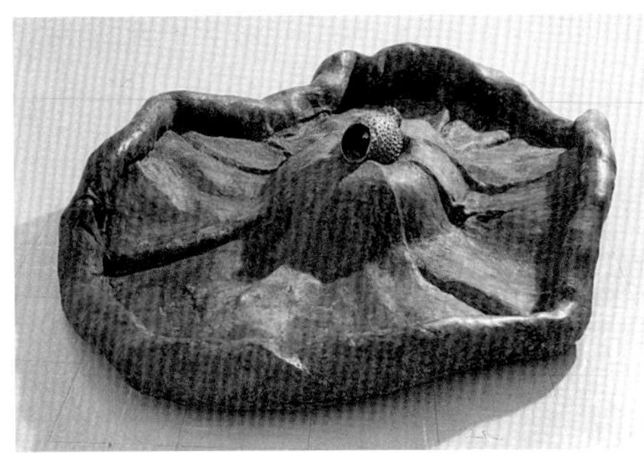

Veronica Ryan
Territorial
1996
Plaster, bronze and wood stain
168 × 457 × 168 cm

and New York. The tension between her childhood surroundings and the world she inhabits now nourishes her sculpture. Ryan admits that the thoughts feeding her work centre on 'disorientation, dislocation/location and a sense of place'.

Another opposition centres on the ambiguity of boundaries, and how they can either encompass or exclude. In *Territorial*, a large work in plaster and bronze produced by Ryan in 1986, the rounded, container-like form at the centre of the sculpture seems at first to be protected. The more we examine it, however, the less sheltered it appears. Raised up on a hump, it looks surprisingly exposed; and the emptiness of its surroundings promotes a suspicion that this isolated form has been abandoned. The unease is reinforced by the strangeness of the mass encircling the form. It lacks clear-cut contours, for Ryan has ensured that the edges of the sculpture have been folded under and rendered invisible. They look unstable and, above all, impossible to define. Nothing can be relied on except, perhaps, the inevitability of erosion and loss.

Elusiveness, Subversion and
Heterogeneity

Whether consciously or not, women artists are often adept at challenging and thwarting any attempt to enclose them within rigid boundaries. They prefer to make their own rules, and the work they produce invariably thrives on resisting facile interpretation. In one of Rose Finn-Kelcey's most celebrated works, an immense and austere aluminium structure dominates the middle of a darkened room. There is nothing oppressive, however, about Finn-Kelcey's minimalism. The main part of her spotlit installation consists of steam, rising from mesh on the floor and swirling towards dispersal in the hood overhead. Reminiscent of an outsize steam-cleaning machine, or warm air escaping into a winter street, her lyrical work replaces sculpture's traditional reliance on solidity with the tantalising evanescence of mist.

In the same elusive way, Finn-Kelcey herself cannot be pigeon-holed. Everything she makes is distinct and unpredictable, the work of an artist who has always refused to be pinned down. In order to maintain the minus 23 degrees centigrade temperature in her wrily named *Royal box*, she makes sure that the door is tightly shut. So visitors can go inside the humming white vault only for a few chilling moments. Once the door closes fast behind you, claustrophobia threatens within this nine-foot-square space. The U-shaped wall of glistening ice-cubes in the centre is oddly seductive, though, and offers to enfold anyone hardy enough to linger there.

As for *Bureau de change*, Finn-Kelcey took her springboard from the sale of Van Gogh's *Sunflowers* painting in 1987 for £24.5 million, then the highest price ever commanded by a work of art. An ingenious reconstruction of the image was laid out on the floor of Matt's Gallery in London, made entirely from £1,000 worth of coins. Beguiling enough in their tonal fidelity to the original, the gleaming pound pieces and tarnished pence looked even more astonishingly like Van Gogh's painting in the video projected by camera and monitor above. No wonder a security guard sat beside them throughout the show, silently protecting an image whose inflated market value has forced it to undergo an ironic yet alluring metamorphosis into hard cash.

Like many artists who now move with such assurance from one way of working to another, Finn-Kelcey cannot be categorised solely as a sculptor. Nor can Hermione Wiltshire, whose work may initially seem removed in its unapologetic sensuality from most of her contemporaries. When she uses finger imagery, in a photographic piece called *My touch*, tactile feelings are aroused at once. The glass covering the photograph of a fingerprint magnifies the image to the point where every line and crease is revealed with the clarity of a police investigation. But Wiltshire takes us in a different direction with her other work. The photograph of a pursed mouth lodged at the centre of *Two points of speech in sight* has the force of an intimate anatomical disclosure. The plaster surrounding it flows with an organic rhythm suggesting the soft insides of a body, and the raised glass lens protecting the mouth image seems to be looking back at the spectator.

Wiltshire has long been preoccupied with the idea of undercutting whatever titillating or pornographic potential her images may possess. In one series of framed photographic works, she juxtaposes the stockinged leg of a mannequin, or a flowing egg apparently covered in goose-pimples, with banal, bijou or hallucinatory objects. She also delights in making the viewer strain to identify the images in her sculpture. The more her work evades recognition, the more intrigued and resolute we become. Even the most chaste gallery-goer becomes aware of the fragile borderline dividing the viewer from the voyeur.

Although teasing comedy plays a part in Wiltshire's work, it is charged with pathos as well. In a memorable installation made originally for the disused Dreadnought Seamen's Mission Hospital at Greenwich, the floor is apparently splattered with drops of water. They sparkle in the light and gradually disclose the penis photographs within the globules of glass. This time, the image's anatomical identity is beyond dispute in every case; but far from celebrating phallic potency, the spilled components of *Seamen* look forlorn. Strewn around as if in the aftermath of ejaculation, they seem just as likely to die as the butterflies whose brief lifespan was explored in an early exhibition by Damien Hirst called *In and out of love*.

Hannah Collins, who has concentrated on black-and-white photography over the last decade, escapes classification even more defiantly. She shares Craigie Horsfield's urge to blow up images to a monumental size, but the results are often far more mysterious. *Legends*, the title of her 1988 publication, hints at the sense of strangeness conveyed by even her most straightforward work. Although the photographs continually hint at narrative, it is always withheld. At the same time, though, Collins insists on drawing us into the worlds recorded through her camera's lens.

The dimensions of her pictures help us to do so. In the room of Collins's work displayed at the Tate Gallery, where she was short-listed for the Turner Prize in 1993, many of the images derived from her exploitation of Istanbul. The most potent was an immense panorama of an empty and dilapidated street. It seemed haunted by all the people who must have passed through, and summed up her preoccupation with the movement of economic refugees from East to West. Other exhibits were more quirky, most notably a surreal picture of an ex-Russian Army rubber boat for sale in a street market. It looked oddly stranded and obsolete, like the country from which the vessel came.

Collins herself seems well aware of the difficulties involved in discovering strangeness among such mundane sources. 'In my search for extraordinary places,' she writes, 'there is the mockery of the everyday.' But she is surely stimulated by the challenge, just as the plate-spinner derives his energy from attempting to prevent his plates from falling to the floor. In one photograph, Collins catches him in action, barefoot and stripped to the waist as he darts eagerly between the plates; at least one of them looks about to drop, like the most precarious pieces in Richard Wentworth's crockery assemblages. But in another photograph the plates all appear to be spinning serenely on their poles, even though the spinner has disappeared and assumed, like Collins herself, an unseen role.

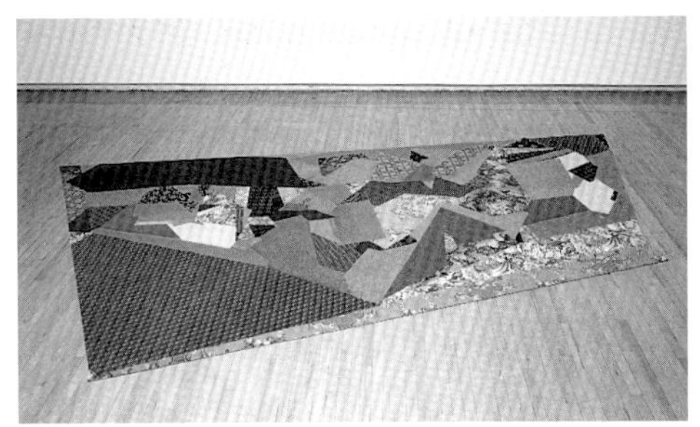

Jacqueline Poncelet
Carpet
1992
Carpeting
512.5 × 280 × 2 cm

Jacqui Poncelet is likewise fascinated by the spectacle of a perilous performance. Her exuberant *Carpet*, a showpiece of cutting and fitting which involved juggling with more than twenty-four different types of material, is a deliberately risky venture. It breaks all the rules about what an acceptable carpet is expected to be. Working with the freedom of a headlong collage artist, she yokes together a deliriously disparate cluster of fragments. They look, at first, as if a bomb had burst on the floor; but the seeming haphazardness turns out, on further inspection, to be based on hairsbreadth calculation. What might so easily have been slapdash and discordant is in reality a sophisticated exercise in virtuoso pattern-making. Taking the conventions of interior decoration as her launching pad, Poncelet subverts them by transforming *Carpet* into a turbulent yet lucidly organised work where sensuality and violence, exhilaration and bewilderment jostle for supremacy.

Born in Belgium, she grew up in the Midlands and started her career by producing modest, rounded pots in white bone china. Although her work was for a while displayed in crafts exhibitions, Poncelet's sculptural ambitions became clear in her subsequent one-person exhibitions. Now she occupies an intriguing and unpredictable position, evading neat definitions in her desire to use disparate materials in unashamedly heterogeneous work. Sometimes, fabric and oil paint are juxtaposed in images which seek to ally the traditions of quilt-making and easel painting. On another occasion, real hair tumbles in anarchy from a bronze, shell-like container closer by far to the conventions of sculpture. But just as carpets fulfil many needs, so Poncelet's diverse output brazenly flouts any attempt to reduce it to a single role.

The Spiritual Dimension

While so many of their contemporaries shy away from religious concerns of any kind, Shirazeh Houshiary and Anish Kapoor have no qualms about moving from materiality towards a spiritual realm. Both artists have confronted, in their highly distinctive ways, the challenge of fusing a non-Western upbringing with the culture of their adopted country. The language they employ has profound links with European art, but it continues to be nourished as well by the very different worlds they knew in childhood. The balance between these two principal sources of imaginative stimulus gives their work a singular tension.

Houshiary has always been proud to proclaim the inspiration she derives from ancient Sufi poetry. It alerts us to the Islamic mysticism fuelling the art of a woman who lived in Iran until the age of eight and subsequently studied in London and Chelsea School of Art. Houshiary's work needs its own contemplative space, and invites us to spend time entering into a philosophy removed from Western thought. Her art acts as an intermediary between body and soul. She produces work to help her search for her true self – a quest bound up with her interest in the Sufi idea that you must withdraw from the world in order to arrive at your essential being.

One of her most memorable recent works is a five-part sculpture called *The enclosure of sanctity*. The large lead cubes are reminiscent of planets, and Houshiary sees them in terms of a central Sun orbited by Mercury, Venus, the Moon and Mars. From the outside, they look sober enough; but once we peer into them, most of the 'planets' become surprisingly complex and rich in colour. Silver foil, copper and gold leaf emblazon the grid-like structures, offering a sense of

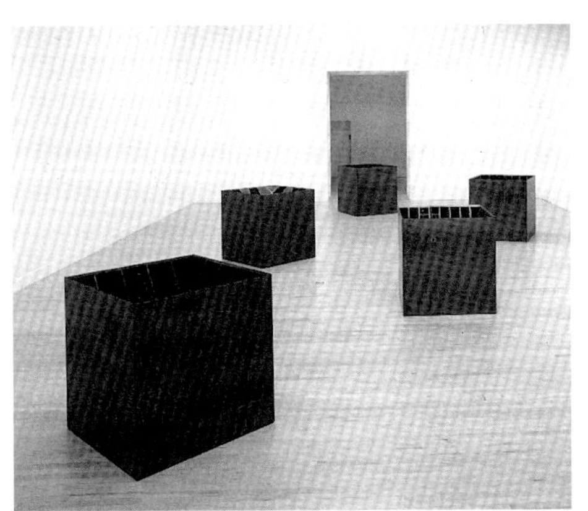

Shirazeh Houshiary
The enclosure of sanctity
1992-3
Lead, copper, silver and gold leaf
Five parts: each 100 × 100 × 100 cm

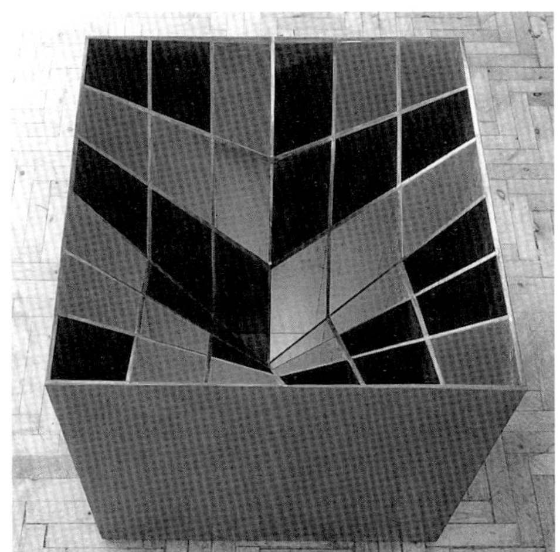

Shirazeh Houshiary
The enclosure of sanctity (detail)
1992-3
Lead, copper, silver and gold leaf
$100 \times 100 \times 100$ cm

radiance after the darkness of the lead containers. Although the grey solidity of the lead certainly protects the labyrinths within, the sculpture can only be savoured by those willing to explore the interiors with care.

A similar commitment is needed when we approach her paintings. From a distance, they resemble black minimal canvases by Ad Reinhardt. Close-to, however, a fine network of pencil lines repeats a Sufi chant in Arabic. They create the ghostly image of a circle whirling inside a square. The extraordinary concentration lying behind these rigorous yet poetic images testifies to the meditative spirit that informs all Houshiary's work.

By using art to move from materiality towards a spiritual realm, Houshiary's work is akin to the concerns of Anish Kapoor. Indian-born but trained in London, where he has lived ever since his student days, Kapoor exemplifies the breadth of interests that sculptors in this country can now encompass. He has links with European artists as diverse as Joseph Beuys, Yves Klein and Ulrich Ruckriem, and yet his concern with metaphysical oppositions is central to an Indian view of the world.

This synthesis of the Asian and European reflects the cultural complexity of an artist who grew up in Bombay before studying in London and settling here. A return visit to India in 1979, just before he embarked on his mature work, marked an important moment of self-definition. For Kapoor, deeply involved by this time with Rothko and Beuys, the trip reawakened his awareness of the duality permeating Indian religious thought. In the shrines to Shiva, he found a nourishing tension between spiritual remoteness and highly charged sexuality. Outside the temples, where powder colour is sold for use in sacred rituals, he discovered another abiding source of inspiration – the realisation that sculpture could be made directly out of colour itself.

After returning to London, Kapoor knew that he could now begin to produce an art that moved away from the concerns of so much contemporary abstract sculpture. The powdered pigment enabled him to deploy colour with a beguiling and sensuous immediacy. His use of brilliant, unadulterated red, yellow and blue marked Kapoor's sculpture out from the prevailing austerity of sculptors who would never have contemplated coating their work with such outspoken hues. His work exerted an instantaneous attraction, and in one sense enhanced the ripe, organic and graspable character of the fruit-like, often openly erotic, forms he favoured. In another respect, though, the sheer luminosity of these shimmering colours moved his work into a sphere far beyond physical gratification. At once desirable and ethereal, tactile and dream-like, Kapoor's sculpture floats between the realms of earth and heaven. Calm and yet profoundly unsettling, it brings the opposite extremes of volume and vacuum, the quantifiable and the unknown, into dramatic confrontation. The reassuring certainty of heavy, boulder-like stone is only evoked in order to point towards the fundamental mystery at the heart of things.

The Human Figure: Presence and Absence

For many centuries, European sculpture remained centrally preoccupied with the human figure. This abiding tradition, inherited from classical civilisation, has been increasingly neglected in recent decades. But the figure refuses to vanish completely. Even when absent, its exclusion from most artists' work need not automatically imply that they are unaware of its importance. And when an exception such as Antony Gormley returns his sculpture to figurative concerns, he does so with a wholeheartedness that can only be described as obsessive.

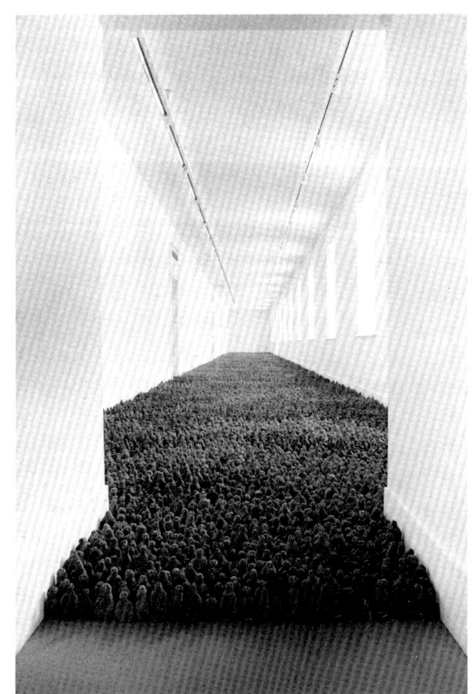

Antony Gormley
Field for the British Isles
1993
Terracotta
Approximately 40,000 figures

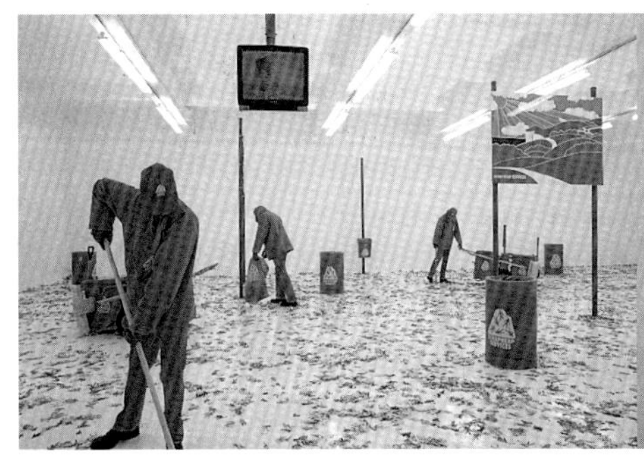

Michael Landy
Scrapheap services
1996
Various dimensions

All the same, Gormley departs from hallowed precedent as well. Instead of inventing form, he relies for the most part on casting his own body in plaster. Such a strategy may sound supremely narcissistic. Rather than producing self-absorbed work, though, Gormley only uses his body as a starting-point. Once the figure has been cast, in lead or iron, it takes on a universal significance. The anonymous face signifies Everyman, not a particular artist. And the limbs are similarly generalised, inviting us to see them above all as containers of feeling. Fingers, toes and other distinguishing features have been smoothed away, by an artist whose passion for simplification is reinforced in the white soldering lines running across the figure without regard for anatomical realism.

Gormley attaches great importance to a 'kind of objective appraisal of my relationship to the world'. Having been brought up as a Catholic in a Benedictine boarding school, he escaped from its doctrinal framework of moral judgements and searched for another world view. 'I want to start with things that just are,' he says, and in this respect his concentration on the figure is a means of arriving at an incontrovertible reality. Gormley's agnosticism will not allow him to entertain the comforting certainties of his childhood faith. Vulnerability is the prevailing mood in *Field for the British Isles*, the grandest and most spectacular work he has so far produced. Filling its barn-like space with around 40,000 terracotta figures modelled by families contacted through local schools in Liverpool, this epic swarm of humanity is at once diminutive and overwhelming. The anonymous people stare up at us. Confined to a single doorway, we return their collective gaze. Towering over them, we could easily conclude that they are frail and defenceless, but there is nothing despairing about them. Their faces are supremely expectant. They generate a feeling of suspense that gives the sculpture its remarkable power. And they cannot be pinned down to a single meaning. Seen as a whole, their bodies come to resemble a colossal carpet, giving off an extraordinary sense of warmth and richness. Just as individual fragility is played off against collective strength, so the muted colour of each figure changes, *en masse*, into a resounding glow.

On the whole, though, the human figure is rarely used by younger sculptors. Although Michael Landy's work offers a far more despairing social diagnosis, he counters gloom with satire. The gaudy attractiveness of his *Costermonger stall no. 3* at first distracts attention from the absence of both seller and clientele but the truth is that the breakdown of this traditional market has turned the sumptuous barrow into a museum piece. The work plaintively asks to be liked in a world that has rendered its social use obsolete. In his most ambitious installation, *Scrapheap services*, the gallery floor is littered with tiny figures painstakingly cut out from discarded crisp packets, burger cartons or beer cans. But the employees of Scrapheap Services, a make-believe cleaning company founded by Landy, stand ready to clear the mess away. The red-uniformed mannequins are silent as they spike, shovel or sweep their way through the detritus. A smoothly persuasive video is also on hand, with a purring voice of welcome and explanation. Scrapheap Services is, apparently, 'the cleaning company that cares because you don't'. Without a trace of genuine concern, the voice observes that 'a prosperous society depends upon a minority of people being discarded'. But this tone becomes principled when it asks: 'Why put up with unsightly people who are a burden on your resources, when you can turn to the Scrapheap Services people-control range of products?'

With the identical nylon-suited disposers at hand, there is no risk of being overwhelmed by these diminutive victims. However inescapably they may besmirch the gallery's white floor, their unwanted bodies will soon be gathered in dust carts, bagged and consigned to the equally red 'purpose-built shredder' dominating the room like a callous, hideously enlarged predator. The menace inherent in its squatting legs gives the lie to the video voice's honeyed tone. Landy calls it The Vulture and ensures that the machine's implacable presence gives the entire tableau a chilling air. The impersonal cleaners, with their corporate clothes and logo-decorated implements, are the anonymous servants of a system whose leaders care more about downsizing than people. Unsightliness is the only fault they can find in unemployment, and the pulverising Vulture can be relied on to reduce all the redundant figures to a state of invisibility.

In Vong Phaophanit's work, the absence of the human figure may well take on an autobiographical significance. Born in Laos, he has not seen his home and family since 1973. As a political refugee he spent student years in Paris before moving to England. Nevertheless, his art proves that the land of his childhood is not forgotten. Memories of that distant world inform everything he produces, and in a 1993 installation at the Serpentine Gallery he evoked this Laotian past with limpid economy and directness.

The floor of his room was filled with rice, shaped into a series of mounds and furrows that stretched away to the far wall like ridges in a ploughed field. But Phaophanit made no attempt to pretend that the gallery had somehow become transformed, through illusionism, into the agricultural terrain of his native country. Instead, he allowed the beds of rice to be illuminated by thin bars of warm orange light. Although their warmth seemed to nourish the 'field' where they were embedded, the light was clearly neon-generated. So organic rice was brought into an unlikely proximity with synthetic illumination, and the two worlds ought to have collided jarringly with each other.

Against the odds, however, age-old rural simplicity and modern urban technology did not conflict. Their juxtaposition was surprising, and doubtless reflected Phaophanit's awareness of divided loyalties deep within himself. Yet the overall impact was unexpectedly serene. Even though the ploughed field emitted a streamlined glow, and could easily have appeared sullied by this alien intruder, calmness prevailed. The misty orange lines induced a contemplative mood, as if the artist was suggesting that harmonious order and fertility might somehow be the outcome of this strange alliance.

Function, Abstraction and Urban Impersonality

Other sculptors of Phaophanit's generation restrict themselves, quite understandably, to a starting point in Western urban society. Because they both exhibit at the Lisson Gallery, Grenville Davey and Julian Opie are often assigned to the same 'school' as the older Cragg, Deacon and Woodrow. Although connections can undoubtedly be traced between them, such category-slotting should be firmly resisted. Davey is his own man, a cool and refined individual who operates on the borderline between functional objects and abstract forms with an independent life.

At times, his sculpture bears a tantalising resemblance to wing-mirrors, teeth or saucepan lids. But it has no real function. Instead, it inhabits a quirky, teasing position. Even as Davey refers to the world of everyday appearances, he reserves the right to explore a more mysterious region where abstraction holds sway. Circular forms dominate the geometrical language he favours. Stripped and elegant, they reflect the amount of fastidious care he devotes to their making. Yet they never become rarefied. Davey ensures that, however exquisite they may seem, these severely simplified objects are not cut off from late twentieth-century industrialised reality. As a result, they have an enigmatic presence.

While Davey's sculpture invites us to identify its origin in the observable world, he always keeps the viewer guessing. In *Common ground*, one of his most impressive sculptures, the form resembles a free-standing counter; but Davey undermines this connection by covering the top of the sculpture with asphalt. At the very moment when we think his work can be pinned down to a representational source, he frustrates our efforts all over again.

Sleek and impersonal, Julian Opie's work has long since lost the individual mark-making he employed when painting his early sculptures in a swift, racy manner. Blank, streamlined and impeccably cool, his containers present a polished front. Their glass, aluminium and stainless steel components look functional but, as in Davey's work, no practical purpose can be discerned. Instead, they remain stubbornly enigmatic. Most of these gleaming boxes and screens seem to have strayed from an airport foyer, and Opie appears most at home when dealing, paradoxically, with impersonal locales.

The same detachment characterised the cluster of brightly painted concrete blocks he assembled on the larger terrace of the Hayward Gallery for his one-person show in 1993. Their primary colours looked cheerful enough, positioned against the backdrop of drab, stained buildings around them. But *Imagine you can order these*, the title of the terrace sculpture, sounded mournful rather than stimulating. Moreover, we could only view the blocks through a gallery window. They remained out of reach, like the archetypal motorway perpetually curving out of sight in the paintings near the gallery entrance.

Here Opie-land was at its most relentless. *Imagine you are driving* urged the caption, but nobody would want to linger unduly on this empty, monotonous road. Black by day and grey-blue at night, the flat expanses of tarmac stretched towards featureless horizons. They did not even quicken interest when set in simulated motion on computer screens, like video games which cast us in the role of driver. For there were no obstacles to dodge, no rival cars struggling for supremacy. Everything was purged of tension, and made as pointless as the concrete racetrack sculptures on the floor.

Some artists are prepared to confront even the most painful aspects of contemporary society, placing its fissures and festering ailments at the very heart of their uneasy work. Like Opie, Willie Doherty has used the act of driving a car as a springboard, but in this instance the result possesses an inescapably political resonance. Still working in his native Derry, a city acutely divided by the 'Irish Troubles', Doherty employs the camera's resources to explore the complexities of life in a fearful city. Through his photographic images, Doherty has highlighted the gulf between Catholic and Protestant areas. He has also deployed words underneath photographic portraits, changing the captions to show how easily the Irish can be branded with stereotypical and misleading identities.

His most widely admired and disturbing achievement, however, is a video installation called, ominously, *The only good one is a dead one*. The room is dark, concentrating attention on two walls where the images are projected. Our eyes move from one to the other and back again, generating a sense of restlessness that grows into outright disquiet after the projections begin. One of them is confined to a view through the window of a parked car, showing the eerie, pink phosphorescence of street lamps in a near-empty part of town. The other lets us look

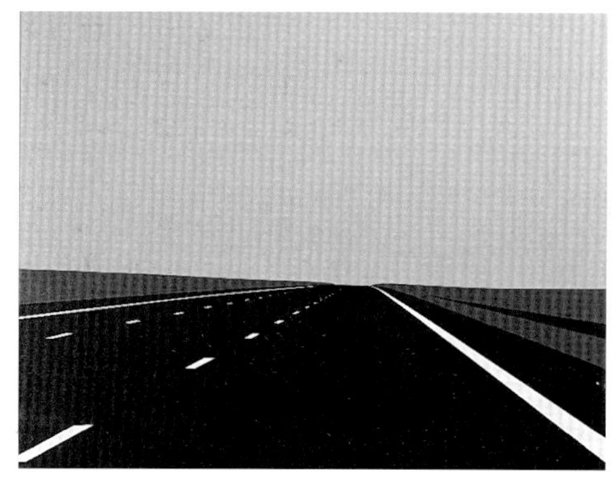

Julian Opie
Imagine you are driving
1993
Acrylic on wood, glass and aluminium
93 × 123 × 3 cm

through the windscreen of a car in motion, its headlights giving the lonely rural road ahead a bleached, menacing ghostliness. Nothing actually happens. But an all-pervasive dread is reinforced by the sound of an unidentified man's voice, quietly confiding his thoughts on victimisation and murderous fantasies. Even the most humdrum journey can, it seems, become a trigger for paranoia in a world riddled with mistrust.

Intimations of Mortality

The waning of the twentieth century has been accompanied in art by a gathering fascination with death. Whether overt or implicit, a preoccupation with extinction runs through much of the work produced by the younger generation. Even in Britain, a country so emotionally inhibited that the grave has long been a taboo area, artists are no longer afraid of the *memento mori*. Their lack of inhibition is in one sense reminiscent of the mood that prevails in Jacobean tragedy, with its elegiac references to blood, bones and human fragility. But there is nothing ghoulish about their approach. Far from indulging in morbidity, they explore the most distressing aspects of existence with cool, alert precision.

Of all the young British artists, Damien Hirst is the most chillingly direct in his central engagement with death. Challenging the belief that anyone who clearly acknowledges human dissolution is guilty of inexcusable gloom, he manages to be frank about mortality without sliding into mawkishness. Hirst is nevertheless the most uncomfortable of artists, and the fact that he presents his death-obsessed findings with calm, surgical exactitude only adds to the disquiet. Look at the pseudo-scientific precision with which he marshals thirty-seven species of dour-looking fish in a work ironically entitled *I want you because I can't have you*. Methodically arranged in perspex cases on shelves, they resemble laboratory specimens intended to prove a researcher's theory. But their only purpose is to emphasise the unfathomable strangeness of life-in-death, as well as subverting the whole notion of finding solace in a bowl of goldfish.

Even when he deals directly with extinction at its most brutal, Hirst remains as disciplined as before. A double glass cube contains the most disturbing of all his exhibits, *A thousand years*. In one half, a neat white box provides a hatching-ground for thousands of maggots. When the bluebottles fly out, though, they find themselves confined by the setting Hirst has devised. All they can do is settle on a repellent cow's head with a hypnotic blue eye lying in the other half of the container. Above this rotting *memento mori* hang the thin tubes of an insectorcutor, attached to a tray littered with dead flies. Plenty more have expired on the floor below, turning the sculpture into a charnel-house.

Mesmerised and nauseated in equal measure, we are forced to ask ourselves why the spectacle is so gruesome. After all, the death of a fly does not normally provoke sympathy in humans. Its lifespan is brief, and Hirst draws attention to that fact as arrestingly as he can. If we find his work cruel, should efforts be made to ban insectorcutors from places where they safeguard our health? The sculpture poses these unsettling questions in a deadpan manner, allowing room for gallows humour alongside the intimations of mortality.

No such levity can be found in Rachel Whiteread's sculpture. But like Hirst and so many artists of their generation, she is preoccupied with transience and loss. In one of her finest early works, the space surrounding an ordinary domestic bath is transformed into solid, four-square blocks of plaster. They encase the bath-shaped void lodged at the centre, its sides stained with rust-coloured streaks that accen-

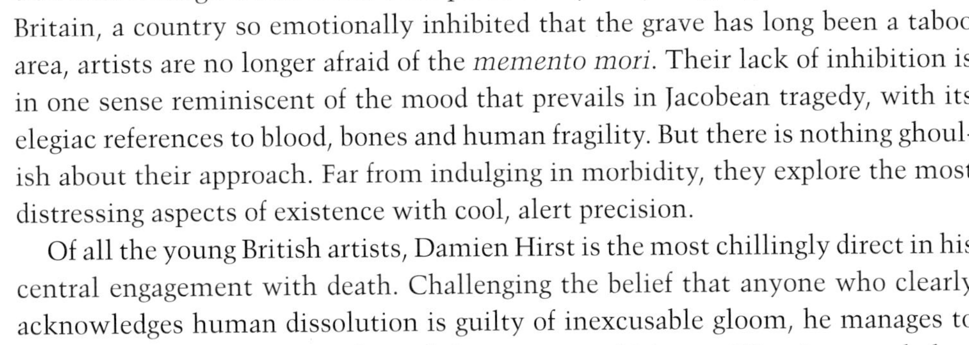

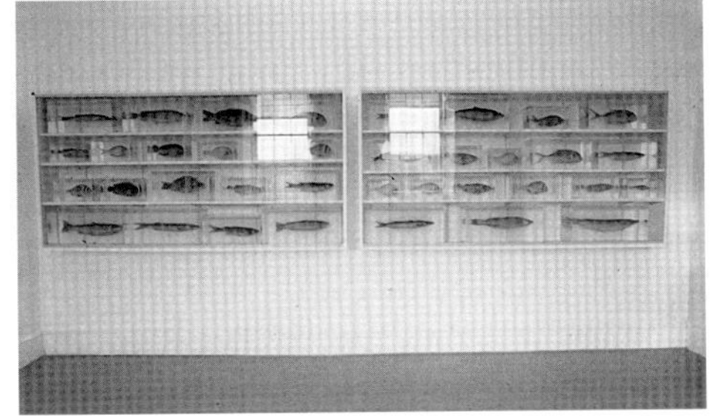

Damien Hirst
I want you because I can't have you
1991
MDF, melamine, wood, steel, glass, perspex cases, fish, 5% formaldehyde solution
Each vitrine: 122 × 244 × 30 cm

tuate the sense of antiquity. This bleached, monumental slab stirs memories of sarcophagi, and its interior certainly looks mournful enough to be fit for a corpse. Similarly the spectre of an unaccountably now-absent bed is powerfully evoked by *Untitled (black bed)*, re-creating childhood fears of nocturnal obliteration.

Ghost is the masterpiece of her early period. Cast in sections from the interior space of a cramped North London living-room, Whiteread's *tour de force* has a melancholy air. The imprints of a window, panelled door and fireplace complete with scorchmarks appear on successive sides of this glacial block. But for all its magisterial presence, the work seems bound up with memories of a past beyond recall. Thin gaps between the sections disclose the emptiness within, buttressed by a steel frame. Bleached, uninhabited and eerily still, *Ghost* finally defies its bulk and becomes as ethereal as a dream.

In her most recent work, Whiteread moves away from her former reliance on found objects. She has started making her own forms, specifically for casting, and also indulges a passion for colour which her earlier work had suppressed. The austerity of white plaster gives way to polychromatic splendour, above all in a superb multi-part installation called *Untitled (one hundred spaces)*. Although hard enough to touch and defined with clear-cut lucidity, these compact resin units seem as edible as jellies. They also look more mysterious than most of Whiteread's work, refusing to yield up their origins as quickly as her early sculpture. Derived from the spaces underneath stools, chairs and tables, they transcend their commonplace origins and assume the four-square magnificence of temples.

All the same, the more disquieting reverberations of Whiteread's art refuse to go away. For the objects gathered together in *Untitled (one hundred spaces)* also resemble caskets fit for cremated ashes, and we can walk up and down their ordered rows like visitors to a military graveyard. The memorialising side of her imagination is as insistent as ever, suggesting that she remains steadfastly attached to the idea of giving permanent, ennobling form to even the most unexceptional aspects of domestic life. She succeeds triumphantly, and her precocious achievement typifies the continuing ability of modern British sculptors to measure up to the highest international standards.

The Survival of a Word

There are some signs, as the new millennium approaches, that 'sculpture' is no longer regarded as an appropriate term even for work centred on three-dimensional forms. In 1997 the Hayward Gallery mounted a major survey of 'The Object in British Art of the 1980s and 90s'. Many of the practitioners discussed in these pages were among the forty-five artists chosen for the show, and their work owed a range of debts to the exceptional vitality of sculptural innovation throughout the century. But the organisers decided to call the exhibition *Material Culture*, even as they explained that it concentrated on 'independent objects, occupying the space of actual things, with which the viewer has first to engage physically in relation to his or her own body'. They went on to admit that 'it would be easy to talk of this as a sculpture exhibition: many of its concerns are sculptural and some of its participants – Richard Deacon and Rachel Whiteread come most readily to mind – are classic "sculptors". But the word has recently expanded its meaning so far as to become almost meaningless.'

In my view, though, expansion need not lead to extinction. Sculpture is in no danger of disappearing. The fact that it continues to undergo momentous and often bewildering changes testifies to vigour rather than redundancy. Far from

lapsing into a complacent reiteration of dull, exhausted formulae, its finest practitioners remain alert, interrogative and audacious. They may well wish to avoid
tying themselves down to an exclusive preoccupation with sculptural concerns,
and shun any automatic loyalty to sculptors' traditional involvement with carving and modelling alone. But that does not mean the word itself no longer retains
its pertinence. The increasingly multifarious activities which can be linked with
the notion of sculpture continue to play a vital role in art today. And the prodigious breadth of approaches explored by the individuals represented in the
Weltkunst Collection proves that they are as eager to pursue renewal as their forerunners at the beginning of the twentieth century, who did so much to widen the
inventive possibilities for sculptural practice in the contemporary world.

Drawing and Withdrawing

Penelope Curtis   The Sculptor and the Drawing

SCULPTORS' DRAWINGS have become a special category. Is this because they are thought to be more 'about' something than painters' drawings (and not just because we can't afford to move or to buy the sculptures themselves)? I think it is, but defining that special quality is difficult. Drawing in general has become more diverse, liberated as it now is from the tradition of drawing from life, or from the Antique; and it may be because of the demise of this shared training that we are now more readily able to differentiate sculptors' drawings from painters' drawings. Now that drawing can be a genuinely free exercise it may well act as a more desirable complement to the practice of sculpture than to the practice of painting. Perhaps sculptors 'need' drawing more than painters do?

We tend to think of drawing as the artist's most private expression. We imagine we feel closest to the artist on the page. Because we presume the lack of external pressures, we imagine that here the artist is alone. This could be particularly true for the sculptor, on whom material constraints are always greater. Whereas painters could almost always paint, sculptors were often prevented from realising their ideas in finished form. But although sculptors' drawings might indeed have been utopian, they have also often been resolutely practical. They were the traditional vehicle – along with the maquette – whereby the sculptor offered choices to clients, provided a guarantee of the final product, envisaged settings, or tried out different options.

Is the pull of sculptors' drawings something to do with the gap between the two-dimensional image and the three-dimensional imagination? The sculptor's drawing may occupy this strange and active space. Such flexibility – half abstract, half real – is echoed in the relationship which sculptors have to the ground plan (for exhibitions or for large-scale sculpture). Such plans are ever present in the artist's consciousness, but despite their familiarity, and the conceptual knowledge of how to read their signs, they only point up the very different nature of space as it is represented on paper.

But most of what we have here in the Weltkunst Collection – and indeed in any collection of recent sculptors' drawings – is neither practical, nor private. These drawings are not, on the whole, intended for clients – or for the artists – to make practical choices about sculptures. They were almost all made as independent works in their own right, finished and suitable for public viewing. Sculptors have in fact developed a much more public drawing than painters.

In the more powerful drawing there is a kind of spatial elasticity which is exciting to observe. But even in other – ostensibly ordinary – drawings there is something about the moment at which the drawing is no longer enough which does indeed take us close, not just to the sculptor, but more importantly, to sculpture. Grenville Davey describes drawings as a way of making and catching decisions for sculptures, which is, after all, what art is about. This is what makes looking at drawings exciting, because sometimes, given the right material, we can see that decision-making at work. Thus the most interesting groupings of drawings are often temporary, and only exist in the sculptor's mind for a brief period. They are always being reshuffled, refiled, and once again rejected. To catch hold not only of the drawing, but also of its topical significance to the artist, demands a collector who is in regular and close contact with the artist, or who comes in at the right moment.

Drawings function as the semi-conscious, as the store pile of imagery which the artist keeps, and periodically reappraises. Most artists live between a fear of losing a good idea, and a wish to surprise themselves by something that was theirs, but now seems suddenly foreign. Almost all these sculptors draw copiously, and then make an initial quality check, discarding those sheets that are definitely bad, but storing most of them in stacks for months before coming back to them. Drawing is at once the clear light of consciousness and the dark record of the suppressed or the submerged. In this sense, it can be seen to cause emergence; to bring out the forms and give them shape on the page. Antony Gormley makes a point of saying how much he likes the word 'drawing' because of its relationship to 'drawing out'.

What is clear is the way we should *not* think of sculptors' drawings. They are rarely drawings for sculptures, nor about resolving forms, and even when they are, they do this in a way that is fluid and fugitive rather than fixed. They are neither preparatory, nor conclusive. They are much more often genuinely complementary in terms of doing something that sculpture cannot; of filling in gaps, of providing another kind of fulfilment. This is why they are interesting; they add texture, colour and difference to the sculptural oeuvre.

It is equally clear that we cannot talk about the Weltkunst Collection of sculptors' drawings, for it does not even pretend to follow the conventional rules of a collection. Though it may set us off along this route – presenting us with a medium produced in one country in a given period – it quickly becomes evident that we are not obliged to assess this collection as we might a public collection, that is, as an attempt to build, cumulatively, a balanced and representative cross-section of a certain 'school'. Instead we should take, and indeed are offered, the opportunity to understand this collection absolutely on its own extremely individual terms. The collection is, in fact, the choice of one man, versed in the world of Old Master Drawings, who has been succeeded since his death by his brother, and it is the result of a series of different relationships with individual artists.

Because it seemed impossible to talk about this collection as a collection, I have instead approached it as a gathering of distinct practices. Furthermore, many of the drawings in this collection were made up to a decade ago; they may represent work that is not simply old, but also definitely past. Indeed, many of these practices now seem historical even to their practitioners.

Some sculptors know very clearly what their drawings are for; others do not. Certainly, for some of the sculptors represented here, drawing has been important – perhaps ironically – in terms of leading them away from form, or at least in terms of opening up that form. Some sculptors do drawings to make their sculptures better – to give them space, life and energy – and afterwards have admitted that their drawings implicitly point at what they felt was wrong in the sculptures themselves.

It is notable how drawings have become more important for many of these artists, and not necessarily because the 1980s boom in the market is over. Deacon is looking with increased interest at drawing; Davey's current fascination is definitely graphic; Woodrow's most vital and self-assured work of recent years has been two-dimensional; Houshiary's retreat from the public arena was marked by drawing and has now moved very resolutely into the two-dimensional; Wilding's return to drawing has been revelatory and inspirational.

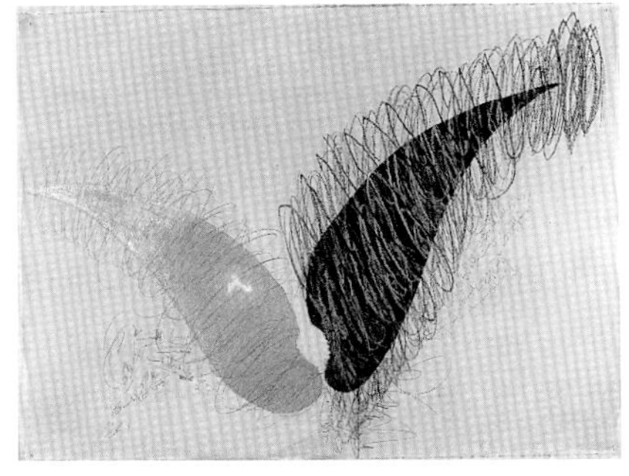

Shirazeh Houshiary
Study: between earth and sky I
1987
Mixed media on paper
56 × 76.5 cm

Although we may say that sculptors' drawings are different from painters' drawings, I am not convinced that we can understand the former in any one way. Sculptors' drawings are as multivalent as art itself, and thus I do not know if they share something greater than what makes them different. Perhaps the notes that follow will yield some clues.

Many sculptors, including several in the Weltkunst Collection, make different kinds of drawings, which exist in a hierarchy designed to suit different purposes. Often, some are public, some are private, and others may exist in a kind of limbo between the two. Most of what we have in this collection represents the 'public' drawing.

Richard Deacon, Rachel Whiteread, Alison Wilding, Anish Kapoor and Edward Allington keep sketchbooks which the public has never seen, and which, at present, they do not intend to make over to public collections. Whiteread, for instance, links this with her deliberate policy of 'keeping hold' of her own work. But all these artists also make a kind of 'public' drawing which is what we have here in the Weltkunst Collection. In contrast, the sketchbooks of Grenville Davey, and to an even greater extent, Hermione Wiltshire, are everyday documents of the most personal kind. Although Davey has let go of his sketchbooks, and although the drawings inside are extremely elegant, they are hardly 'public'. He has not exhibited them, and they do not claim public space as do those of others.

Inside the Sketchbook

Grenville Davey's nine sketchbooks range over nearly a decade, from 1985 to 1994. He has drawn most days, at all kinds of times, in the studio, in pubs, before going to bed, while waiting, or when an idea is waiting. At present he is interested in establishing drawing as a more formal part of his routine – with its own space and time, with more gaps between drawing and sculpture. Davey dislikes the notebook mentality, and deliberately loosens the pages from their bindings. The ones here have been put back together again. Although some have only a few pages, others have around fifty or even a hundred. They contain drawings that relate to many of his sculptures, laid out sequentially, without words, rather like a phrase of music which is repeated with many slight variations. They are mostly drawn in an unvarying black line, but with a grace and economy that makes them beautiful. Occasionally one is surprised, amid this sober recitative, by a sudden incursion of a flight of fantasy – a Baroque teapot, a Norman castle or a Gaudi-like architectural scheme. They may represent a love of the curvaceous which lies underneath the severe discipline of his sculpture, but they also reveal Davey's interest in the entrance into a form.

Davey draws until he has to make something, that is, up to the point when the drawing begs the sculpture, when it can no longer answer questions by itself. This is the end of the line, the final catch perhaps, of the genesis of the idea. Eventually, out the other side, Davey continues to think of his sculptures as being like drawings, whereas he also knows they tell you more than a drawing can.

Although these sketchbooks have been reconstituted, Davey prefers to work with loose pages. He packs the drawings away in his plan chest, puts the good ones on the walls, and comes back later to surprise himself. He likes his memory to play tricks, and believes that the drawings are the most effective way for him to store things away. They can be cleverer than he can.

Grenville Davey
Untitled
1988-9
Ink on paper
30 × 21 cm

Hermione Wiltshire's sketchbooks are rather like exercise books which accompany the artist when she is 'at work'. They comprise thumbnail sketches of ideas that come in bursts, irregularly. They are like a diary, or even more like an album, sufficiently important to come back to retrospectively, pasting in notes or significant ideas recorded elsewhere at other times, made expressly for subsequent inclusion. They record ideas for sculptures in a note-taking form, with an explanation, recording an idea that cannot be adequately captured in the image. Some of the ideas are, as Wiltshire notes here, 'very difficult to draw'.

The notes are quite colloquial, as if we were actually having a conversation with the artist. She herself sees them as notations on 'personalities peopling her mind'. This storehouse of ideas is current for some years, and during this time Wiltshire will return to them, until they become outdated and she is ready to put them away altogether.

As with Davey's drawings, on these pages one recognises many sculptures that were subsequently realised, in more or less similar form. While both Davey and Wiltshire talk of reaching the point when the sculpture is needed, the point of needing the sculpture to make a decision seems to arrive more quickly for her. Wiltshire's method of fabrication depends on the subject, whereas Davey's is a consistent line. Sometimes a few pages show a whole range of sculptures waiting to be made for the next exhibition (and indeed the July 1990 notebook correlates to her exhibition at the Riverside, and the December 1991 with that at the Lisson Gallery).

Whereas Davey's notebooks contain almost no words – for his drawings are about drawing – Wiltshire's are just as much about symbol and content. Words often provide variations, but they also unpick the visual form, noting possible connotations. Connotations lead on to visual parallels and puns. Words progress suggestively in an organic chain, and so do the images. Words also denote ideas for accompanying sounds, though this is, as yet, an area still to be explored.

Rachel Whiteread's drawings are slow and beautiful productions which are as solid and slow as her sculptures. Whiteread began as a painter, and this comes through not only in her interest in colour and texture, but also in her defining her drawings as 'thinking spaces'. The graph paper gives her a coloured ground on which to work, and the materiality of her media – tippex, resin, rubber – seems effectively to slow down the eye as it travails over the page, and evokes her own working over of its surface. Tippex's opaque viscosity works to conceal, and Whiteread uses it also over photocopies of her photographs. This actualising of an idea by the business of drawing is important for her, and she does it even if mechanical or electronic drawings have already been made. The drawing bridges the gap between the actual space and the imaginary space.

The drawings by Whiteread in the Weltkunst Collection were made while she had a fellowship in Berlin. Though the herringbone parquet in one of the Weltkunst drawings is the parquet from Berlin, most of the features are more typical than specific, and in any case are not drawn from the motif. They represent a period of quiet time away from the everyday business of London. Such drawings emerge from interludes of reflection, and come also to represent such reflection.

Rachel Whiteread
Floor
1993
Correction fluid and ink on graph paper
122 × 45.5 cm

Although Richard Deacon makes two kinds of 'public' drawings, generative and non-generative – the former not really represented here, but known through the Tate's *Orpheus* series – their linear quality is much the same. The majority of Deacon's public drawings are working drawings in which he works out measurements, sections and quantities of material, either for himself or for others. They appear to betray little of the personal. Though we recognise the shapes as Deacon, the lines and the handwriting seem ubiquitous.

Deacon nevertheless makes almost all his technical drawings himself, and besides, he points out, to look for the 'signature' passage – the passage that is more Deacon than another – is wrong-headed. He has made his practice successful – and this is particularly true for his monumental practice – only by making all its links his own. This may warn us off that tendency to think that the tentative or doubting line is necessarily more revealing of individual character than the line that is assured. Funnily enough, Deacon defines the recognisability of his drawings as lying in their poor quality, and the niceness of the information they carry.

The bulk of Deacon's drawings in the Weltkunst Collection relate to Toronto's *Between the eyes*, and to British Telecom's *Body of thought*, two large urban commissions. They are representative of Deacon's way of working on such projects – and documenting such projects, retaining his notes from beginning to end – and these particular projects exemplify a certain moment, around 1990, when a group of sculptures for urban spaces (Vienna, Southampton, Warwick) came to fruition. Broadly speaking, the cities' mass provided the foil for open structures, and these were developed with clay maquettes, open models, and site models, at either 1:20 or 1:100, as well as with photographs. The two series here allow us an unusually extensive view across a full range of developmental drawings towards one project. The 12 British Telecom drawings show the disposition of sections, with measurements of joints and spaces. The 45 drawings for Toronto, from 1987 to 1989, are perhaps inevitably more varied. They vary from small figures to larger sections, from the doodle to the plan, but all focus on the depiction of a pinch and a twist in a single three-dimensional body. They look at the creation of a shape from both the outside and the inside.

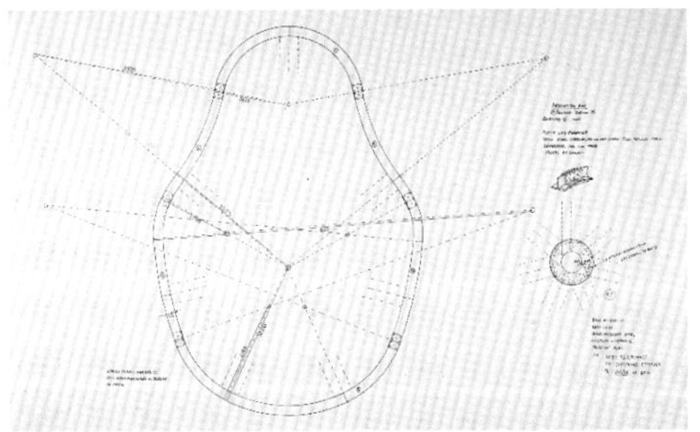

Richard Deacon
Between the eyes
1990
Ink on tracing paper
48.5 × 84 cm

Anish Kapoor questions the term 'drawing' at all, and points out that what his 'drawings' give him are the qualities of painting: colour, liquidity, mixing, light. They give him the pictorial, the frontal, which is so much at the heart of his three-dimensional work. Indeed he questions whether he even makes 'sculpture' but rather colour and space. If we were to attempt a more meaningful split than sculpture/drawing, we might think instead in terms of the outer and the inner. For Kapoor the drawing is the view from the inside, moving from the eyes to the interior, from the visual to the visceral. Perhaps we might even think of the drawings as the insides of his sculptures?

Kapoor's works on paper are a parallel activity, as much public as his sculpture. He makes them every day, one or two daily. He throws none away, but shows in public those that clearly emerge as good. Others he may try to rework. They are also an enduring activity, which has gone on since well before the sculpture, and which he imagines going on after. Moreover, they are central to his expression. Thus, whereas for some the Weltkunst Collections represent a closed moment, for Kapoor these drawings are part of a continuum.

Kapoor too keeps private sketchbooks, which depict objects in space. The

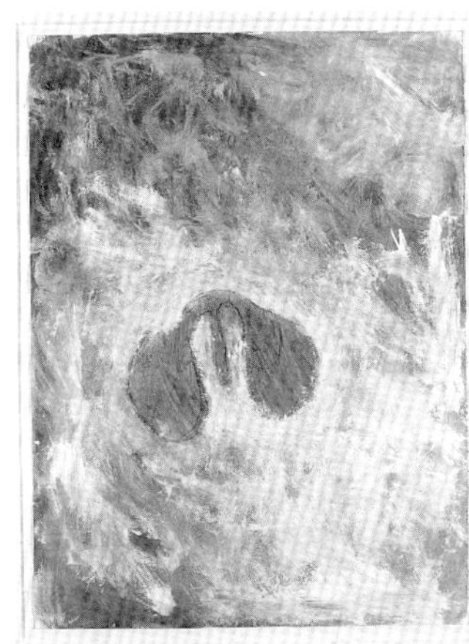

Anish Kapoor
Untitled
Undated
Graphite and gouache on paper
52 × 39 cm

'drawings' that he makes, drawings proper, remain on the walls of his studios, or were once on the surface of his stones. He links drawing with other methods of keeping his practice lively, other kinds of 'irritations', like photography, video, oil painting, and he reminds us not to look at drawing in isolation, as the single complementary activity to sculpture.

In and Out of the Light

Alison Wilding began to make drawings – single drawings apart from her notebook – in 1988. She was impelled into making a series of 'Angry Drawings', 16 in all, and surprised herself with the result. Nevertheless, she sat on them for ages before releasing them to her gallery. Keeping back her drawings is something Wilding does quite deliberately, making some especially to lay down for the future, even describing these as bottles of wine, some of which will mature well, while others will need to be thrown away. A few drawings will be ready to go public at once, whereas most are consigned to the litter bin. Wilding will go back to the stacks of earlier drawings to look for surprise, but also to test them, to see if they are still in some way relevant, if they still touch her.

Wilding draws when she feels a kind of craving, a need for what is, in some ways at least, a known activity. This need may last several days, like an interlude that parallels her sculpture. Although drawing has come sporadically, it has done so with increasing frequency, and recently has echoed mind-images or memory flashes that might be going through her own brain; and while Wilding is perfectly conscious of the rhythm of her practice, and even of its double style – clean/dirty – she would like it to have greater regularity, and suggests this might come if she had a dedicated space. Drawing became more important to her when the fabrication of the sculptures was removed from her own studio. She drew, therefore, when she felt alienated or distanced from her work, or when she needed to reassure herself that she knew what she was looking for. Drawing is also the way to let something out. Sometimes the vocabulary in the drawings echoes that in the sculpture; sometimes one prefigures the other. The current transparency of her drawings is prefigured by the increasing transparency of the materials of her sculpture, but looking at her drawings helps to explicate the pool-like imagery of her recent work, and focuses attention on its auras and aureoles.

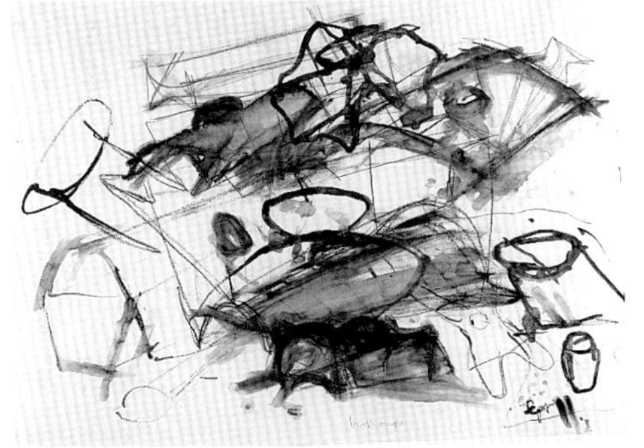

Alison Wilding
Untitled
1988
Charcoal and oil crayon on paper
42 × 59 cm

Balancing Mind and Body

For a number of sculptors the drawing has been of tremendous importance in distancing them from the battle of making the shape to fit the subject. Shirazeh Houshiary recognises the vital role played by drawing in bringing her to an understanding of the true subject of her quest, which was in fact resolutely anti-object. The drawings she makes now are working drawings for other people to follow, while her own primary activity has transferred to painting, to a rigorous but restorative practice involving the hand, the sign and the surface.

The drawings she made in 1987-8 were made in tandem with sculpture. Though the practice was simultaneous, drawing was not used to resolve the forms, and if it looked like form, it was not about form, but about space, movement and energy. Thereafter, it was by withdrawing to an exclusive practice of drawing, with a complete cessation of sculpture-making, that Houshiary was able to reorient her practice. The result of this two-year hibernation was the show of green drawings at the Lisson Gallery in 1992.

Drawing can exactly echo the body and its movement in a way that making sculpture cannot. With Kapoor, Gormley and Houshiary the viewer is confronted by that physical relationship. Houshiary likens her drawing to dance, and one senses that pace and rhythm: the quick and the slow. Indeed she likes to work to music, and it echoes in her work. This interest in movement was something that led Houshiary away from her sculpture, and more and more into the activity on the page. Drawings carried both the hot and the cold, the passion and the discipline and, more importantly, allowed the artist to lose herself within them in a way that sculpture, because it is so hard, and always in some way other, never could.

Night Thoughts

While for some the drawing is resolutely conscious, for others it is a way of winding down, an almost trance-like activity in which one allows the residues of the day to emerge and develop a possible form. Drawing is a night-time activity for Antony Gormley. Gormley uses chance, and defines drawing as a way of finding the subconscious and regaining the conscious. Much of his work depends on his understanding of our original habitat as a 'primal pond', and the page itself reappears in this light. Gormley enjoys drawing immensely, and describes it as a relaxation. However, like others, he also regards it – or making time for it – as a mark of a kind of artistic good health. Gormley's ideal routine would be to round off the working day with some time in the drawing studio, drawing late into the night, perhaps throwing the drawings away next morning. Gormley makes a basic distinction between those drawings with nice ideas, and those which are nice drawings. He, too, keeps sketchbooks, in which he has notes and drawings about his sculptures and has rarely shown these.

Gormley separates his drawing practice from his sculpture, and suggests that if he is successful it may be in a space somewhere between the two. Whereas his sculptures have to be completed by the spectator's empathy, his drawings are more clearly about his own urge to find some kind of embodiment of his position in space. They, too, show the male figure, the artist himself, and are about that consciousness being pulled both on to the page and beyond it. Perhaps the drawings, in being unbounded, convey more effectively Gormley's interest in our potential to be at one with the elements than do the closed sculptures.

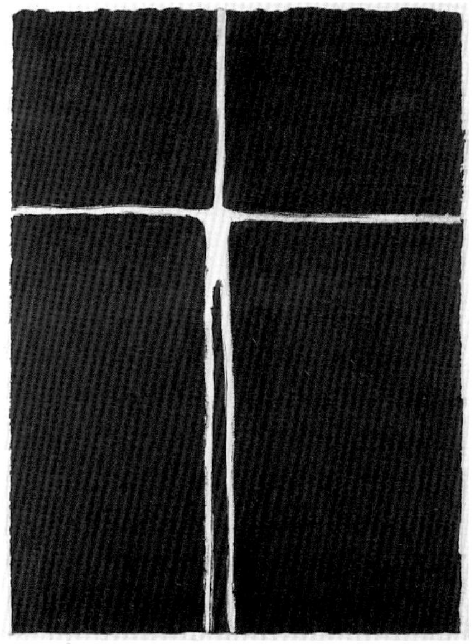

Antony Gormley
Space
1980
Oil and pigment on paper
38 × 28 cm

Daily Practice

For others, drawing is the daylight discipline, the quotidianal routine which must be exercised in a conscious way. Edward Allington makes himself draw: it is a deliberate strategy of production which in its turn starts to depersonalise the very drawings that seem to be quintessential 'of him'. And yet, though his drawing is absolutely conscious, the word 'residue' reappears in discussing his approach. For although Allington's drawings are not related to his sculptures, they deal with its excess, the stuff the sculptures did not require.

While Allington draws daily, making himself achieve a turn-out of around one finished drawing a week, others – like Whiteread – know that every now and again they must come back to drawing, seeing it as crucial to the health and development of their ideas. For her, the slowness, the almost mechanical longueur of the act of drawing, brings with it the maturation and realisation of the rightness of certain projects.

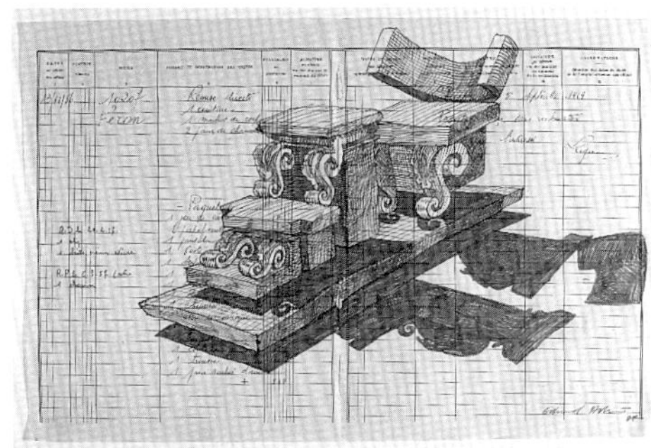

Edward Allington
After Piranesi I
1987
Sepia ink on used ledger paper
26.5 × 42 cm

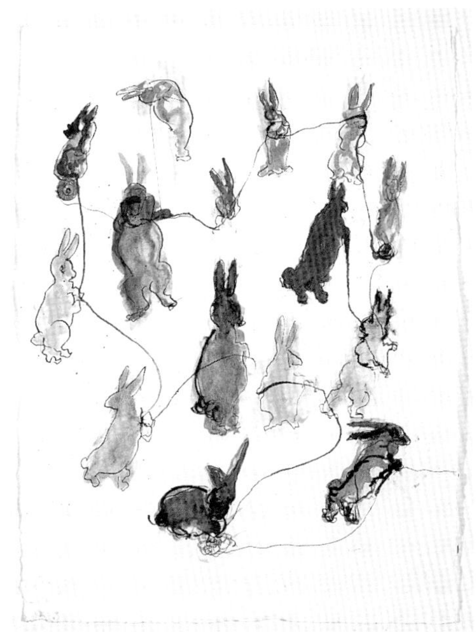

Lucia Nogueira
Untitled
1992
Graphite and watercolour on paper
38 × 28 cm

Allington's drawings are not for sculpture, though they bear his handwriting as strongly as, and probably more strongly than, any of his three-dimensional works. They are strangely of him, and not of him. Their characteristic of something that emerges fully formed is enhanced by his use of other people's ledger and old exercise books. The white forms seem to hover on the page as if they had been mysteriously beamed in from above. They are at once immediately recognisable as 'Allington' and yet the fact that they always do look the same reveals their programmatic basis.

Lucia Nogueira is represented by only a few watercolours in the Weltkunst Collection. Although she makes many such consistently beautiful works which stand alongside the sculptures as a parallel activity, one of the ways in which they differ from the sculpture – which is mostly monochromatic – is in the rich density of their hues. In her sculptures Nogueira tells stories around a room or a field, and her drawings tell stories across the page. Many of them use animals – elephants and rabbits, snails or bears – linked or isolated, superimposed or separate, to convey lightness or weight. They suggest a concentration of the same physical forces which produce the dispersion of her installations.

Nogueira has been drawing in the same way, at the same scale, ever since she was a student. She devotes days to her drawings, hides them and returns some weeks later to finish them off. She draws within both two- and three-dimensional mindsets and combines the conscious and the unconscious: hard work and doodles. For her, drawing is the natural way of thinking – of clarifying her concept. The sculptures and their installations come later, when she has refined that concept out of a process that begins with reading, continues into drawing, and ends in sculpture. This process might be compared to a kind of gradual clarification by which intuition is captured through reading certain key texts, followed up by means of drawings on the page, and finally emerges into the three-dimensional world as everyday objects begin to take on a new character. It is through this process of gestation that Nogueira is able to recognise everyday objects and claim them for herself. Nogueira's screen is blank – the sky, the page, the gallery, the ice rink – and across it coloured markers – flag, kites, fluff, or lines – mark the limits of space coming in and out of focus.

Squaring the Circle

Of all the sculptors in this group, Bill Woodrow probably makes the most self-contained drawings. Drawing, however, is absolutely central to his sculpture, and it is evident that his sculptures were effectively derived from drawn objects. Transposing and remaking is in both; he takes an object and camouflages it in another; he draws an object and veils it in others. It is notable that when Woodrow's sculptures were closest to drawing, he made few drawings. Does he now make so many more because his current sculptures have lost that cut and paste storyline? He certainly draws more when sculptures are away being cast, although it is also broadly true that the sculpture now embraces a more catholic range of fabrication.

Just as Woodrow used ready-made objects as the base images for his sculpture, so he takes images as they are already 'set' on the pages of magazines (the *National Geographic* in particular), copies them freehand on to the page, and then reconfigures their space. The scale is important – or rather playing tricks with scale –

and as we used to see scales incongruously juxtaposed in his sculptures, so now one reason for the *National Geographic*'s fascination is its own juxtaposition of panorama and close-up.

Having placed an object on to his page, Woodrow then fills in the page to give it a setting, and to develop the story – its narrative potential. It is not so much a *horror vacui*, but rather a determination to bring the composition round until he considers it successful. We can see that for Woodrow drawing is something he wants to get right. He doesn't throw drawings away, but that is partly because he doesn't like to let that be necessary, he enjoys making every piece work. The inherent interest of 'getting something right' is harder in sculpture, but therefore more interesting, and this may account for the pre-eminence sculpture continues to enjoy. Getting things right is of abiding interest; and is part of the reason – the different reasons – for making drawings and for making sculptures.

Certain common threads – reasons, attractions, explanations – have emerged in discussing drawing with these sculptors. They may not stand out clearly from the separate individual sections, so perhaps it is worth summarising some overall impressions. They can even be listed.

Sculptors draw:
–   what they cannot make
–   to alleviate the tedium of making
–   so that others can make
–   to do quickly what sculptures do slowly
–   to restore intimacy
–   to verify or restore their subject
–   to imagine shapes without making them, and then make them when they can no longer imagine them
–   to learn or to store, to remember and to forget
–   to get what they cannot get from sculpture: colour, fluidity, chance, distance, forgetfulness.

One thing is abundantly clear; these drawings do have to be discussed separately. They cannot be seen as 'explaining' the sculptures, nor can they be seen as secondary. Their status is shifting, and in some cases has come increasingly to the fore. Drawing has accompanied, marked or caused important shifts in sculptural practice.

Most sculptors have made drawings for as long as they can remember, and certainly before they made sculptures. Drawing is loved for its freedom, its intimacy, its directness. It has few complications. We are perhaps being wrong-headed in enquiring into sculptors' drawings. The drawing is the most natural – the first – expression. The question may be rather, why do their authors then move on to make sculptures?

With very many thanks to the sculptors, to whom I talked on the following dates in 1996: 10 June: Edward Allington; 11 June: Richard Deacon; 4 July: Rachel Whiteread; 19 July: Shirazeh Houshiary; 11 September: Anish Kapoor; 13 September: Grenville Davey; 16 September: Bill Woodrow, Antony Gormley; 4 November: Hermione Wiltshire; 5 November: Alison Wilding; 30 January 1997: Lucia Nogueira and to Wiltshire and Wilding for earlier discussions.

PLATES

All measurements are provided
as height × width × depth.

Caption entries compiled by
Catherine Marshall, Ronan McCrea
and Declan McGonagle.

Rose Finn-Kelcey

Bureau de change
1987
Coins, wooden floor,
spotlights, viewing platform,
closed circuit TV system,
security guard
229 x 152 cm

The installation *Bureau de change* was conceived at the time of the notorious Van Gogh *Sunflowers* sale in 1987 when the painting was sold to the Yasuda and Marine Insurance Company of Tokyo for £24.5 million – the highest price ever paid for an artwork.

In *Bureau de change* £1000 of different denomination coins are arranged into a 7.6×5 feet image of *The Sunflowers* by Vincent Van Gogh laid out on an interposed wooden floor with irregular edges. The gold, silver and copper coins are similar to the tones in the original painting. Says Finn-Kelcey:

'It's very important that I have a range of tones and colours in order for the image to be read. Some of the coins are quite dirty to reflect that the money has been in circulation and passed through people's hands. Once the piece is finished the money has to be bagged up, taken to the bank and goes back into people's pockets.'[1]

The 'Sunflowers' are spotlit, and re-presented through a closed circuit TV system. The monitor is visible, suspended from the gallery ceiling. The work also shares the floor with a seated uniformed security guard on duty. This tableau can all be seen by the viewer who is invested with a greater sense of importance via a specially raised viewing platform. The artist explains:

'I wanted to give the viewer the optimum position from which to see the work, because the work is on the floor, you really need to look down on it to suggest that it's come from the painting. I also wanted to emphasise the relationship between the subject and the viewer and to give the viewer a sense of importance, of being raised. I've been able with the attendant and the surveillance to emphasise the preciousness of the work. But the surveillance is also there to re-present the image – the image on the monitor is almost like the painting, some people come in and think it's a pre-recorded image of the actual painting and it's only when they see the camera they realise that it's a live image that's relayed to the monitor and so again the image has undergone another transformation through electronics as opposed to metal.'

This installation, similar to other works by Rose Finn-Kelcey, confronts the relationship between the real and the illusory. The presence of the guard, another human being within the construction of a tableau, locates the work somewhere between an installation and a performance, but also introduces an unsettling reality into the artifice of artistic constructions.

The version of *Bureau de change* in the Weltkunst Collection is the 'Extended Version', using sterling coinage exhibited at Matt's Gallery, London, 1988. The 'International Version' of *Bureau de change,* shown at the New Museum of Contemporary Art, New York in 1990, used sterling, dollars and yen coins to make up the image of Van Gogh's *Sunflowers.*

[1]This and following quotation in an interview with artist on documentary film *Bureau de change,* Weltkunst Foundation Archive.

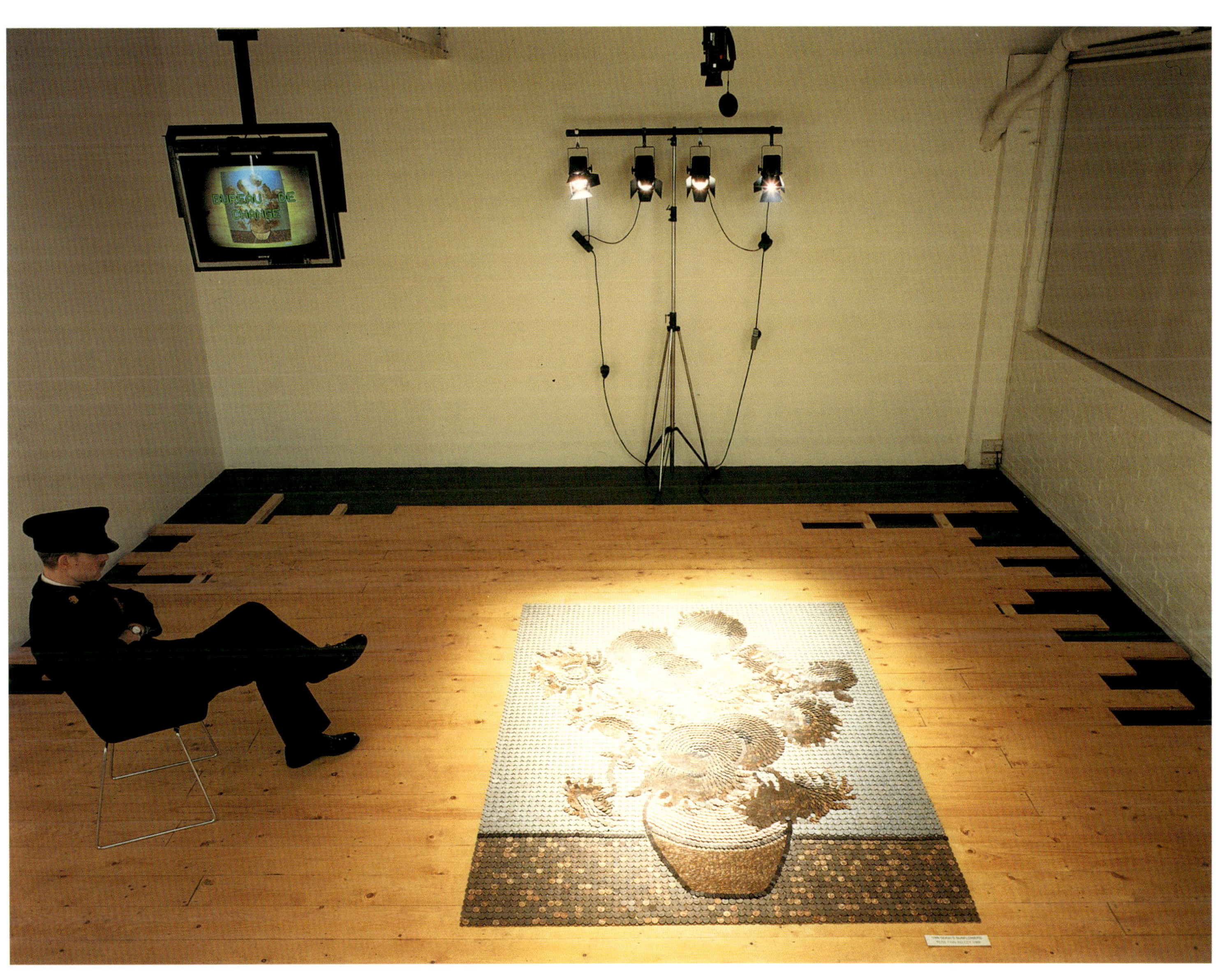
BUREAU DE
CHANGE

Antony Gormley

Seeds
1986
Lead bullets
Unit size: 3.5 cm (length) x 1.1 cm (diameter)

Seeds consists of a small pile of solid lead bullets. These
are cast from an American-made 38-calibre bullet mould.
Gormley's paradoxical juxtapositioning of the potential for
life with the means of ending it is his way of making an
ironic comment on the fact that, as he says, 'human beings
can not only work to feed themselves but also work to kill
each other', which he feels is a kind of comment about
humanity at the end of the twentieth century.

Seeds relates to earlier works by Gormley, such as
Natural selection, where small objects – tools, fruits,
vegetables and weapons – are encased in lead.

With *Seeds,* however, Gormley for the first time made
solid lead objects instead of the usual lead outer 'skin'.
He says:

'What interested me was the idea that the bullets were made to
penetrate the skin, yet were made from the material I'd been
using to re-make the skin of the body. I think it's important that
they are at rest . . . which is the way that gravity allows things to
have a kind of structure which reinforces their inertia or their
benign state. This is in distinction to how they would be, were
they fired from a gun.'[1]

[1] This and subsequent quotations by Antony Gormley in conversation with
Ronan McCrea, The Irish Museum of Modern Art, 1996

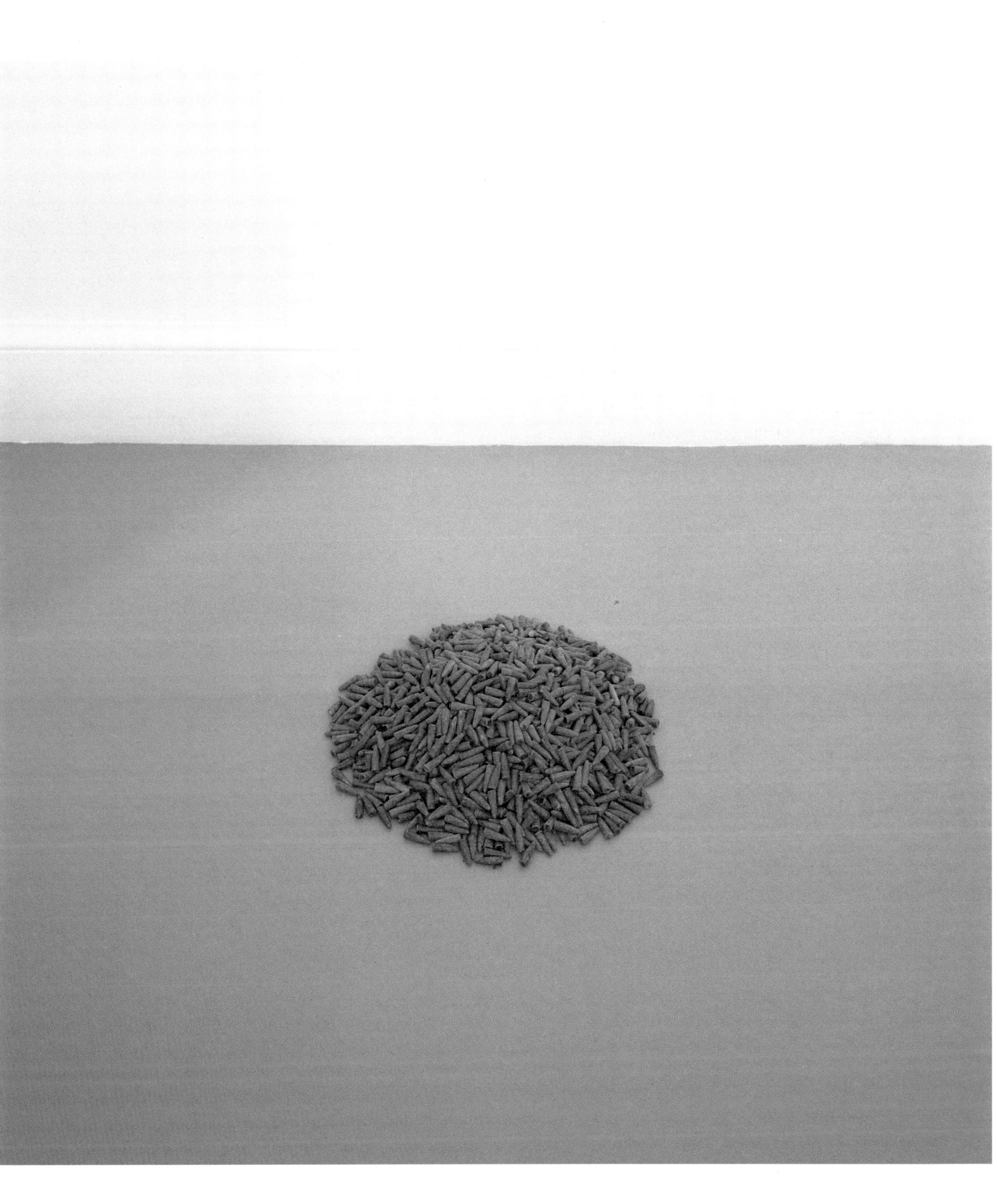

Antony Gormley
Sick
1987-9
Lead, fibreglass, plaster, air
192 x 51 x 77 cm

Antony Gormley's sculpture takes its starting point from the presence of the body or human form.

Sick is an early example of the 'body case' sculptures, cast in lead from the artist's own body, for which Gormley has gained wide recognition. Using his own body in the casting process is important to Gormley:

'It's my closest experience of matter. It's a very simple thing to say but in fact it's the truth. I regard my body as the vehicle through which all my impressions of the world come, and equally I want to use my body as the vehicle through which anything that I have to communicate with the world can be carried.'

The title of the work reminds us of the toxic nature of the material from which it is made and which is used to line coffins, yet also forms a protection against radio-activity. The absolute stillness of the pose suggests sickness or disease, disorientation arising out of the way the figure projects over empty space, defying 'normal' gravity laws. Gormley suggests:

'The work has an effect on your feeling about the stability of the room. The position of the figure is one of pleading or supplication, associated with the Christian tradition that has framed Western societal development. . . . Like a lot of the works from around that period that stand on the wall, it inserted itself into the architecture on its own terms.'

The sculpture, while being an object in space, is not separated from the world of the viewer by the traditional sculptural device of a plinth and yet there are many contradictions inherent in the material, pose and its position in space:

'The whole idea is about disorientation, to make you feel less certain about the narrative that has brought you to the place where you confront the work . . . the way it is fixed on the wall is very important in that the head is where the head would be were it standing, but it doesn't stand . . . it stands on the wall as it were.'

Antony Gormley sees a definite relationship between *Seeds* and *Sick*, both of which were made at the same time and exhibited together at the Salvatore Ala Gallery in New York. He sees *Sick* as referring to a state of being that is prevalent in society, coexisting with the violence implicit in *Seeds*.

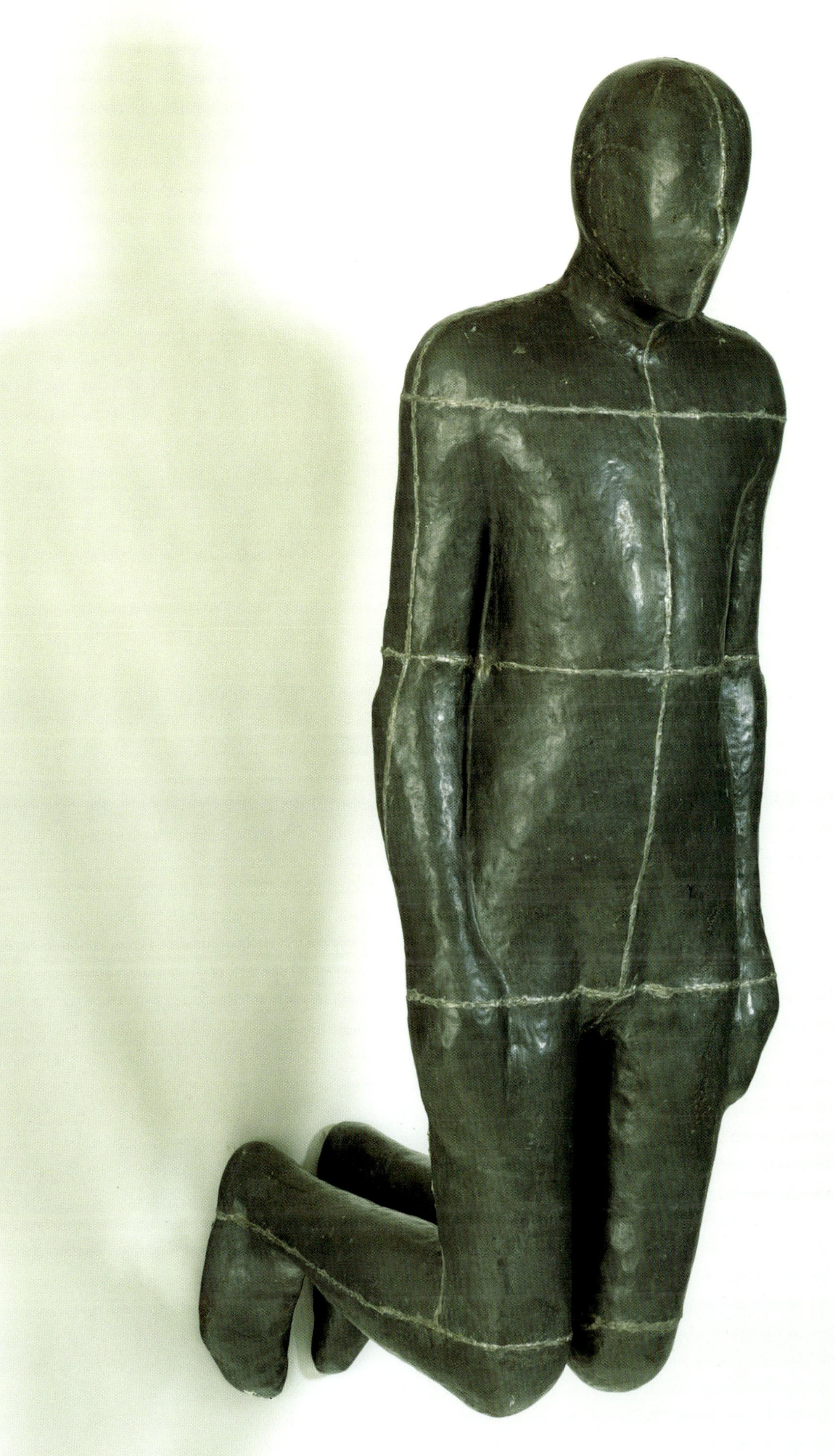

Hamish Fulton

Fourteen works
1982-9
Fourteen offset lithographs in portfolio case bound in black buckram
(Note: This work is also entered in the section 'Works on Paper' on p.120 as it is classified by the artist as a sculpture and also as a work on paper.)

Fourteen works was conceived between 1982 and 1989 by the artist as a series of walks in places as far apart as Australia, Nepal, Portugal, Britain and Canada. *Fourteen works* is sculptural because it is spatial. The space it inhabits is the mind and spirit of the viewer which is triggered by the textual configuration of signs and ideas in the prints. The work is made on behalf of nature of which humanity is, of course, one part.

Fulton's early works often take the form of photographs with texts. On a walk, he would take/make one image which would represent the whole journey. These were also recorded in his notebooks. The artist has said that 'his artform is the short journey, made by walking in the landscape'. His walks, undertaken since the early 1970s, originate in a concern for the land and the landscape – what today is referred to as 'environmental concern'. Fulton presents the increasingly difficult possibility of a human connection with nature, made actual by the walk. Several prints record journeys literally, although the map and its implied prescriptions in *Fourteen coast to coast walks, British Isles* 1971-87 is unusual and untypical.

While the model of the figure with notebook and/or camera in the landscape is akin to nineteenth-century projected global exploration and classification, Fulton's work carries none of the innocence of that period. There is a sense of urban noise, psychological and actual, shadowing the walker, on which he would like to turn his back.

Fourteen works was published in a single portfolio of prints in 1989. When produced in this form *Fourteen works* was the largest collection of prints he had made. The form of each of the offset lithographs is based on notes made by the artist during each of the walks. There is a direct relationship between the form of the immediate experience, its notation and the final artwork.

Individual titles, dates and sizes:

1. *Untitled*. Australia, 1982. 46.5 × 111 cm

2. *Mountain skyline*. Nepal, 1983. 86.5 × 99.3 cm

3. *Untitled*. Alberta, 1984. 72 × 101.6 cm

4. *Seven winds*. Scotland, 1985. 107 × 82.9 cm

5. *Untitled*. Japan, 1986. 98.1 × 68.9 cm

6. *Untitled*. Brittany, 1987. 47 × 110.7 cm

7. *Untitled*. Twenty-one-day walk, 1987. 38.2 × 111.8 cm

8. *Fourteen coast to coast walks*. British Isles, 1971-87. 98.3 × 70 cm

9. *Full moon*. Kent, 1988. 72 × 99 cm

10. *Rock fall echo dust*. Baffin Island, 1988. 104.2 × 88 cm

11. *No thoughts counting seven paces on Senjoh Dake at sunset*. Japan, 1988. 60.4 × 101.7 cm

12. *Twenty-one walks walking from one to twenty-one days*. Various countries, 1971-88. 70.6 × 111.8 cm

13. *Dead dogs*. Portugal and Spain, 1989. 80 × 111.8 cm

14. *Untitled*. Nepal, 1989. 78.7 × 95.8 cm

ROCK FALL ECHO DUST

A TWELVE AND A HALF DAY WALK ON BAFFIN ISLAND ARCTIC CANADA SUMMER 1988

Anish Kapoor

Wound
1988
Limestone and pigment
308 x 432 x 331 cm

'I don't want to make sculptures about form, but about belief, or about passion, about experience that is outside of material form.'[1]

In *Wound* three large pieces of limestone sit flat on the floor. The forms are roughly shaped, with the marks of both the quarry and the subsequent carving present on the surface. Carved out along the axis of the stones are curving cavities which are coloured with a deep red pigment. A long ridge-like form sits vertically on the wall. This is entirely covered in pigment which is spread on to the wall and floor. Says Kapoor:

'One of the reasons I have always used pigment is that it has an incredible materiality, a real physical presence, a real "hereness". But it is also made of nothing. It is made of infinitesimal particles that in a sense are nothing. So it is physical and air at the same time.'[2]

Wound can be seen as a transitional work in Kapoor's oeuvre. In earlier work loose pigment was used to disguise the identity of the material and its surface. Later the material, such as stone, is often evident, the dense pigment present in an interior space cut into the material, creating an experience of a void. *Wound* is also perhaps untypical in that the artist's hand is visible in the manufacture of the work. Chisel marks are present in the carved-out concave areas, whereas in earlier works the surface was completely covered in pigment and in later works interiors are bored into the material without leaving obvious traces of carving. This also marks the development of a way of working with concepts of interior and exterior: 'I have always engaged with interiority, that which is inside. Interiority has now become evident, where in the early work it was implied.'[3]

Germano Celant suggests that *Wound*

'is a dialectic between inside and outside, where the stone is "wounded" and displays a pair of open wide lips to the viewer's gaze . . . carrying on the artist's concern with the mechanism of life as a play of antagonistic poles like Eros and Thanatos. . . . Nature shows that the inert – stone – can be reanimated, discovering a lost spiritual and fleshy potency.'[4]

[1] Interview with Iwona Blaszczyk, *Objects and Sculpture*, London, 1981
[2] Interview with Stephanie du Tan, *Journal of Art*, November 1990
[3] Interview with Constance Lewellen, *View*, vol.VII, no.4, San Francisco, 1991
[4] Germano Celant, *Artist as Sacerdos. Anish Kapoor*, Thames and Hudson, 1996

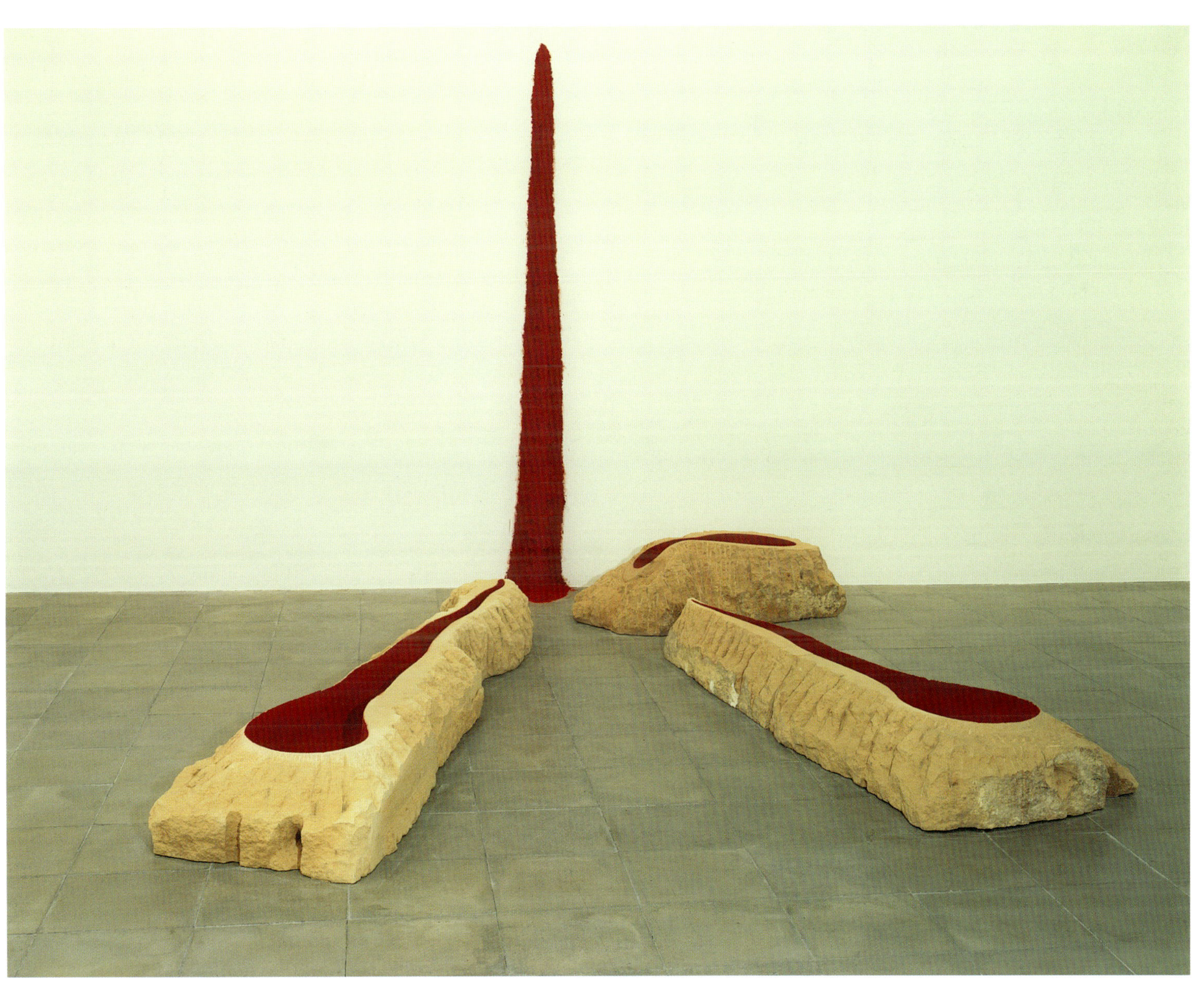

Jacqueline Poncelet

**Clay, bronze, wood
and fabric**
1988
Clay, bronze, wood, fabric
96 x 191 x 32 cm

The pair of sculptural objects in *Clay, bronze, wood and fabric* combine the materials of wood and bronze and the two classic sculptural processes of carving and casting. They are organic, visceral forms placed on a rectangle of patterned curtain fabric. There exists a tension between the conflation of these sensual sculptural forms and the floral pattern of the cloth. David Ward considers that Poncelet's work manifests 'a frank and imprudent sexuality in the confluence of form, material, and importantly surface pattern.'[1]

Poncelet comments:

'I think this piece inhabits a space in the same way that painting does, exactly because the objects are on that piece of cloth, so it's not an independent object in the way a sculpture normally is. It actually has clearly defined boundaries that imply that it doesn't exist beyond the edges of that cloth. After I made this piece I went on to spend most of my time painting and then later I went back to working with carpets, specifically with that idea in mind of defining the territory that objects survive in. The other thing about the pattern was that it's quite shimmering in the same way that the work is, so in a sense if you could see the work two-dimensionally you'd see echoes of the objects in the pattern'.[2]

Patterned fabrics and carpets are used extensively in Poncelet's work. The artist comments on the material in this piece:

'The fabric is a curtain. The pattern is important because I wanted it to be something that had a history . . . and it's a very conventional piece of English fabric, it has a lot to do with a particular period of interior design. You know the way the English are such pirates. It is a Persian pattern that's been literally adapted in an English manner.'[3]

Perhaps this pattern stands as a metaphor of cultural containment of the 'Other': 'Nature', the female, and the 'exotic Persian' all within the repressive propriety of the English interior.

Poncelet's work can also be placed in an area of feminist practice 'that refuses to observe the boundaries between what has conventionally been regarded as craft and fine art'.[4] Within the traditional hierarchy of decorative art at the bottom and the human form or expressive gesture at the top, Poncelet's practice addresses the role of decoration in both defining social space – the question of what should go where – and how 'the decorative' can create and manipulate space, volume and surface.

[1]Spotlight Series, Arts Council Collection, 1994
[2]In conversation with Helen O'Donoghue, The Irish Museum of Modern Art, 1995
[3]Ibid
[4]Press release for *The Decorative Sublime*, Museum of Modern Art, Oxford, 1995

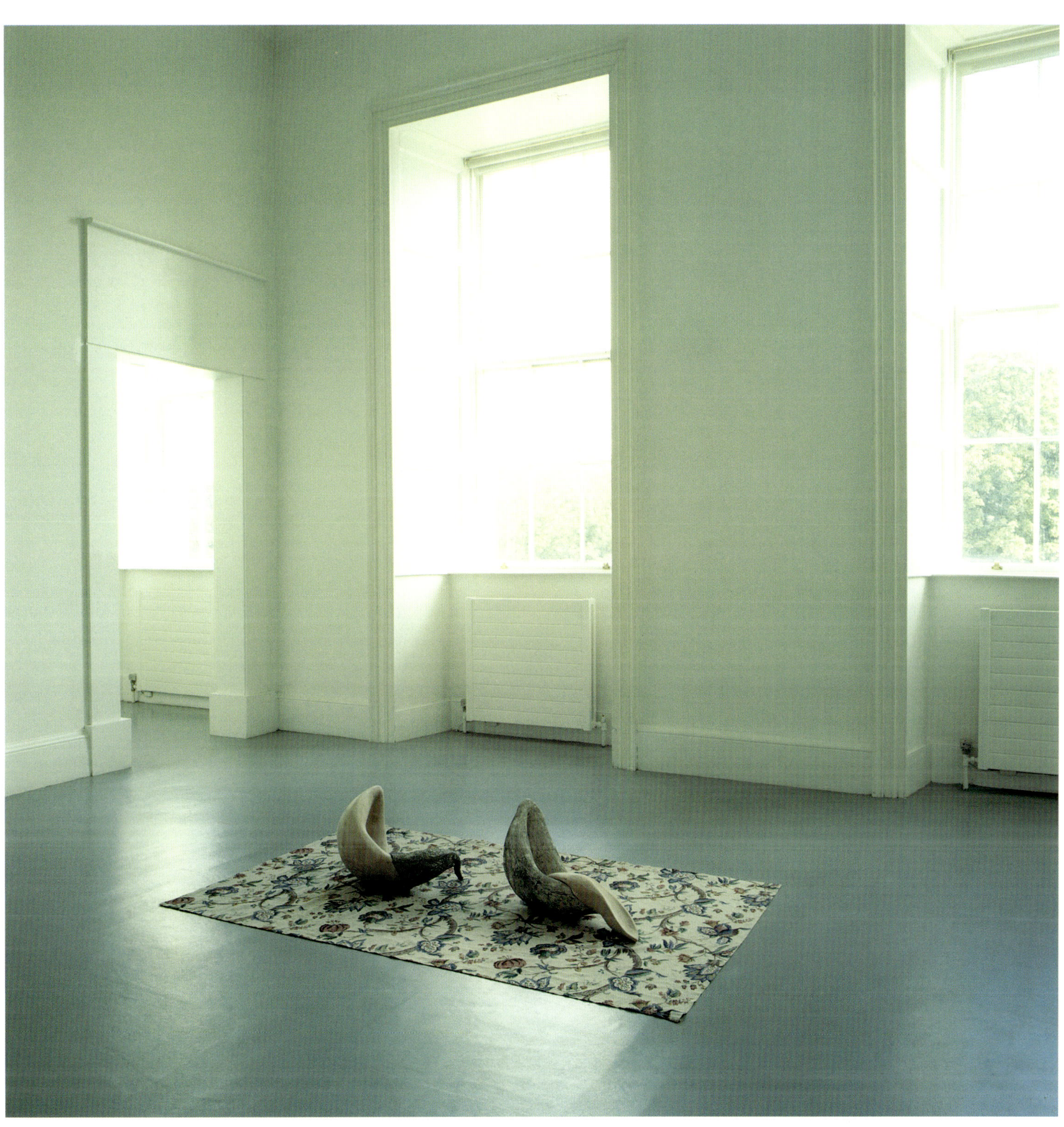

Alison Wilding

Stormy weather
1987
Galvanised steel, oil paint
and bronze
225 x 115 x 170 cm

The relationship between process, materials and form were central to Alison Wilding's concerns in creating *Stormy weather*. The work explores the physical relationship between two sheets of metal which are free-standing, one element of which is slim and upright, the other broad and, according to Wilding, 'sort of kneeling'. A third contrasting element, a cast bronze plate approximately 3 cm thick, lies on the floor in the space between the two vertical elements. The surface of the metal is marked and textured in a way reminiscent of sand washed by a recent tide. References to water in one sense or another have been features of Wilding's work, since she finds it 'an amazing medium and element that I never use and yet I often allude to'.

The meteorological title was chosen to 'bring to the piece the idea of the elements' but also to invest the work with a psychological dimension which suggests a kind of state between two objects or two people, which Wilding sees as 'some kind of stand-off'.[1]

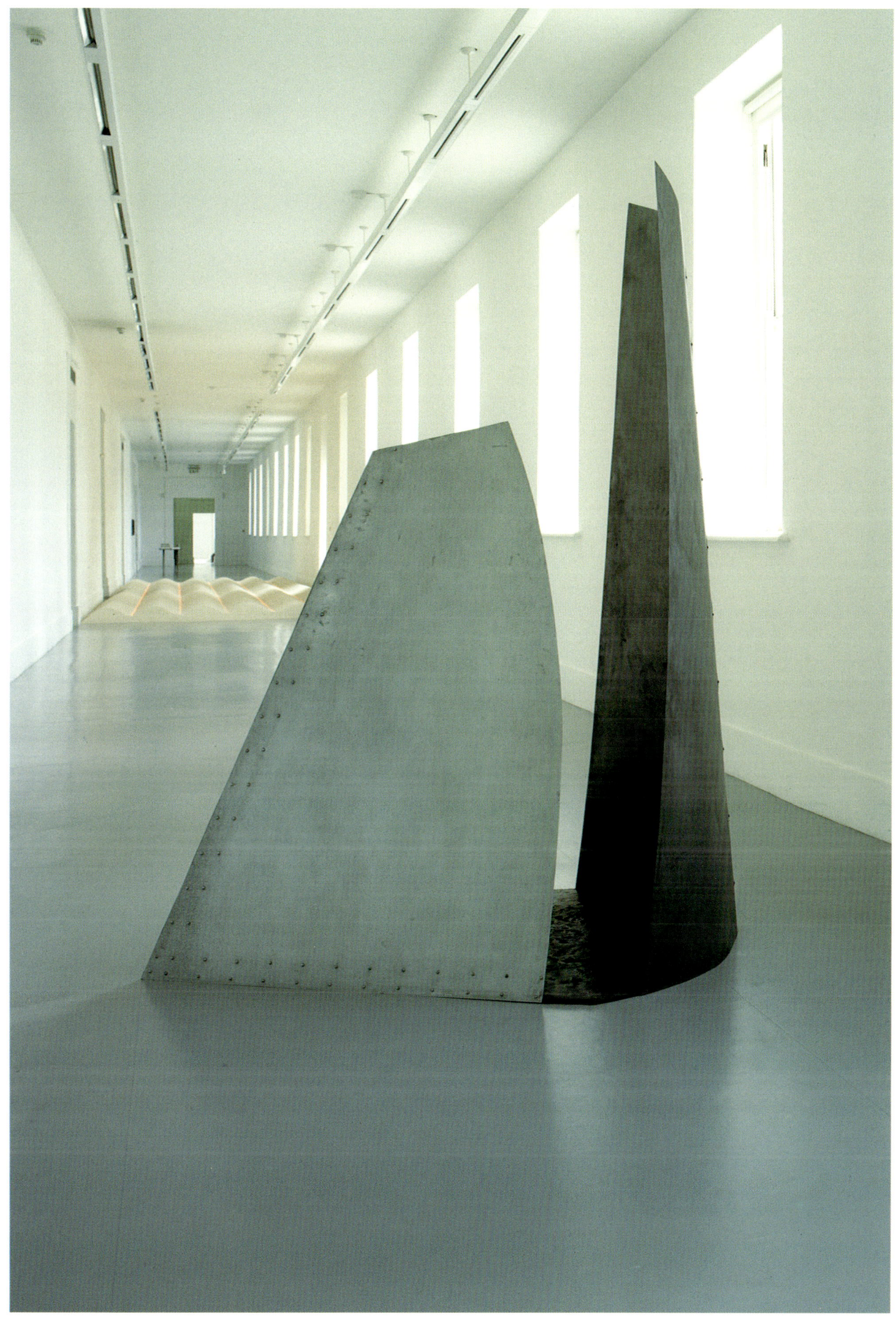

Alison Wilding
Into the dark
1986
Limewood, various pigments,
lead
12.5 x 19 x 5.5 cm

Into the dark is one of a number of wall-mounted
sculptures by Wilding. 'This piece is about getting to the
inside of the work and what is revealed when you get
there.' In common with other work of this period, this
sculpture started with the notion of trying to get to the
centre of the piece of wood which, for the artist, formed a
'kind of excavation to find the heart of it'. The form has
been carved through the centre, creating a hollow space.
The naturally pale wood is coloured with graphite and oil
paint. The space at the top is plugged with cast lead poured,
when molten, on to the wood. While Wilding's work is
resolutely abstract there are often figurative allusions
present. For instance, in this work, Wilding sees
anthropomorphic implications when the sculpture is
viewed from the front. 'It had the look of a classical bust,
which is very severe without a head or neck. . . . There
is only this opening with a puddle of lead.' Another
consequence of casting with lead is that when viewed from
beneath, the surface of the lead is suggestive of a nut or a
seed. As Wilding says: 'It's almost organic, like seeing the
inside of a natural form, whereas from the outside, the
piece is very severe.'

This work, in common with *Stormy weather,* engages
the viewer very actively. Wilding insists that to experience
the work fully the viewer must make an effort to get
involved: 'You have to enter it in some sense . . . it isn't
about making a reading from fifteen paces and walking
away.'

<hr>

[1]This and other quotations from Alison Wilding in conversation with
Ronan McCrea, The Irish Museum of Modern Art, 1995

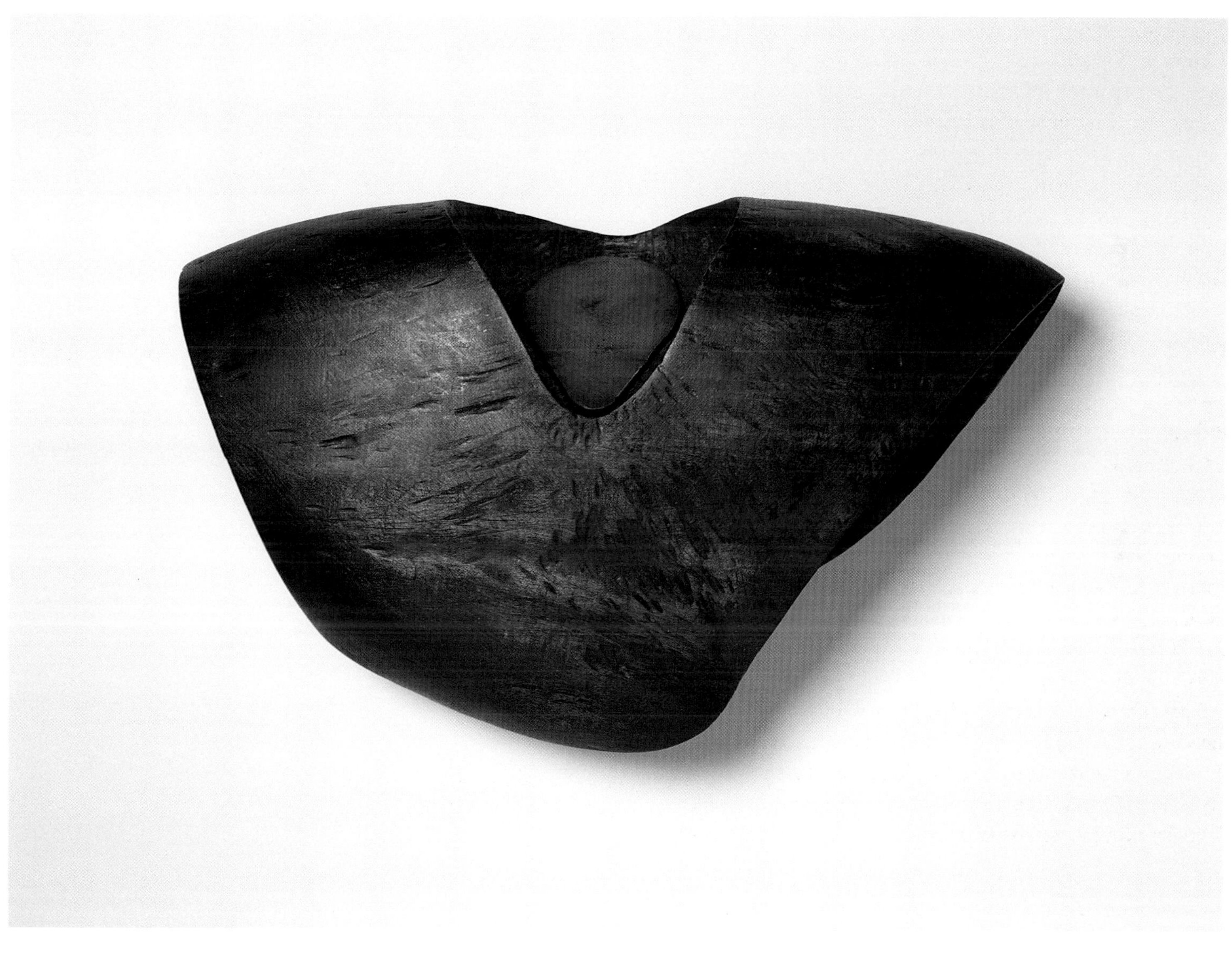

Richard Wilson

**She came in through the
bathroom window**
1989
Mixed media (installation at
Matt's Gallery)

She came in through the bathroom window, a title taken from the Joe Cocker song of the same name, was conceived as a site-specific installation at Matt's Gallery, London in 1989. Wilson's work involved the removal of a section of a steel-framed window from the wall of the gallery, repositioning it inside the room. The trajectory from its original position to the new location inside the gallery was enclosed by a box-like construction. The top and bottom of this construction was made from soft-board panelling fitted into a metal framework and the sides from heavy plastic tarpaulin.

Wilson states:

'It's an installation piece not an object. I like activating architectural spaces as sculpture; the space, the window and the remaining area around the window will be part and parcel of the total experience as the viewer comes into the room.'[1]

This alteration to the gallery changes the relationship of the inside and outside, as Michael Newman has noted in his catalogue essay on Richard Wilson:

'It's as if the outside had been dragged into the interior space; and conversely, as if the interior were the outside of the space defined by the removed window and the structure added by the artist.'[2]

Following the invitation to make a work at Matt's Gallery, Wilson sought to create a work specifically in contrast to his much acclaimed installation *20:50*. In this 1987 work the gallery became a half-filled container for a lake of used sump oil, which the visitor experienced by walking along a narrow steel walkway built like a trench into the centre of the oil-filled room. The black liquid acted like a perfect mirror of the space above.

'In the oil piece *20:50* people were amazed by the sense of illusion, the psychological experience of seeing the reflection of the gallery architecture in the oil, something that wasn't real. In *She came in through the bathroom window* the point of the piece is its total physicality, the fact that the window has been removed and relocated and the viewer can touch and see through it. The work has an incredibly physical presence.'[3]

The process of working is important for an understanding of *She came in through the bathroom window*. Wilson begins with a series of drawings and maquettes. A feasibility study is carried out to ascertain engineering and financial viability. Throughout this process the work changes, for example in relation to the use of suitable materials. The final position for the window was chosen by the artist after mounting the removed window on a portable gantry and experimenting with different locations.

Regarding the ownership of *She came in through the bathroom window*, a site-specific work, Robin Klassnick, director of Matt's, in interview before the acquisition, likened the transaction to buying the rights to a play:

'If someone wanted the piece, Richard could use any particular window (it could even be in a house); it's the idea of pulling the window indoors. The idea behind this work is for sale.'[4]

Two drawings and two working maquettes for *She came in through the bathroom window* are owned by the Weltkunst Foundation Collection in addition to archive material.

---

[1] Interview with Robin Klassnick, *The Late Show*, BBC Television, 1989
[2] Michael Newman, *From the Fire to the Light*, Exhibition Catalogue, Matt's Gallery / Museum of Modern Art, Oxford / Arnolfini, Bristol, 1989
[3] Interview, BBC Television, 1989
[4] Ibid

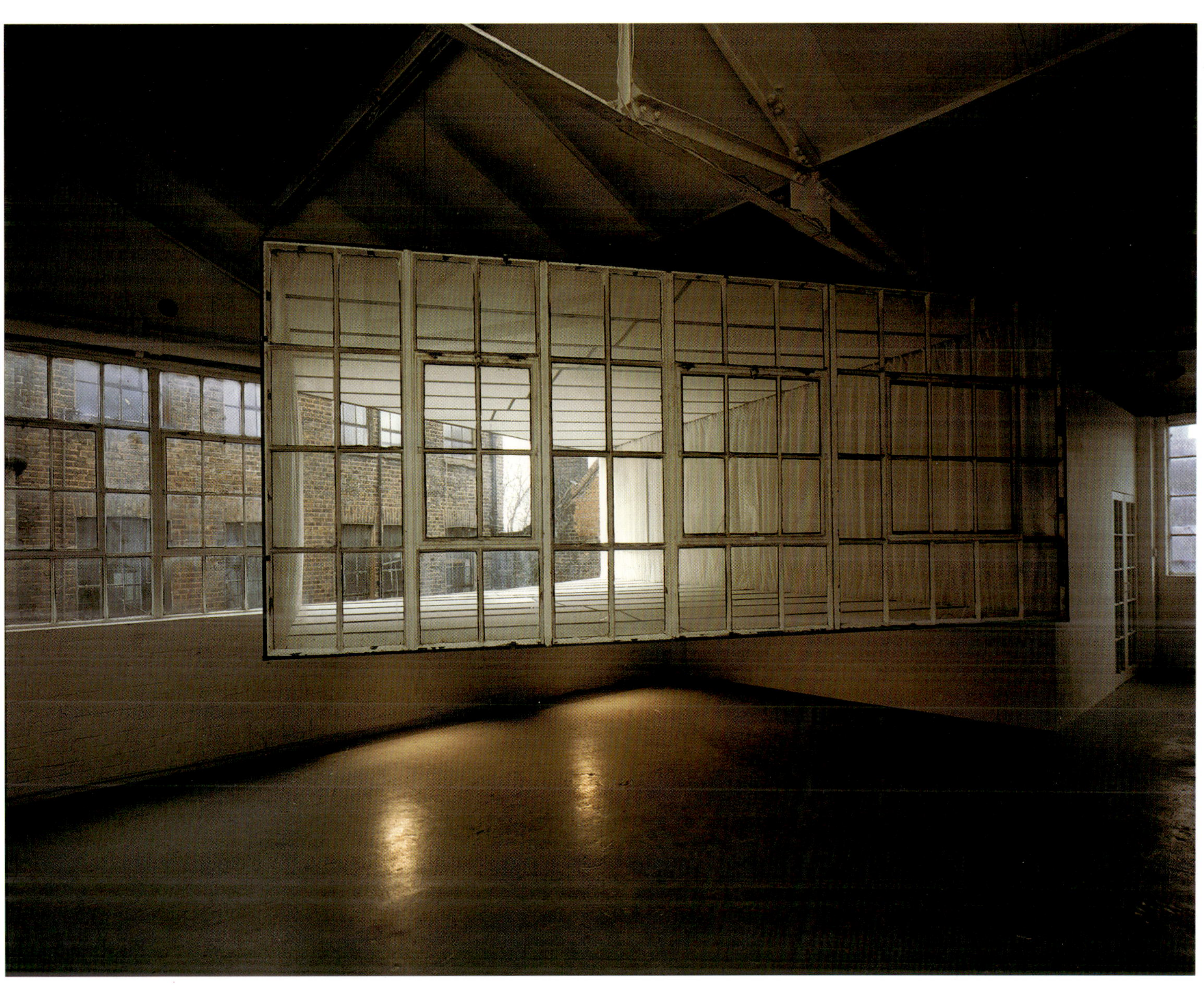

Tony Cragg

Untitled
1988
Bronze
210 x 210 x 285 cm

Untitled is one of a series of large- to medium-scale bronze sculptures by Tony Cragg, the forms of which are derived from scientific laboratory vessels. Unlike other cast bronze works in this series which include two-part sculptures featuring a pipette and a flask, this work has a singular element taking the form of a glass bottle or flask. The work reveals Cragg's ongoing interest in science and technology and the world of manufacturing. This is expressed by the use of a diversity of materials with a conventional commitment to sculptures as objects complete in themselves.

The sculptural dynamic of *Untitled* seems to articulate the position of the gigantic vessel in two positions, upright and lying on its side. The sweeping contour or 'open lip' articulates all the dynamic points in between these two static positions. Cragg notes:

'At the point at which Einstein said there is no such thing as matter, he didn't talk about the particles of things, he talked about things being a chain of events. . . . The sort of work that has occupied me since the mid-1980s is work where the substances develop a body – things like bottles, containers just wrap around surfaces. They become metaphors for bodies of some kind.'

In his 1995 monograph on Tony Cragg, Germano Celant has linked this shift in Cragg's work (in which *Untitled* is included) with processes of casting: glass, bronze, aluminium cast iron that

'lead him to favour masses and membranes. By eschewing fragmentation and segmentation (in his earlier work) the telluric force of the material builds up and forms solid heavy entities'.[1]

These works lead to notions of transformation and alchemical processes and a consideration of the vessels used in these processes, such as test-tubes, pestle and mortars and wombs in gestation. Celant sees Cragg's more recent interest in organic forms, fissures and cavities as a natural development of this investigation. Cragg states:

'My whole activity is governed by three thematic areas of which the most important one is that of my relationship to the natural world. I also want to have a relationship with the objects and materials around me. And this, which includes the ever growing non-visual information world as well, is the second area. The third constitutes itself out of these two. It has to do with the way functionalism shapes the man-made world'.

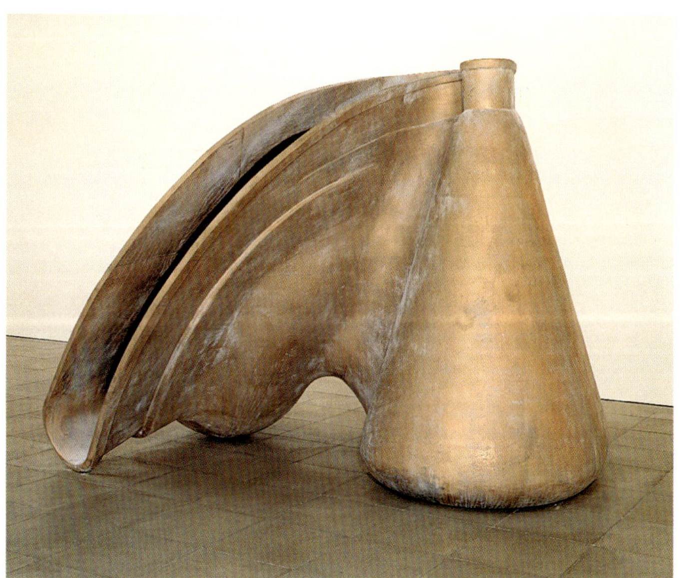

---

[1]Germano Celant, *Tony Cragg*, Thames and Hudson, 1995

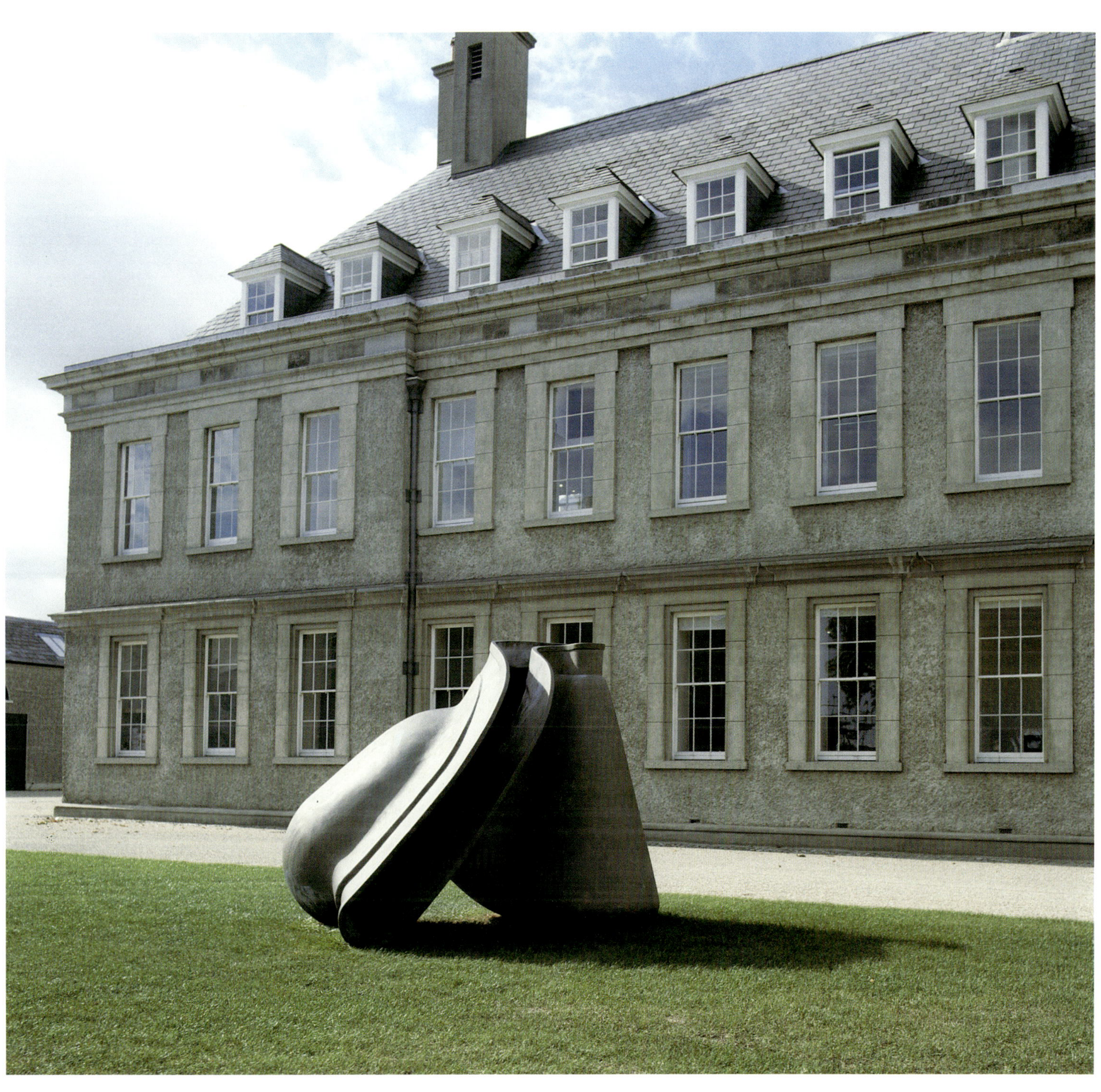

Bill Woodrow

In case of
1988-90
Glass, plastic, wax, coins,
water
84 x 70 x 51 cm

In case of consists of a tank aquarium or glass box filled
with water with a pile of clear plastic cutlery on the
bottom. Floating on top is a block of wax imprinted with
the shape of a key. Inside the tank float two turtles made of
glass, one 'diving' at an angle and one resting at the bottom.
An axe made from glass leans against the side of the tank
and inside the head of the axe is a number of coins.

Woodrow notes that this sculpture is unusual for him in
that it is made almost entirely from glass. It is one of three
or four sculptures made in 1988, during a visit to the glass
school in Pilchuck near Seattle in the USA.

'Well it's called *In case of* which is a reference to those cases with
a hammer which say "In case of emergency break glass". The axe
is glass, nearly everything is glass so it's very fragile. So in a sense
not only would the aquarium shatter if you hit it with the axe but
the axe would also break, so it's a sort of balanced situation . . . it's
a comment on many things, from environmental pollution to how
consumerism fuels that (problem) and the necessary but
apparently futile attempts that humans make to sort things out.
Now these efforts have to be made and I support them fully, but
sometimes one has to think about what environmental activists
do . . . and their effect seems so minuscule, that one can get
depressed about it. The work is in some way about all those
things. The axe is non-functional, the actual cutting blade is full
of money which is a reference that maybe finance and money is
one way that we can deal with environmental problems, that the
axe is the emergency hammer if you like, or it could also be seen
the opposite way in that the currency is the problem, the gold
underlies all the problems. The work flicks back and forth
(between these readings) all the time . . . and I don't want to
dictate how people respond to it.'[1]

---

[1] Interview with Helen O'Donoghue, The Irish Museum of Modern Art,
1995

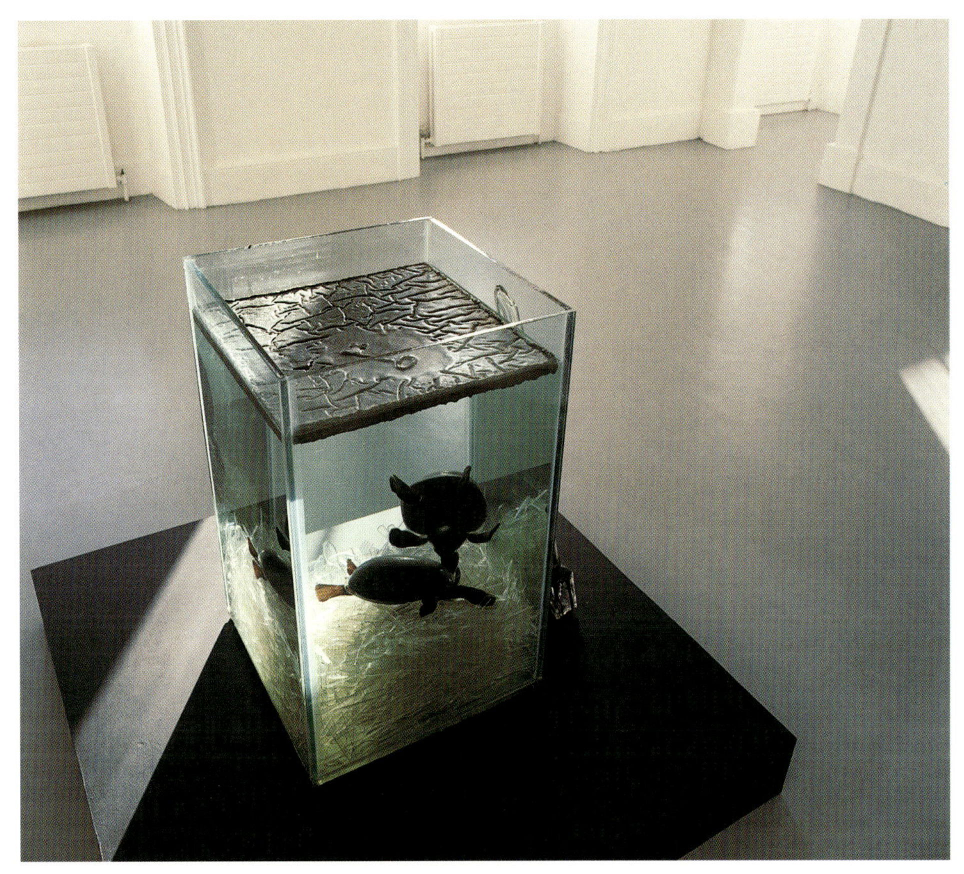

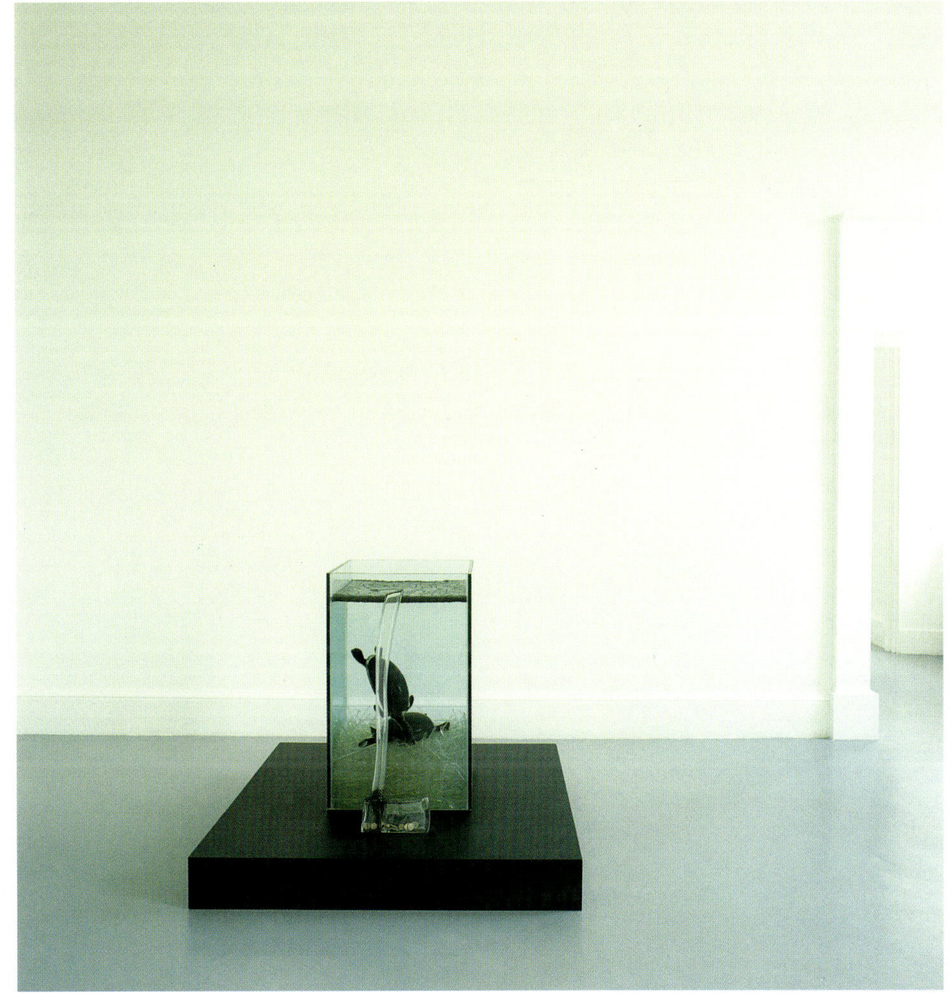

Grenville Davey

Fat edge
1989
Rusted steel
183 cm (diameter) x 31.5 cm (depth)

'I looked at the ceiling. "There is little to be seen there," I said, "except a blue bottle that looks dead." The sergeant looked up and pointed his stick. "That's not a blue bottle," he said. "That is Gogarty's oathouse".'

Flann O'Brien, *The Third Policeman*, MacGibbon and Kee, 1967

Grenville Davey's sculpture has an ambiguous quality, belonging neither to the world of functional objects nor the world of pure form, Charles Hall suggests that Davey's work

'occupies a paradoxical territory. The sculpture doesn't exactly look like anything, it just gives the impression that it might do'.[1]

Fat edge belongs to what the artist terms 'a family of works'. These works, including a floor sculpture *Plane* (1989), are essentially 'overscaled' in terms of their relationship to their referent image. The form of *Fat edge* does not derive from a specific object so much as from the dynamic of the surface of steel being displaced on an enlarged scale, and as with much of Davey's work, *Fat edge* sits between categories. Tim Marlow suggests:

'*Fat edge* contains the idea of a parallel physical and mechanical gesture, the work suggesting both a giant light switch and the brush of a thumb or finger across a steel disk. Like other works . . . it demands an act of positive perception in order to realise the gesture and in this respect the viewer takes control.'[2]

Fat edge is one of a number of works that take the circle as a starting point for the development of the sculpture. Davey sees the motif of a circle in his work as somewhat of a generalisation. Geometric or Platonic perfection is not Davey's ambition. The sculptures push against the formal rules they seem to follow. While constructed with exacting craftsmanship, circles are, more often than not, ellipses. The depth of edge on *Fat edge* is thicker on one side of the circle than the other. The geometry can be seen as imperfect. The circle seems to manifest itself with built-in 'faults' that the artist admits in the work are 'easy to pass over'. The circular motif can be read as a sort of framing device or edge that is often the starting point for the work.

Previous works in this sculptural 'family' were constructed in hardboard, the surface evenly painted in often neutral colours. The artist regards these works as theatrical and they struggle to maintain some sort of (sculptural) authority. *Fat edge* was planned as a hardboard work and a full-scale version in this material was constructed by Davey; however, the opportunity to fabricate the work in sheet steel opened up possibilities for manipulating the surface qualities of the material. This was the first work by Davey to be fabricated in sheet steel. The rusted quality of the steel was developed by the artist in a similar way to the treatment of the surface of a painting.

[1] Charles Hall, *Art Review*, London, 1992
[2] Tim Marlow, *The Parallel Gaze*, Grenville Davey Exhibition Catalogue, Musée Départementale de Rochechouart; Württembergischer Kunstverein, Stuttgart

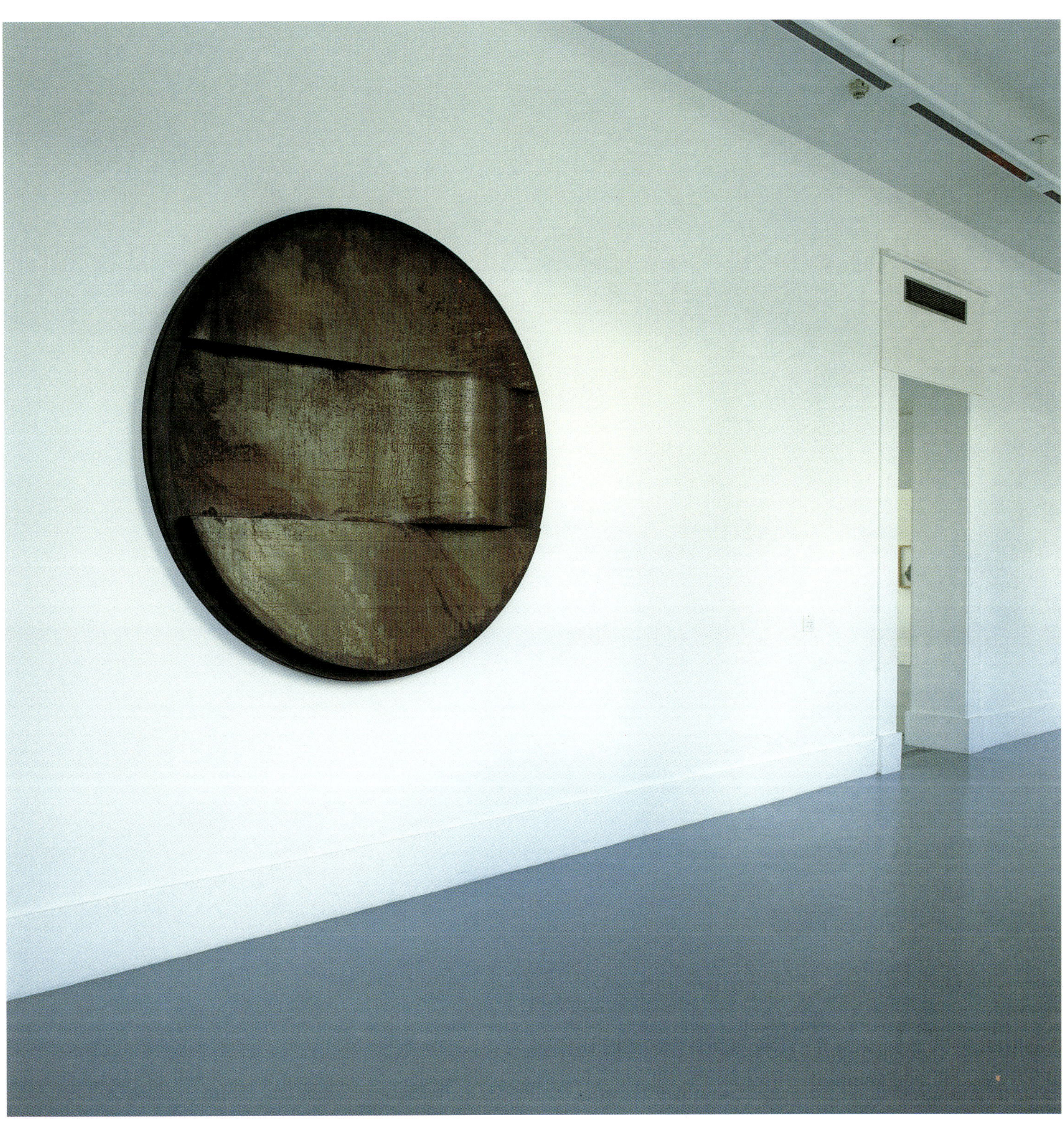

Edward Allington

**Three steps towards
the sea**
1985
Leather bound book, wood,
bronze
Various dimensions

Three steps towards the sea is one of a series of works where sculptures are concealed within books. Allington terms this series 'Book Works, or Concealed Bronzes'. Old ledgers are a source of paper for Allington's drawings. The paper in this book was unusable but the spine and covers were suitable for the artwork. The three bronze elements were loosely modelled from sea shells in wax and cast directly as unique bronzes.

Allington's work addresses questions about the setting for modern sculpture. In *Three steps towards the sea* he fantasises about an 'ideal space for his work hiding on a library shelf for illicit enjoyment',[1] as an alternative to its 'natural' home in the gallery or museum.

James Roberts notes that in the twentieth century 'high' art and sculpture in particular have become increasingly locked into placement in the spaces of the art gallery or museum. The scale of post-war sculpture relates to that of the purpose-built art gallery space. This, however, has not always been the case. In the eighteenth century, with the rise of the 'Gentleman', connoisseur collections of antiquities, paintings, medals and curios were incorporated into the decorative interiors of homes.

Allington states:

'The thing that fascinates me about the small bronzes in general is that they are sort of awkward, sort of muck down on genre and part of the thing that really fascinates me about them is that they belong in the home, not in the art gallery. It's the sort of object that isn't proper art anymore.'[2]

Three steps towards the sea can potentially exist in different modes of display or of non-display – a hidden state. Allington says:

'I am fascinated by the idea of smuggling and also by the idea that most of the time works of art are hidden in boxes or crates [in storage]. I am also fascinated by notions of what pleasure is in relationship to works of art.'

He perceives a link between pleasure and secrecy or invisibility in this work:

'In many ways I'm trying to negotiate what I feel to be one of the most important aspects of conceptual art. I see my practice as a direct result of my admiration for the conceptual art which came together in the late Sixties and Seventies, and one thing that is so important about that contribution is that it brings [out] those things that are invisible, those things you make in your mind, where one's pleasure in something isn't just to do with materials. It's to do with a lot of other things.'

Asked how he chose these shell-like forms to use in this bookwork, the artist replies:

'It's a sort of case within a case . . . shells or containers are like garments, they are like clothes, there is a certain amount of poignancy to them.'

---

[1]Appendix. *Edward Allington: Pictured Bronzes*, Exhibition Catalogue, 1991, Kohji Ogura Gallery, Nagoya, Japan. Essays by Shin Ichi Nakazawa and James Roberts
[2]This and other unattributed quotations from Edward Allington in an interview with Ann Davern and Helen O'Donoghue, The Irish Museum of Modern Art, 1966.

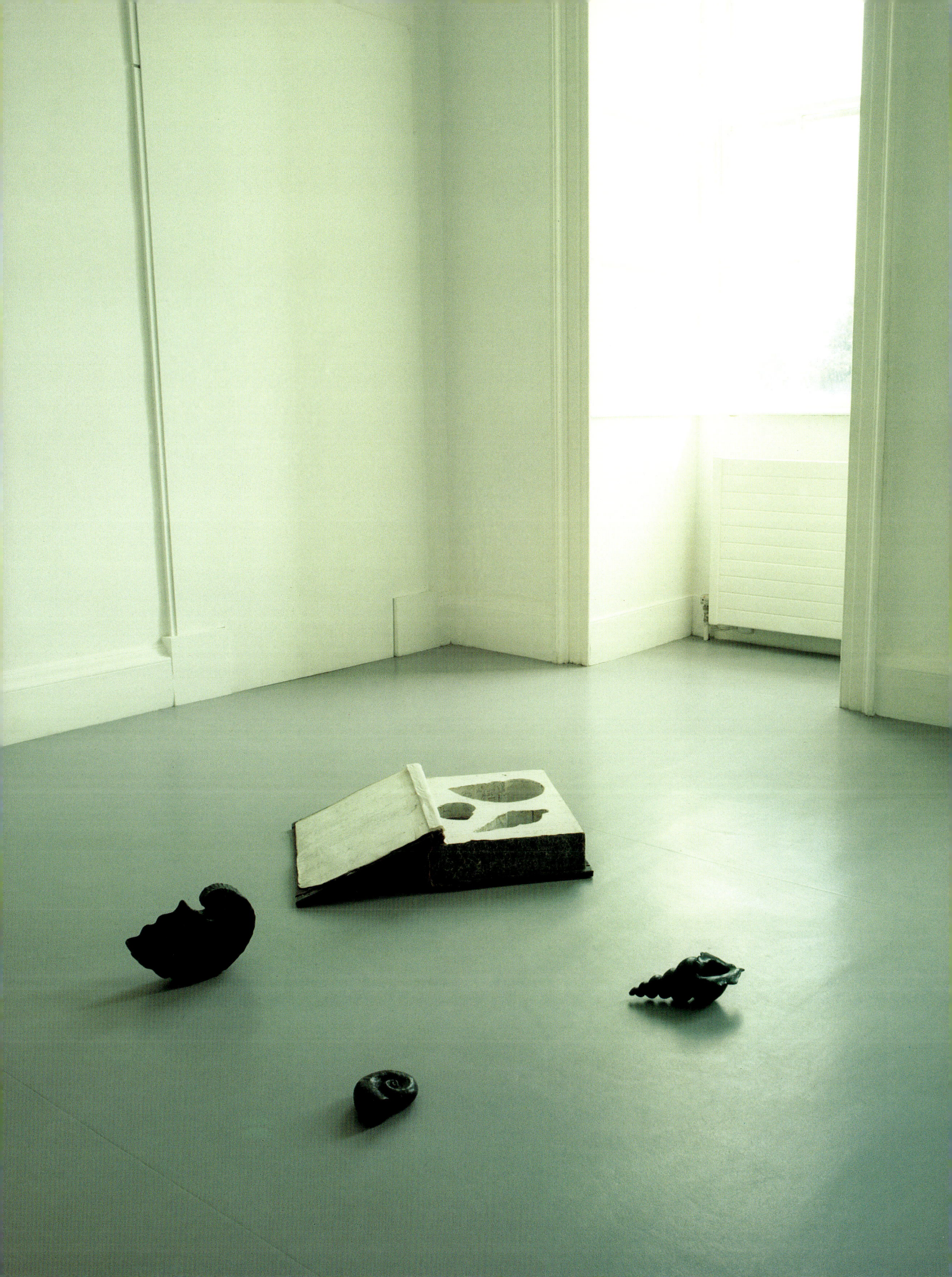

Edward Allington
¹ **Salammbo**
1985-6
Bronze
Edition of 6
18.5 x 25 x 15.5 cm

Edward Allington
² **The source**
1986
Bronze
Edition of 6
22 x 20 x 16 cm

Edward Allington
³ **Caritas Romana**
1986
Bronze
Edition of 6
17 x 30 x 23 cm

Edward Allington
⁴ **With hidden vessel**
1986
Bronze
Unique
29.5 x 30.5 x 18 cm

Salammbo, Caritas Romana and *The source* are from a series entitled 'Bronzes for the Bureaux'. As this title suggests, their intended 'home' is a site on a bureau in the home. The small scale of the sculptures reflects this.

The titles were inspired by popular nineteenth-century works of literature and art – Flaubert's *Salammbo*, *The source* by Ingres, and cultural objects such as the *Roman Charity*. Allington thought of them as enhanced by discussion and transformed into 'true curios'.

Allington explains this development in his practice, as follows:

'In the latter part of 1984, my natural inclination towards using only the most basic of materials began to be eroded by a growing fascination for that intriguing aspect of eighteenth-century taste, the arrangement of Renaissance or Baroque bronzes in curio cabinets or vitrines, which had developed from a manner of collecting into a well defined genre: the small art bronze.'

The small bronzes became a vehicle through which Allington could investigate the autonomy of the art object, in particular its independence of architecture.

'The real point of interest is that despite their profoundly physical presence, most sculptures are completed by a leap of the imagination, which pictures them in their most ideal setting – such as a museum or art gallery – rather than in storage or within a private home. The small art bronze seemed to embody these processes with unusual transparency, and with the added satisfaction that accompanies miniaturisation. The perception of the small art bronze as being anachronistic and decorative rendered the genre even more attractive. I decided to produce a series of works in bronze for the plinth, the desk and the shelf, and to do so with all sincerity and seriousness. Aware that such an endeavour would seem perverse if not absolutely absurd, I tried to say as little as possible and started work with great enthusiasm.'[1]

With hidden vessel, along with a number of other works, *Lamia* and *Euridike* and *The Horn and the Scythe* (not in the Weltkunst Collection), make up a series entitled 'Luxuskabinettstück'. 'These works were intended as unique, luxurious objects, made with the unspoken intention of placement in a vitrine or study of a connoisseur.' *With hidden vessel* represents an increase in scale from some of his previous bronzes which allowed him to 'get a different type of voluptuousness into the formal qualities. It was also the precursor or prototype for the next series of works, the "Pictured Bronzes", where the unspoken intention of the sculptures' placement becomes explicit.'[2]

---

[1] *Edward Allington: Pictured Bronzes*, Exhibition Catalogue, 1991. Appendix. Kohji Ogura Gallery, Nagoya, Japan
[2] Ibid

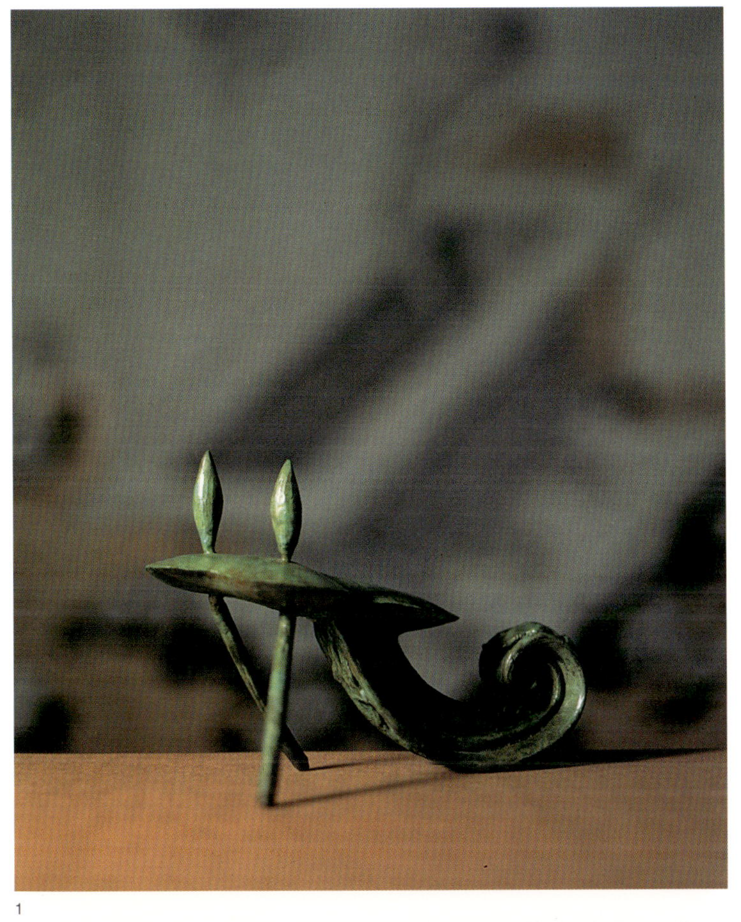

1

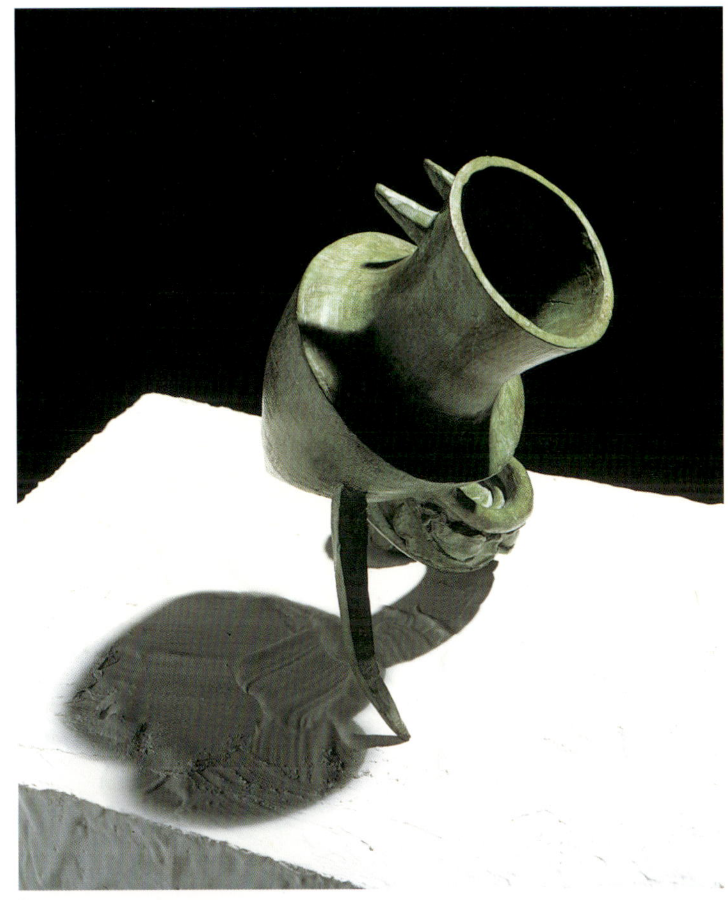

2

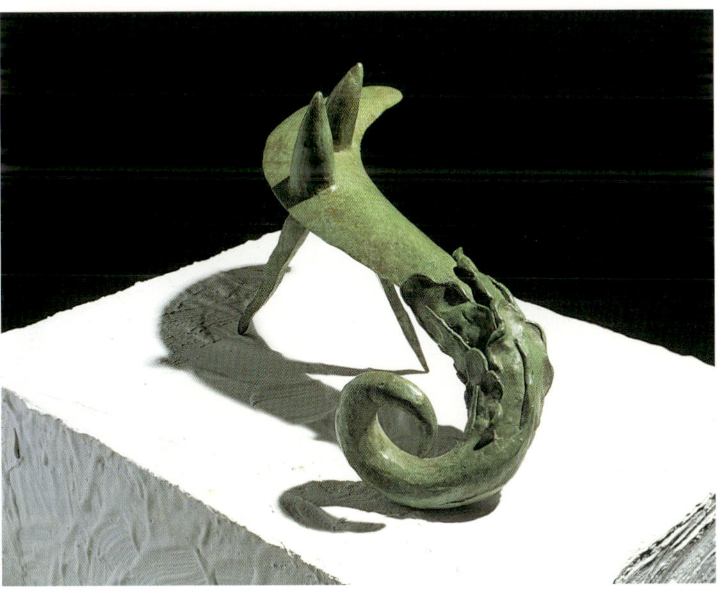

3

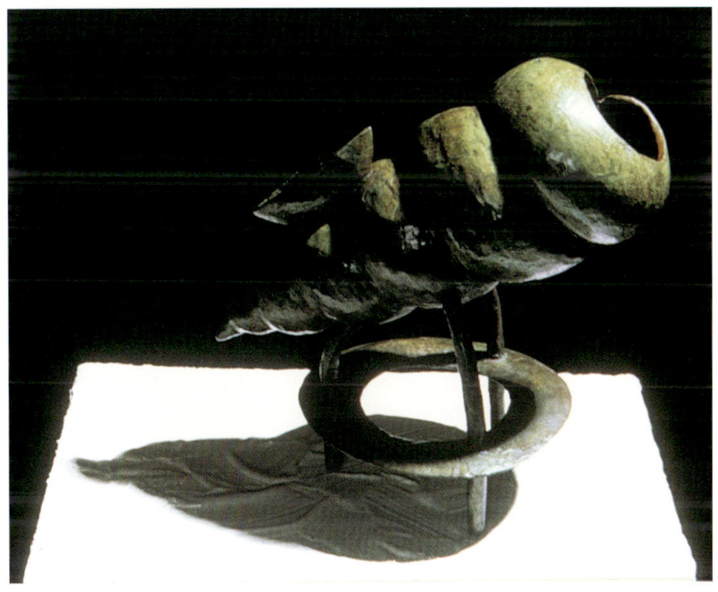

4

Edward Allington
[1] **Queen of torments**
1990
Edition of 6
Framed cibachrome
photograph, bronze, shelf
Photograph: 79.5 x 62 cm
Bronze: 32 x 39 x 35 cm
Shelf: 10.5 x 41 x 41 cm
Installation: 203 x 132 x 41 cm

Edward Allington
[2] **Queen of proofs**
1990
Edition of 6
Framed cibachrome
photograph, bronze, shelf
Photograph: 83 x 66 cm
Bronze: 31 x 49 x 52 cm
Shelf: 13 x 51 x 51 cm
Installation: 203 x 132 x 51 cm

Queen of proofs and *Queen of torments* come from the series of works by Edward Allington entitled the 'Pictured Bronzes'. This body of work continues the artist's interest in questions raised in his previous works. Allington states:

'The small bronze typified an important problem in sculpture generally, which is – where do we meet art? Where does it exist? Most works of art are usually pictured in some kind of way, usually by a catalogue photograph. Such photographs depict the world at a different time, and thus seem to depict the work's actual or ideal state . . . that space is usually the gallery or museum space – the installation shot for example. The work has gone out of the studio into that space and it is photographed there, and that seems to represent the apex of existence . . . I started thinking about fictionalised, idealised spaces that these objects could be placed in, and to photograph them there, and the photograph would somehow place them in time and space but quite fictionally.'[1]

The chosen location for the bronzes is intended to place and picture the piece in the imagination as an ideal setting for the object. Working with photographer Edward Woodman (who takes the photographs in these works), Allington removes an existing ornament from the chosen setting and replaces it with the bronze, which is then photographed. The completed work comprises the bronze, displayed upon a white shelf in the gallery, with a white-framed photograph of the work in its ideal setting. Thus pictured, the bronze is complete.

Queen of proofs and *Queen of torments* both feature bronzes photographed in nineteenth-century neo-classical-style settings. Electric light fittings and the presence of a telephone reveal the contemporaneity of these spaces. The titles of the works come from a book the artist read on torture. The 'Queen of Torments' is the name historically given to the rack and the 'Queen of Proofs' is a term for the confession extracted under torture. These devices have their origin in ancient Greece and Allington sees this as underlining the connection between concepts of high civilisation and acts of barbarity.

<hr>

[1]Interview with Joanna Lowry, *Creative Camera*, June/July 1996

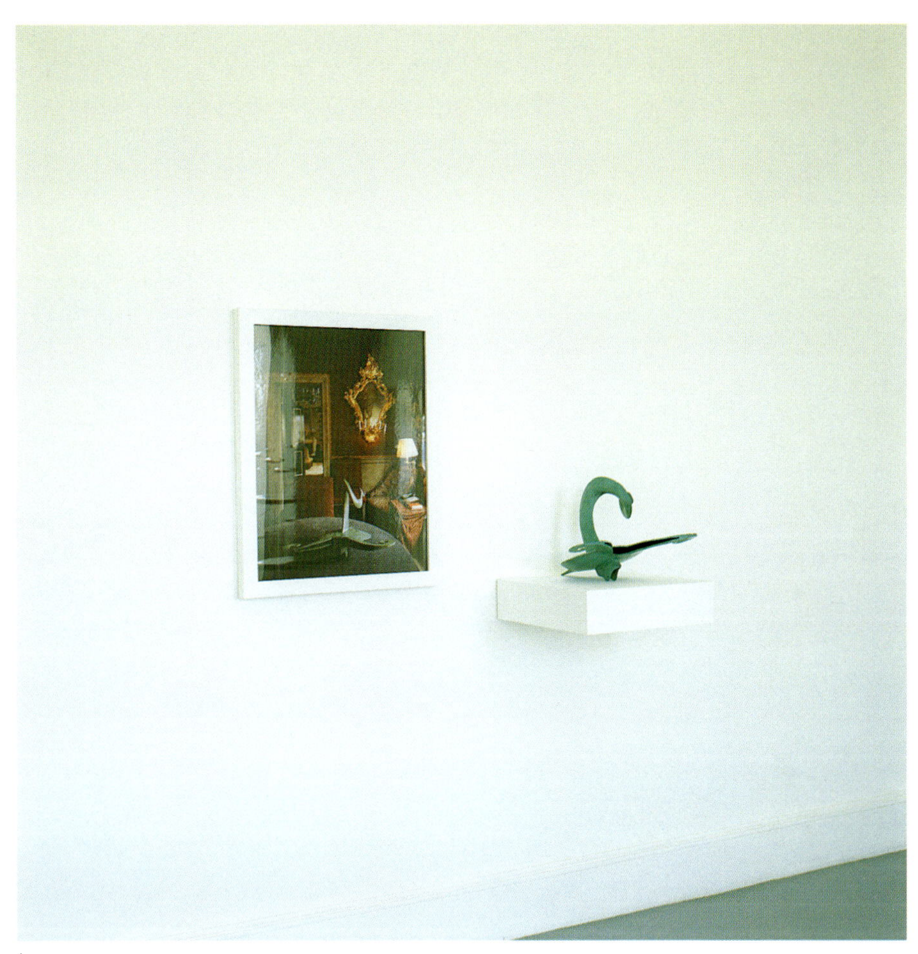

1

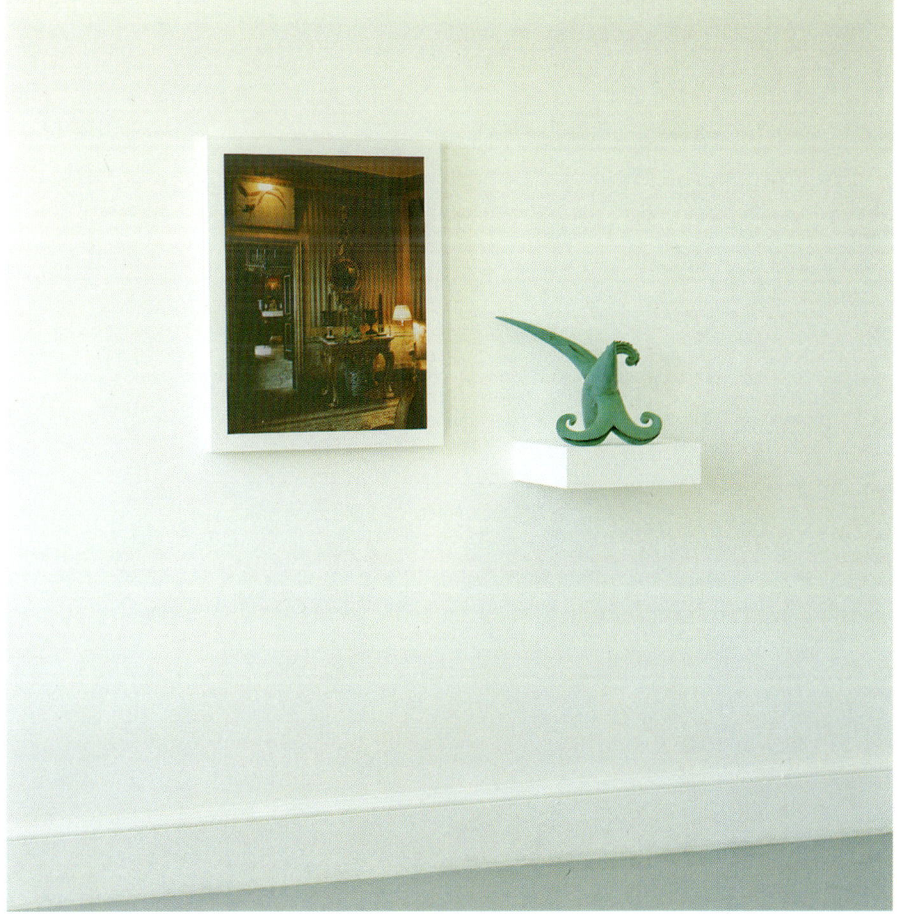

2

Richard Wentworth

The five works by Richard Wentworth in the Weltkunst Collection span the period 1982-8 and reflect the range of his sculptural concerns during that time. While sharing a common modest scale, the works show a diversity of materials and procedures present within the vocabulary of Wentworth's sculpture.

'I live in a readymade landscape and I want to put it to work',[1] Wentworth is quoted as saying. He often chooses artefacts of industrial production that can be described variously as man-made, hand-scale, domestic or generic. Wentworth also feels drawn towards things that are at the end of their life. These everyday objects are manipulated and juxtaposed and 'marriages' of seemingly unconnected things occur in the works. However, in contrast to traditional Surrealist juxtaposition, Marina Warner points out that 'Wentworth brings home the value of the disregarded, without spoiling the special quality of their ordinariness.'[2]

Wentworth recalls an interest in heraldry during the time many of the works were made, and notably the heraldic devices that bring together completely disparate symbolic motifs on to one coat of arms. While the metonymic motifs in heraldry may amount to vanity or wishful thinking, Wentworth sees anthropomorphic qualities in his works, much closer to the frailties of lived human condition. 'My work usually involves an element of failure. . . . I would make an argument with the proposal of a perfect world and simultaneously try to offer an admission that perfection, that ideal is very vulnerable.'[3]

Language is a vital source of inspiration for Wentworth's work. The relationship between a thing and its name is not for him a transparent business and his sculptures play with the process of naming. Resonances and slippages in language, between sign and signified, are part of Wentworth's often paradoxical titles. He comments:

'There are, like tunes, words and phrases that seem to 'stick' but I don't have a rule. I like the act of naming (and the immediate anomalies it generates) but I just want things to be apt, and this can be more or less impacted, compact, onomatopoeic.'

In *Glad that things don't talk*, a rubber overshoe sits on an oval rubber mat. A lead ball is tethered to the back of the shoe. A small wedge sits under the toe of the shoe and another under the mat. 'The lead ball has got plenty of gravity in it and in some way most of the time I do enjoy gravity or use it in some way.' Wentworth recalls someone aptly describing the work as 'the shoe being extrovert and the ball holding it back', adding: 'It's as if it does not quite have the courage to do something, which is a common human condition, where you think of doing something but didn't quite make the move.'

The title *Glad that things don't talk* relates to this sculpture's possible narrative interpretation, which Wentworth is keen to avoid, adding: 'This work is very nearly narrative and then it isn't.'

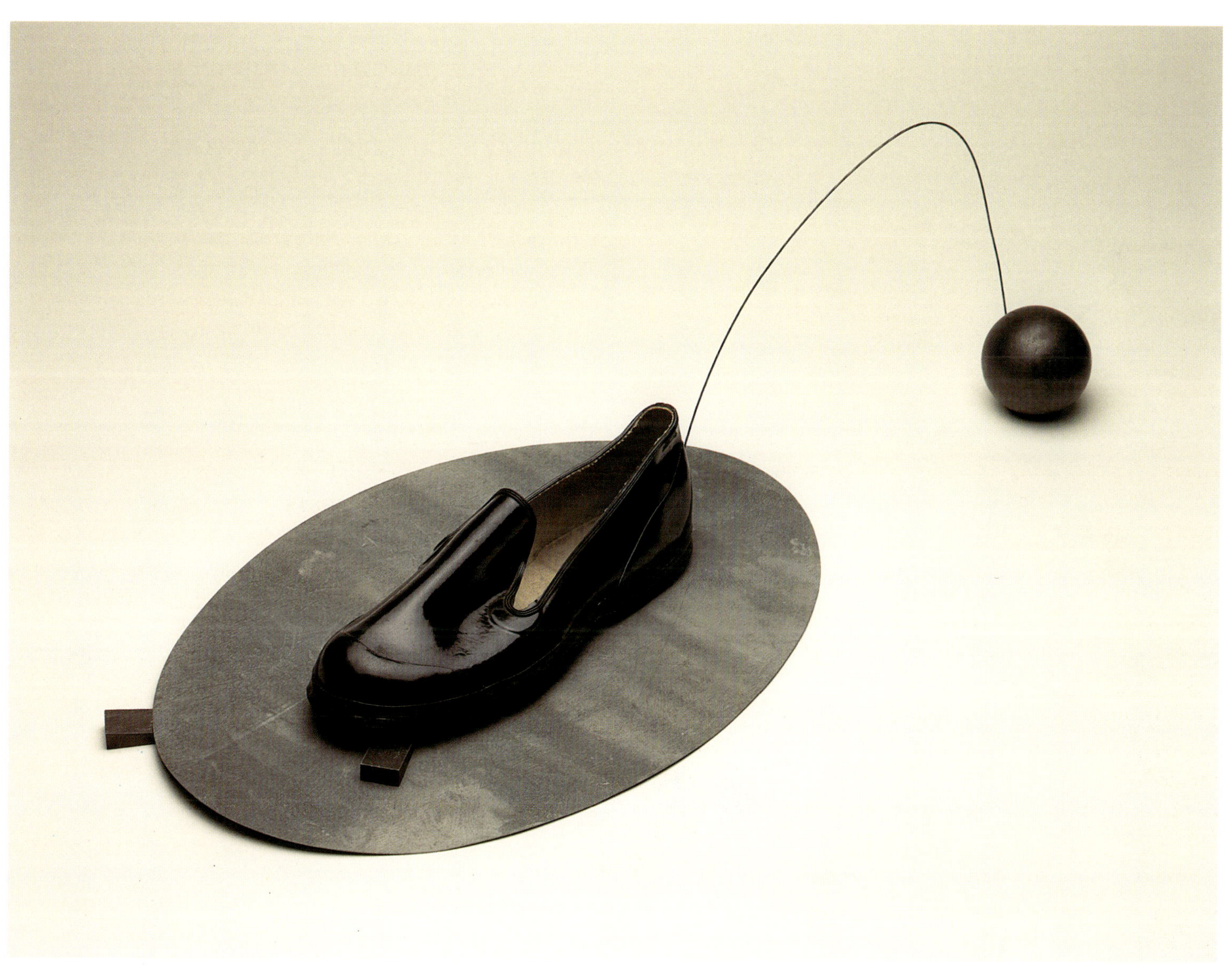

Richard Wentworth
Heist (for S.E.)
1983
Linen, duckdown, gilded lead,
tinned steel
60 x 90 x 65 cm

Richard Wentworth
Logo
1986
Concrete, steel, rubber
38 x 41 x 36 cm

The forces of gravity are at work also in *Heist (for S.E.)*
(1983). The long handle of an institutional-sized ladle,
'ridiculously big and heavy even before it's filled with
anything' is made to stand erect, by virtue of the weight of
a gilded lead ball completely filling the cup. Wentworth
acknowledges the sexual connotations of the handle's angle
which reaches the crotch height of the average viewer.
Wentworth sees the pillow as the place where we sleep, yet
here it functions as a kind of plinth or base for the other
elements, offering them up to the viewer like a jewel on a
cushion. The lead ball is gilded. 'I am interested in the
almost childlike idea that if it is gold or shiny it must be
valuable,' says Wentworth. 'It's pushed to the point of
almost being vulgar but also it's at the edge of being
desirable.'

Logo (1986) involves the transformation of an abandoned
office letter tray by filling the spaces that once held paper
with cast concrete. While this may have something to do
with Wentworth's admission of having no aptitude for
organising paperwork, the result is that a slim piece of
office furniture becomes a formidable block. The strip of
tyre on which it sits, once released from its regular
enclosed circular form, 'acts a bit like an animal, flipping
about, having a life of its own when you try to handle it'.
The tyre is folded in on itself and held in place by the
weight of the other object. In a reversal of the classical
sculptural formation the unruly element plays the plinth
to the rectangular block.

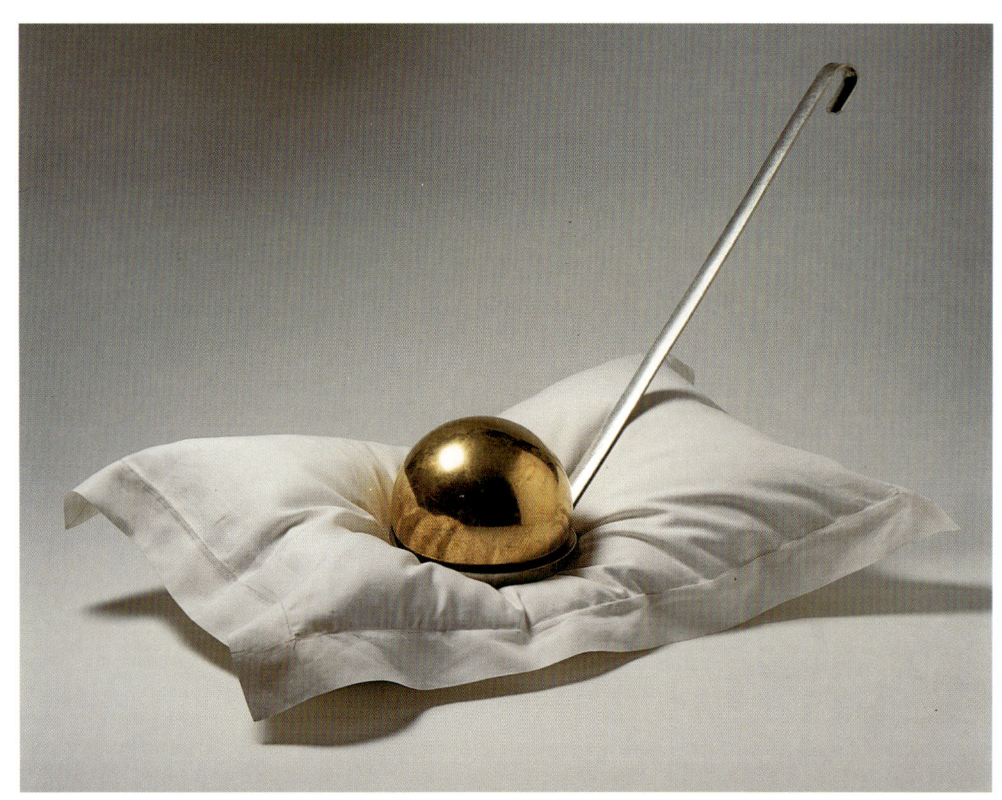

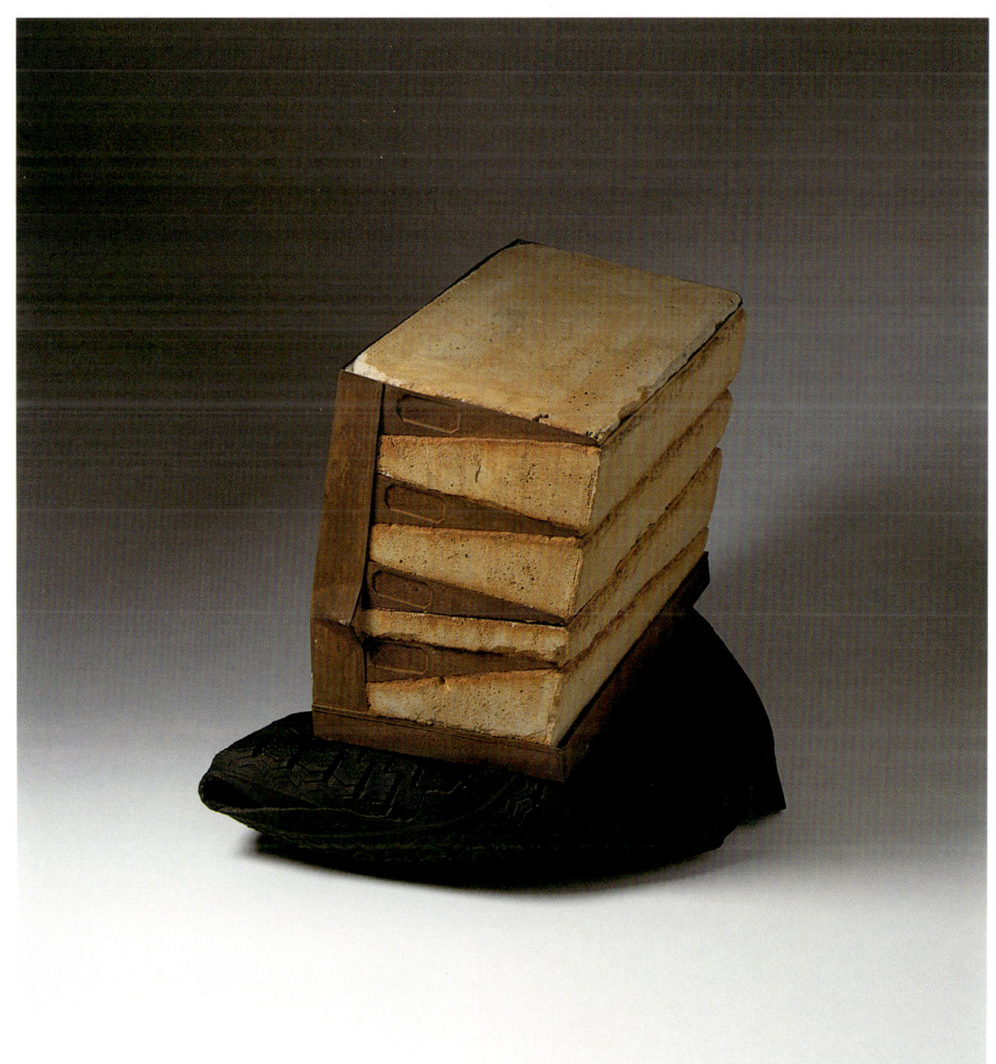

Richard Wentworth
Gosse
1984
Galvanised steel and
aluminium
28 x 66 x 48 cm

Richard Wentworth
Preserve
1987-8
Steel, concrete, dud light
bulbs
35 cm (height) x 44 cm (diameter)

In *Gosse* (1984) an electric fan propeller is fitted to the
inside of a galvanised steel bath. The title refers to the
French term for a lad or boy and this piece was made at the
time Wentworth's first son was four years old. The artist
was interested in how a child plays and interacts with
objects in his world, particularly the transformational
aspect of instantly creating and metamorphosing things
that surround him. In this way, through the power of
imagination, a bath would become a boat. Denying the
obvious image of a boat with the propeller on the outside
of the bath, the propeller in *Gosse* is on the inside with
the bath water.

Preserve (1987-8) features non-functioning light bulbs
which often appear as emblematic objects in Wentworth's
sculpture. In *Preserve* they are contained in a wire basket
capped by a lid of concrete which threatens to bear down on
their (supposed) fragility. In fact, the concrete is cast on to
the wire lattice holding the concrete lid in place. The title
Preserve plays on the American term for 'jam' which is also
a slang word for a predicament. The contents of the basket
are sealed up in their container for safe keeping. Wentworth
also refers to the concrete cap as a reference to an atomic
silo. Marina Warner suggests that this work and a similar
work, *Hurricane* (1987) (in which the concrete fills three-
quarters of a similar wire basket bearing down on a fewer
number of bulbs), 'strike a darker note, a conflict of
textures, thin against thick, fragile against impervious. . . .
Preserve evokes the catastrophe of Chernobyl, the concrete
entombment of the radioactive wasteland.'[4]

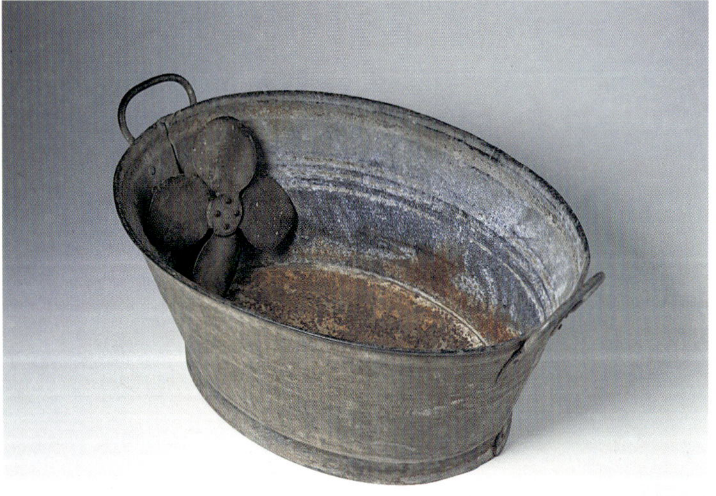

[1] This and other unattributed quotations from a conversation with Ronan
McCrea, The Irish Museum of Modern Art, 1997
[2] Marina Warner, *Richard Wentworth*, Thames and Hudson, 1993
[3] Interview with Bill Furlong, *Audio Arts Magazine*, vol.14, no.4, London,
1995
[4] Marina Warner, op. cit.

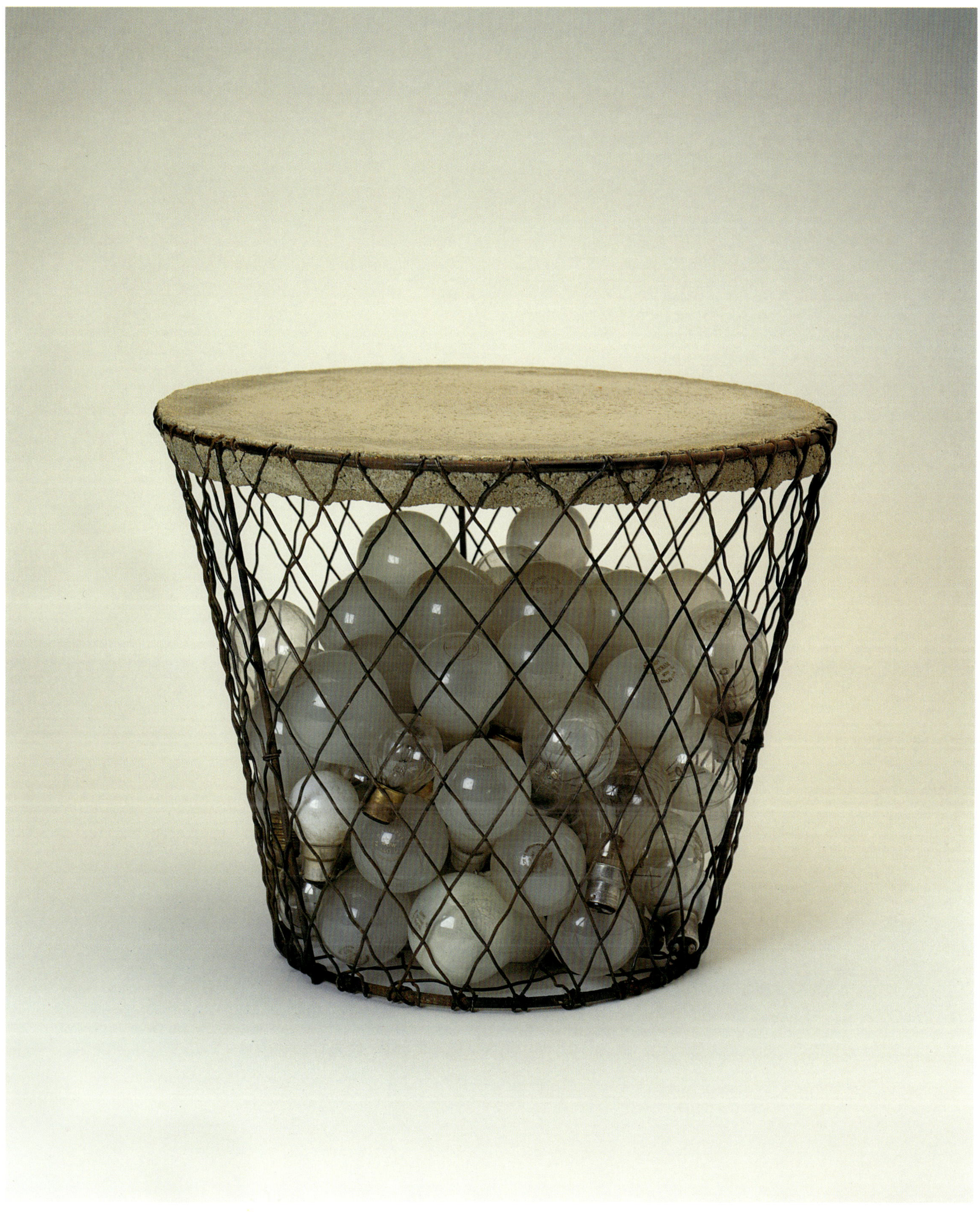

Veronica Ryan

Cavities
1988
Lead
Depth of each object approximately: 28 cm
Overall installation length: 1342 cm

Cavities was made and installed in the lawns at Fellows Garden, Jesus College in Cambridge University in 1988 as part of Veronica Ryan's 1987-8 residency at Kettle's Yard Gallery. The work exists in two versions, the first *in situ* in the lawns together with its associated documentation, and the second, as shown since, with the vessel-like lead foil objects flattened and box-framed for presentation in gallery contexts. Both strategies of presenting work have been present in the artist's practice. Veronica Ryan has described her work as representations of 'dislocation/location and disorientation . . . the sense of a different place as my home was present in early childhood as a result of stories from my grandmother'.

'Boundaries, territories, place, dislocations, memory have been some of the continuing preoccupations in my work. The form and structures often have the sense of alluding to remembered and fleeting memorabilia. These remarkable things might have been the result of decayed fruit, and the remaining husks and seeds on the ground. The first experience of eating a sugar apple was terrible nausea and sickness from the perfumed fruit. It is primarily the experience and not the representation which the work is concerned with'.[1]

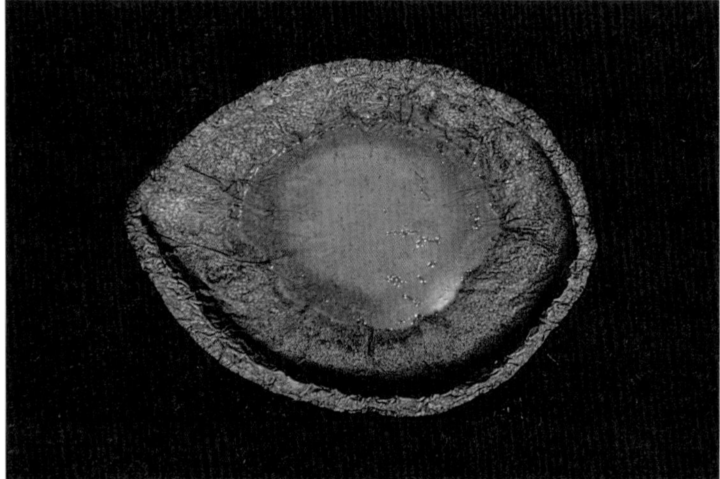

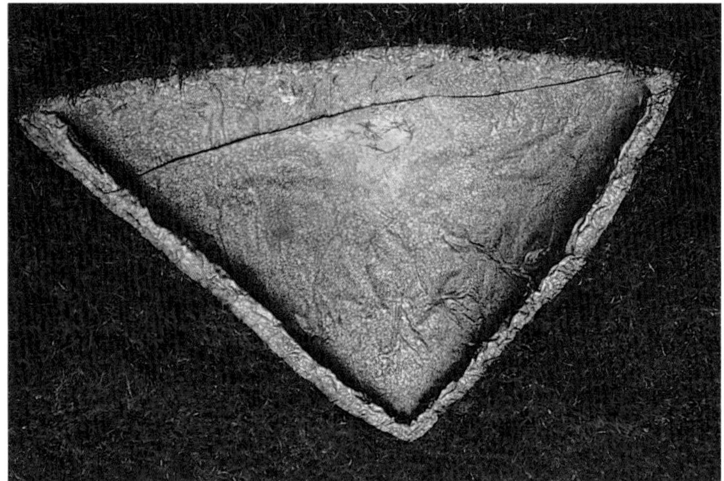

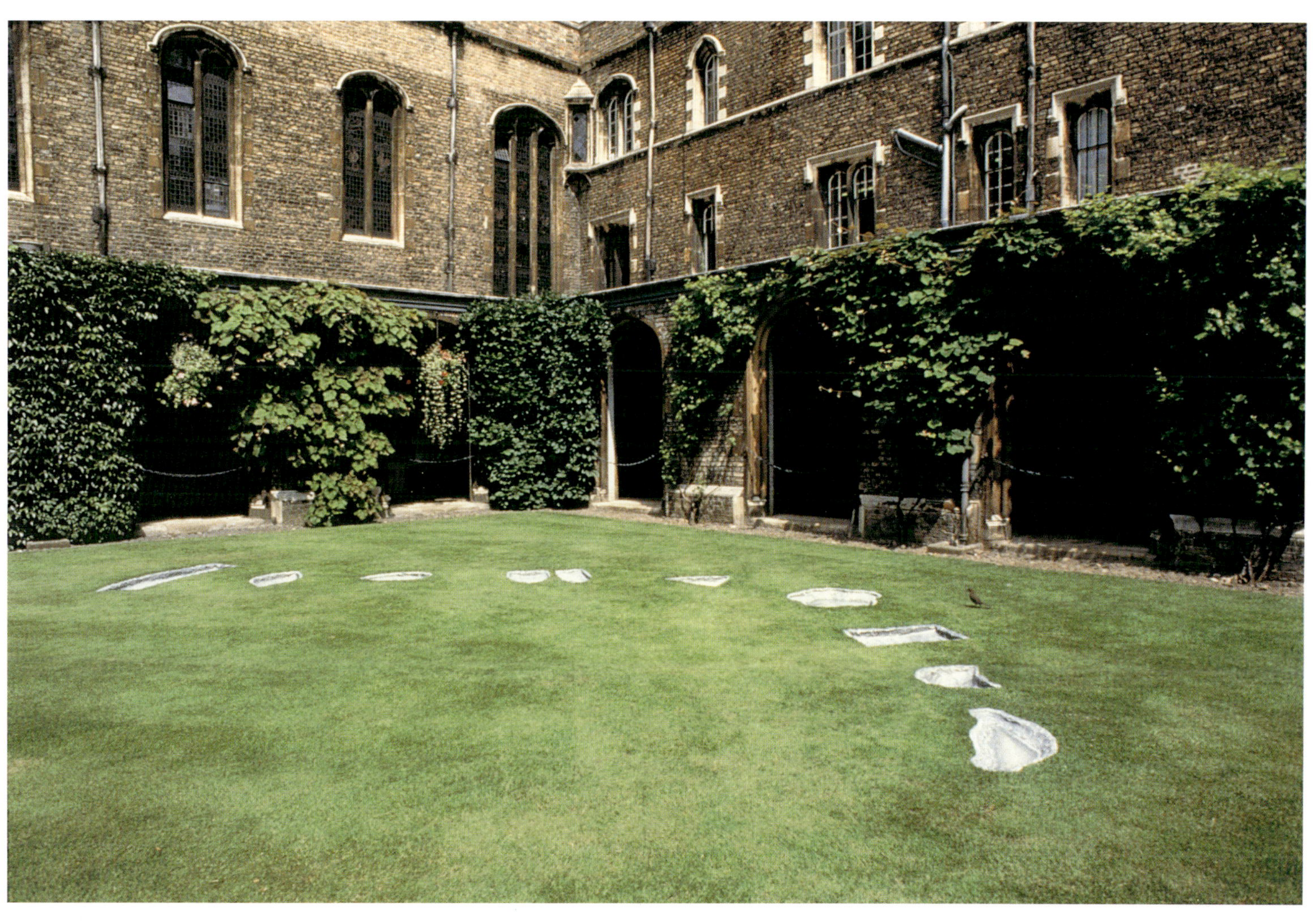

Veronica Ryan
[1] **Surfacing**
1988
Bronze
66.5 x 127 x 7.6 cm

Veronica Ryan
[2] **Perforations**
1988
Bronze
52.4 x 40.6 x 23.5 cm

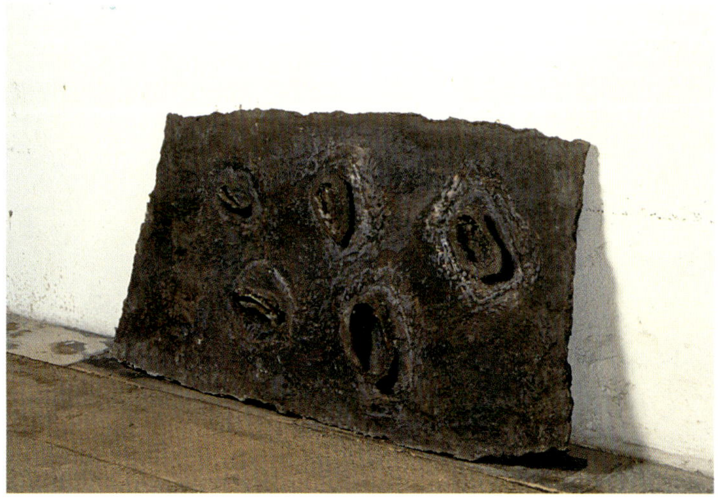

1

Cavities, like *Perforations*, is typical of her work in that period, resembling bowls, gourds, organic forms, pods and seeds which have the familiarity of things drawn from a deep well of associations and meanings but are non-specific. *Perforations* is also reminiscent of the base for one of the oldest board games in the world, common in sub-Saharan Africa. In *Cavities* the working processes hinted at with the vessel form are contradicted by the perforations in the lead. No liquid could ever have collected in these objects, for any purpose. Their contradiction of function holds the piece outside considerations of craft or utility despite their hand-built nature. *Surfacing*, cast in bronze, is like a fragment of an organic entity, removed from its source.

[1]Veronica Ryan from *A New Necessity*, Exhibition Catalogue, The First Tyne International, Gateshead, 1990

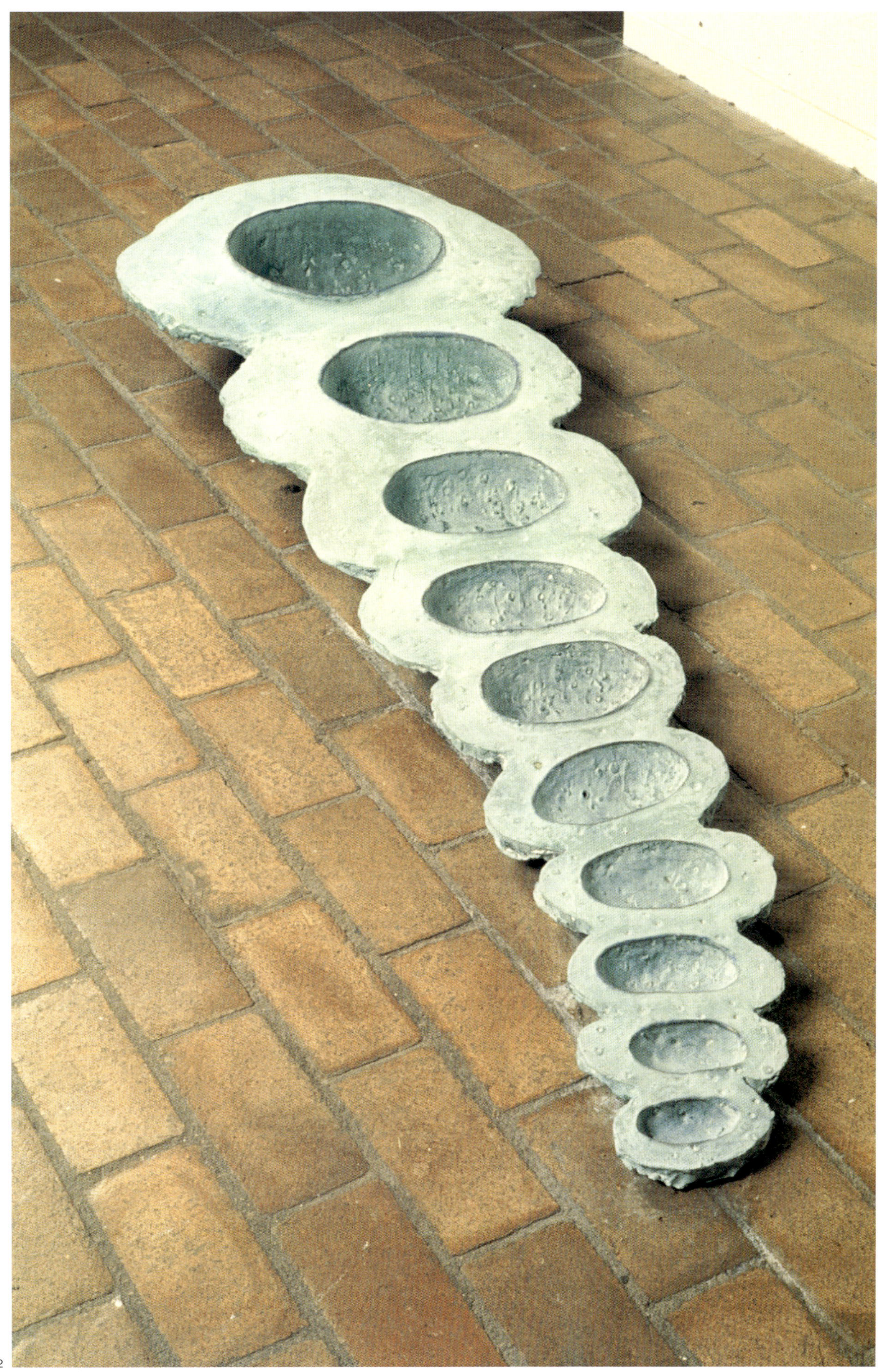

2

Richard Deacon

Lock
1990
Hardboard, epoxy, vinyl,
aluminium
215 x 380 x 255 cm

Lock is made from layers of laminated hardboard. On one 'side' of the form is a layer of vinyl floor covering material (lino). On the other is sheet aluminium. The work is constructed of two similar interlocking open-form elements. They were built as mirror images of each other or as the artist puts it, 'like a pair of gloves'.

Deacon chooses his materials very deliberately. Apart from their formal properties he is interested in the uses to which they are normally put:

'The first time I started making laminates, what interested me was that structurally it (the process) has a slightly non-specific character, (and) that it was bendable and therefore distortable. I was also interested in the patterning of domestic materials.'[1]

The pattern on the surface of *Lock* looks like marquetry. The viewer is surprised to discover that its printed pattern is from a piece of floor covering:

'These insets are set into the surface, they're not on the surface, so that it's as if they have been exposed rather than imposed. There is a suggestion that the material, the laminated material has kinds of things in it, which could be revealed.'

Deacon explores ideas about depth in this piece, the physical depths of the material, the illusionistic depth of the inlays, the reflective depth of the aluminium:

'Depth itself is something which is very difficult to determine. It's a subjective phenomenon rather than an objective phenomenon. And the notion of distance is something that is built on experience, so with *Lock* I was trying to put, as it were, the three different ideas about distance or depth into the material. I've become quite intrigued by what constituted distance and by inverse, what constituted personality or individuality.'

The title refers to the way the pieces fit together. There is a closeness – an onomatopoeic relationship – between 'lock' and 'look':

'And also when "Lock" is a description of a physical object and one action and also is a way of describing. . . . You can use it to describe the way people look at each other "their eyes locked" in relationship to looking. It implies a sudden kind of concentration.'

Deacon's sculpture *Lock* is the last in a body of work that involved lamination as the form of construction:

'I decided to stop making "laminates" during the making of *Lock*. I decided this because I was getting too good at it. I've always been slightly careful to avoid over-identification with particular materials or procedures.'

---

[1] This and subsequent quotations in an interview with Ann Davern and Helen O'Donoghue, The Irish Museum of Modern Art, 1996

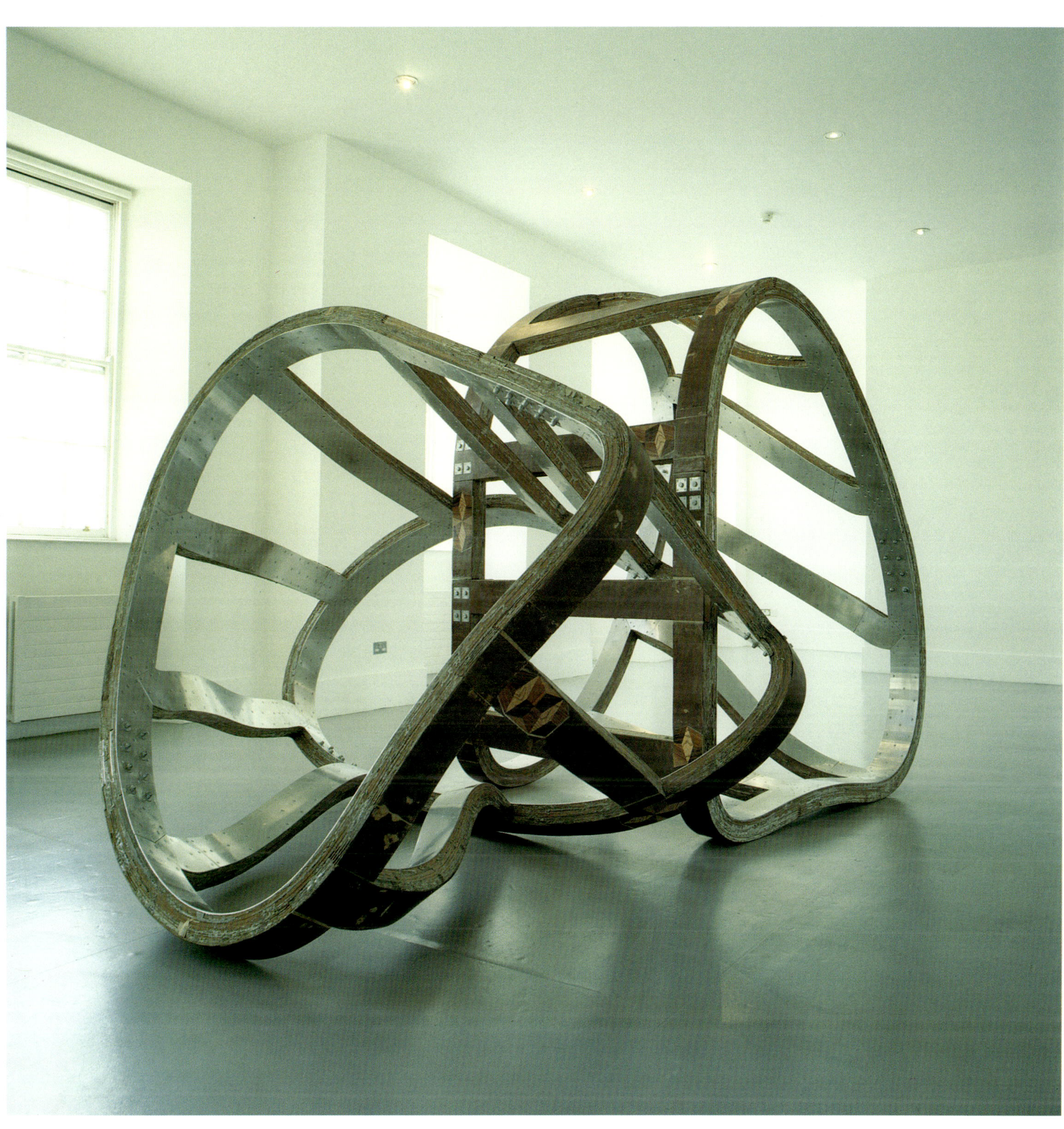

Eric Bainbridge

Occurrence on an endless column is one of many sculptures by Eric Bainbridge that consist of forms of everyday objects rendered on a different scale and covered in fake fur.

Driven by a sense of fun, Bainbridge covered an animal form in spotty fur fabric and was fascinated by the way the original form was concealed by the thickness of the fur while the spotty pattern made the contours less legible:

'So I realised I'd a very different object. It was the potential for the skin to disguise the form underneath, also what was interesting was that fake fur was a quintessentially synthetic twentieth-century material.'[1]

The forms themselves in *Occurrence on an endless column* are from various sources. The two animal forms are based on actual objects – small souvenirs – and these are contrasted with some seemingly abstract forms. The square element, however, was derived from part of a child's building-block game:

'In this work the thing that is highlighted is the play between things that are very figurative and seemingly abstract.'

Occurrence on an endless column is a reference to the famous *Endless column* by Constantin Brancusi. The notion that this might be merely a section of an endless column or that this kind of activity could go on forever interested the artist. There is a deliberately obscene aspect to the work. The donkey 'mounts' his companion but there are no holes to allow for the completion of the sexual act. Paradoxically the abstract forms are holed – a reference to earlier work in which connections or their absence was a theme. Instead, what is offered here is what Bainbridge describes as 'an impossible kind of coupling':

'I think the element of taste is something that interests me a lot which is related very much to the idea of the reduction of traditional quality (in art). I think I'm interested in a kind of equalising of things. I tend to believe less and less in the qualities of high art. I'm less interested in preserving those attitudes. I think a toy or a souvenir donkey is not necessarily less interesting than anything else, simply because of its supposed lowly position. I think we don't look at it, we kind of recognise it for being part of a category and then deal with it. It's more problematic when one actually starts to look at the languages, looks at the ideas of idealised nature that are depicted in these kinds of things.'

[1] This and subsequent quotations in an interview with Ann Davern and Helen O'Donoghue, The Irish Museum of Modern Art, 1995

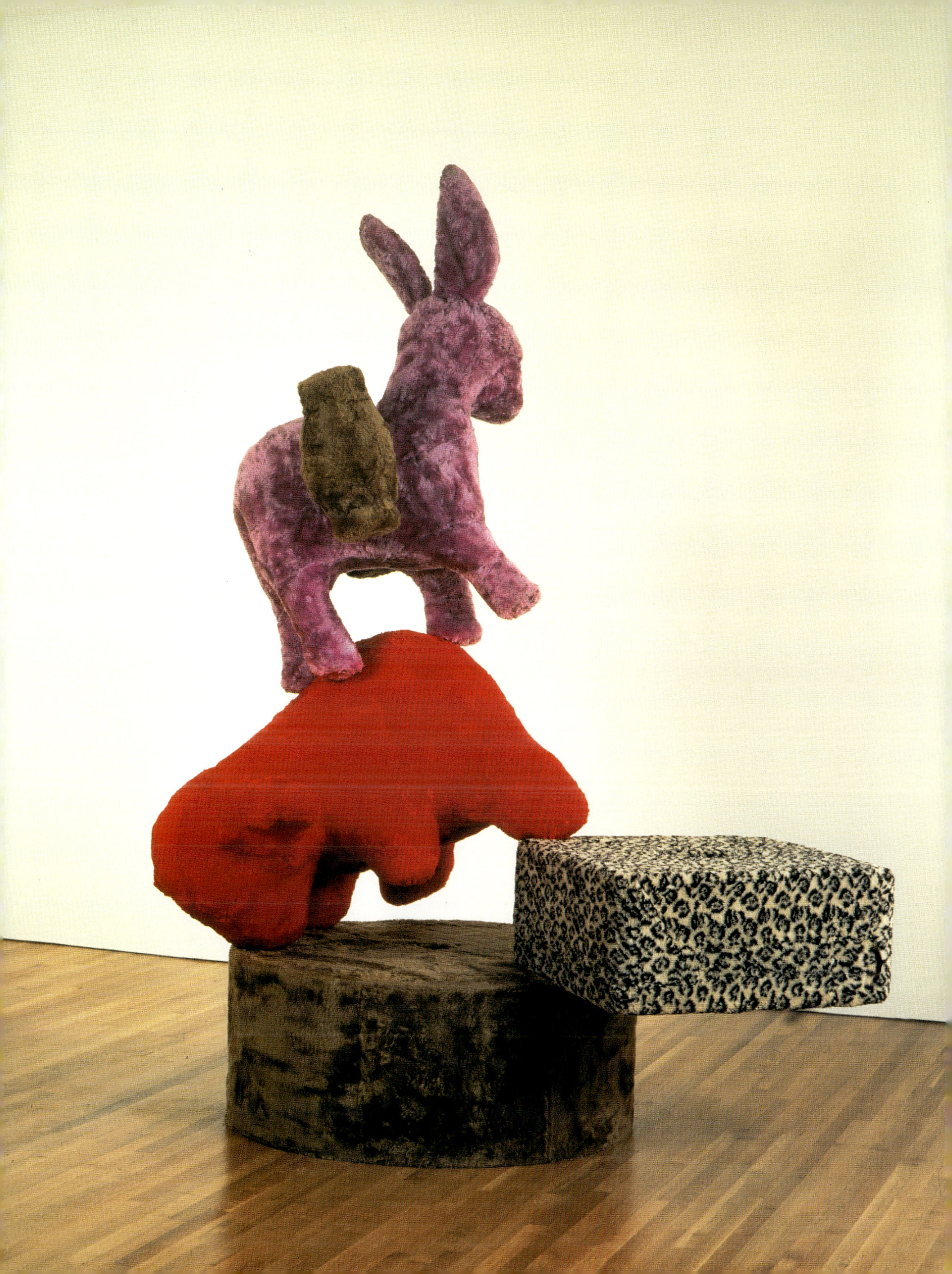

Hannah Collins

Platespinning
1991-5
Silver gelatin print, mounted
on cotton
287 x 365 cm

Hannah Collins has described the powerful large-scale, black-and-white photographic images of this period, which are mounted on linen, as both 'sculptural and pictorial'.

For many artists black-and-white photography is more real because it is a step away from legible appearance. In a world of colour, black and white can focus perception and concentration.

Platespinning is shown unstretched, pinned to a wall and allowed to hang like a banner. The work has an architectural presence which includes the viewer in its field of vision rather than vice versa. Collins's works, especially the large-scale photoworks, are made with the viewer's relationship to the image in mind. The viewer is physically and psychologically part of the work.

In this piece the platespinning activity is already underway but the spinner is absent. In another related work (called *The platespinner*), the spinner is present but the theatrical act is familiar enough for us to understand that the plates can only be kept spinning by an increasingly frenetic human intervention – if chaos is not to result. The metaphor is universal. The spinner of the plates, who is absent here, could also be read as the artist who engages in an activity which is directed towards an audience. When the work is shown, the only human presence is that of the viewer.

In a later series of works exhibited in 1996, Hannah Collins dealt directly with situations in eastern Europe which are on the borders and margins of society. Collins believes that art can represent the interface between personal histories and the culture in which we live. *Platespinning* predates the eastern European images but their sense of edginess, of things tottering towards the brink, is prefigured in this piece.

It is, therefore, a pivotal work in that it also includes the state of vulnerability established in previous pieces, which dealt with abstracted interiors and landscapes and which consciously embraced categories of traditional art – something true of all her work.

Platespinning nevertheless describes an event, not just a state. The act is on stage and the viewer is the audience. With its heavy blackness, in which the plates spin in a shallow space that has an unspecified, displaced quality, the work confronts the viewer with a powerful metaphor, already current in society, for uncertainty, insecurity, inevitable changes. In fact, the work suggests the tendency for all things to degrade and move toward chaos.

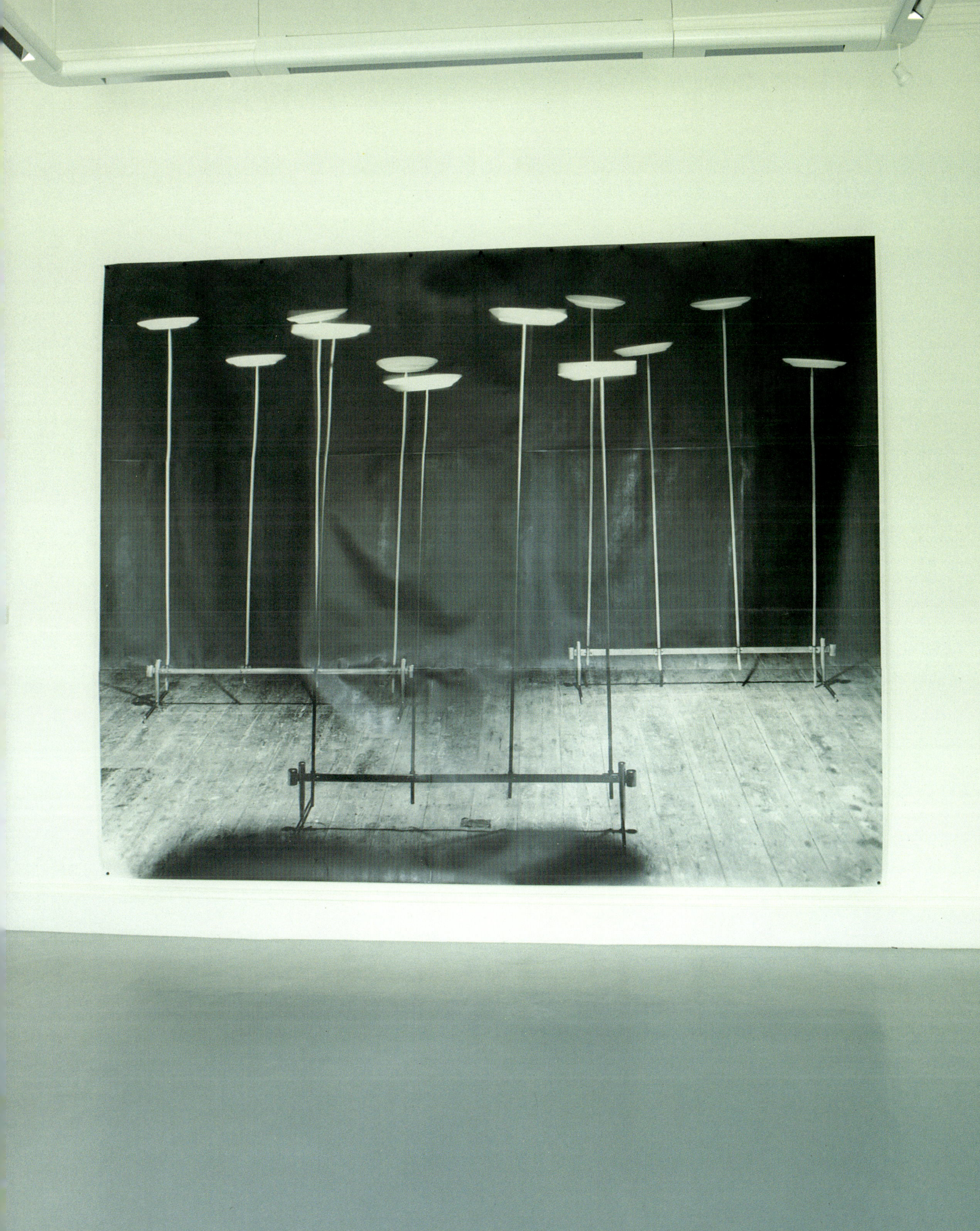

Art & Language

Incident, now they are, next
1993
Oil on canvas on wood with
enamel on glass and mixed
media
Seven panels of various dimensions
Dimensions when assembled
147.1 x 137 x 171.5 cm

Art & Language currently designates the collaborative artistic and literary work of Michael Baldwin and Mel Ramsden. It also identifies written work of these two in conjunction with Charles Harrison. The name is derived from the journal *Art-Language* first published in 1969. Art & Language had its origin in the work of Terry Atkinson and Michael Baldwin (from 1966) in association with Harold Hurrell and David Bainbridge, who were the original editors.

Incident, now they are, next takes the form of a polyptych painting, consisting of seven panels. These are arranged in a three-dimensional, box-like composition so that for the most part, the front of the paintings face inward. Each panel is made of a braced plywood surface, over which canvas is stretched and painted. Laid over this is a sheet of glass, painted on the inside face. Behind the glass surface lies a painted rendition of Courbet's *Origine du monde*.

Michael Baldwin explains:

'The paintings are in a series called *Incident, now they are, next*, and they consist of an image derived from Courbet's *Origine du monde* (*Origin of the world*) which has been variously cut up by us. That image is then masked by pink glass and the pink glass has a message, a little greeting in the centre of the paintings; the little greeting reads "hello".'

Commenting on the selection of this image for their work, Baldwin states:

'It is a voyeuristic image of a woman. *Origine du monde* has a long history of being masked. Courbet painted it for a collector and it was exhibited in a private residence. It started life masked by an another painting which depicted a castle in the snow. It then was shown with an André Masson over the top . . . then acquired by Masson's brother-in-law, and finally when he died it reappeared in the world. It's a strange sort of fugitive story of an indecent image. Now what is rather significant about this indecent image is that some argue it is the ultimate painting inasmuch as painting involves a kind of voyeurism. Therefore this truncated image of the female torso in sexual parts is in a certain sense the psychoanalytic apogeé. But the fact that this painting had been concealed, or masked, was one of the things that drew us to it, because previous to becoming involved with that particular image, some of our paintings had a history of being laminated and covered by other things. And we started to wonder about the "figure". The "figure" is as scandalous a topic for painting as it is possible to encounter.

'Possibly one of the easiest ways to get a grip on this work as a polyptych is to imagine it as dismantled; as a painting that ought to be flat on the wall and has been dismantled, and in a certain sense *déshabillée* (a state of undress); not ready to be seen, which twists it round back to the paintings, so it might be argued that in a way you see the back of the paintings, which is a condition in which it does not wish to be seen.'[1]

---

[1] Interview with Helen O'Donoghue, The Irish Museum of Modern Art, May 1995

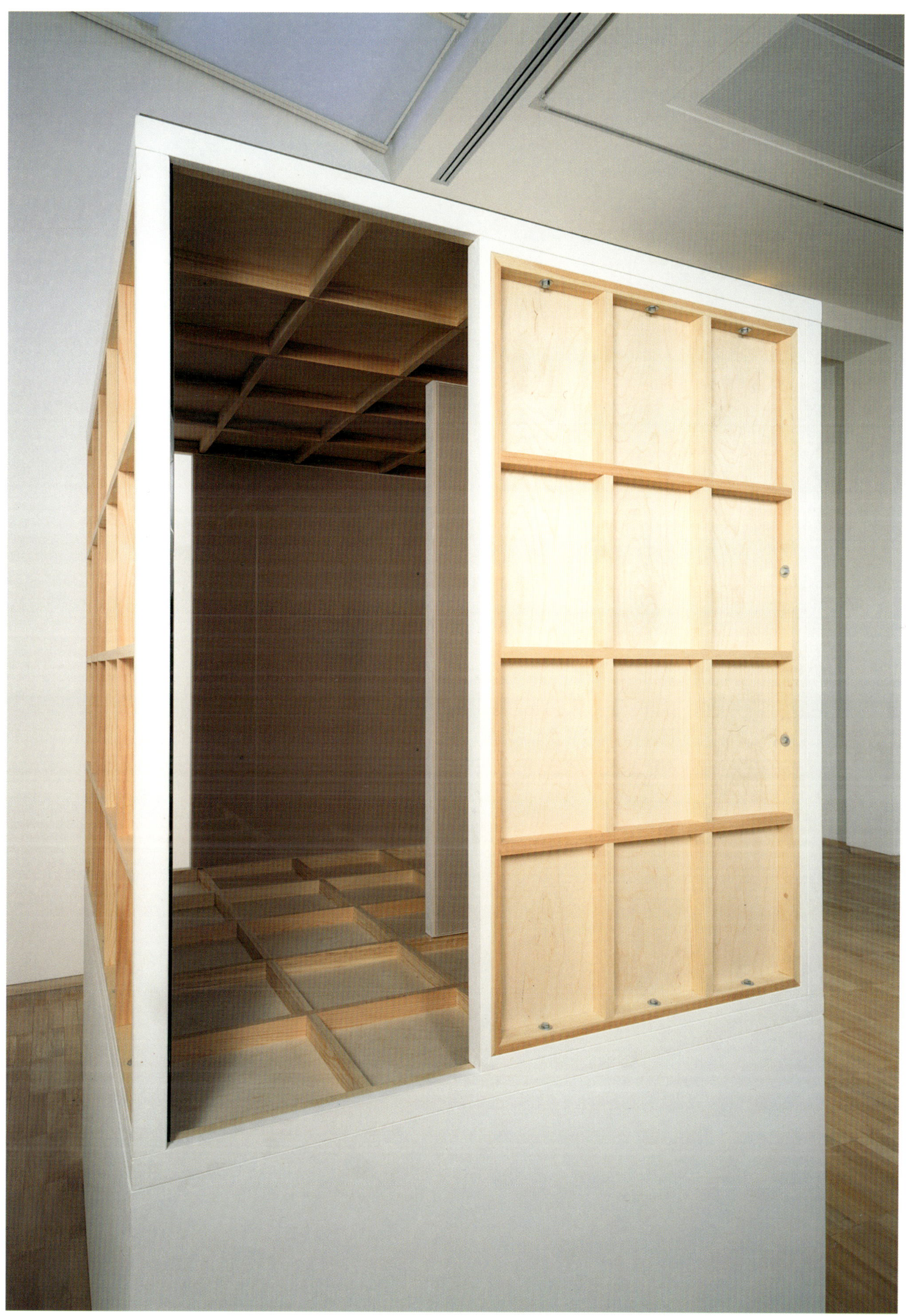

Hermione Wiltshire

Seamen I
1992
Cibachrome photographs,
glass
Various dimensions

The entire floor surface of a room or corridor is covered in blue marbled linoleum. From a distance the viewer sees 'droplets' of clear glass covering the floor. Only when walking among and standing over the glass globules does it become apparent that each one contains a photograph of a penis.

Seamen 1 was originally installed in 1992 at the Dreadnought Seamen's Mission Hospital at Greenwich, London, which for over 400 years treated, among others, sailors who had contracted sexually transmitted diseases on their travels. The blue-marbled linoleum in one of the wards provided a sea-like environment appropriate to the hospital's name but it also evoked the achievements of another sailor, Christopher Columbus, whose voyage to America of 1492 the artist wished to commemorate.

Wiltshire sees the work in terms of an heroic all-male world of both courage and foolishness, tough and admirable, yet a world that denies the expression of similar attributes to women. For her the droplets are like a huge fleet crossing the ocean:

'A large quantity of "seamen" has been ejaculated across the floor, splattering the walls. It is a huge fleet traversing the ocean. It is (also) a spray of tiny droplets of liquid landing on a surface for a moment, as if on their way somewhere else. The transformation from the abstract and metaphorical vision to the explicit photographs of erections is the twist of the piece. The extreme literalness of the images serves to extend the metaphor.'[1]

The shiny glass surfaces and the play of light on them obscure the photographic images underneath, a device that enables the artist to seduce the viewer into the work:

'If you (the viewer) see the photographs too soon, if you can identify what they are too soon, the transformation, the double reading, does not work. So you have to be blinded initially, seduced by the beauty of it and then you discover what you are looking at.'

[1] This and other quotations from Hermione Wiltshire in conversation with Ronan McCrea, The Irish Museum of Modern Art, 1997

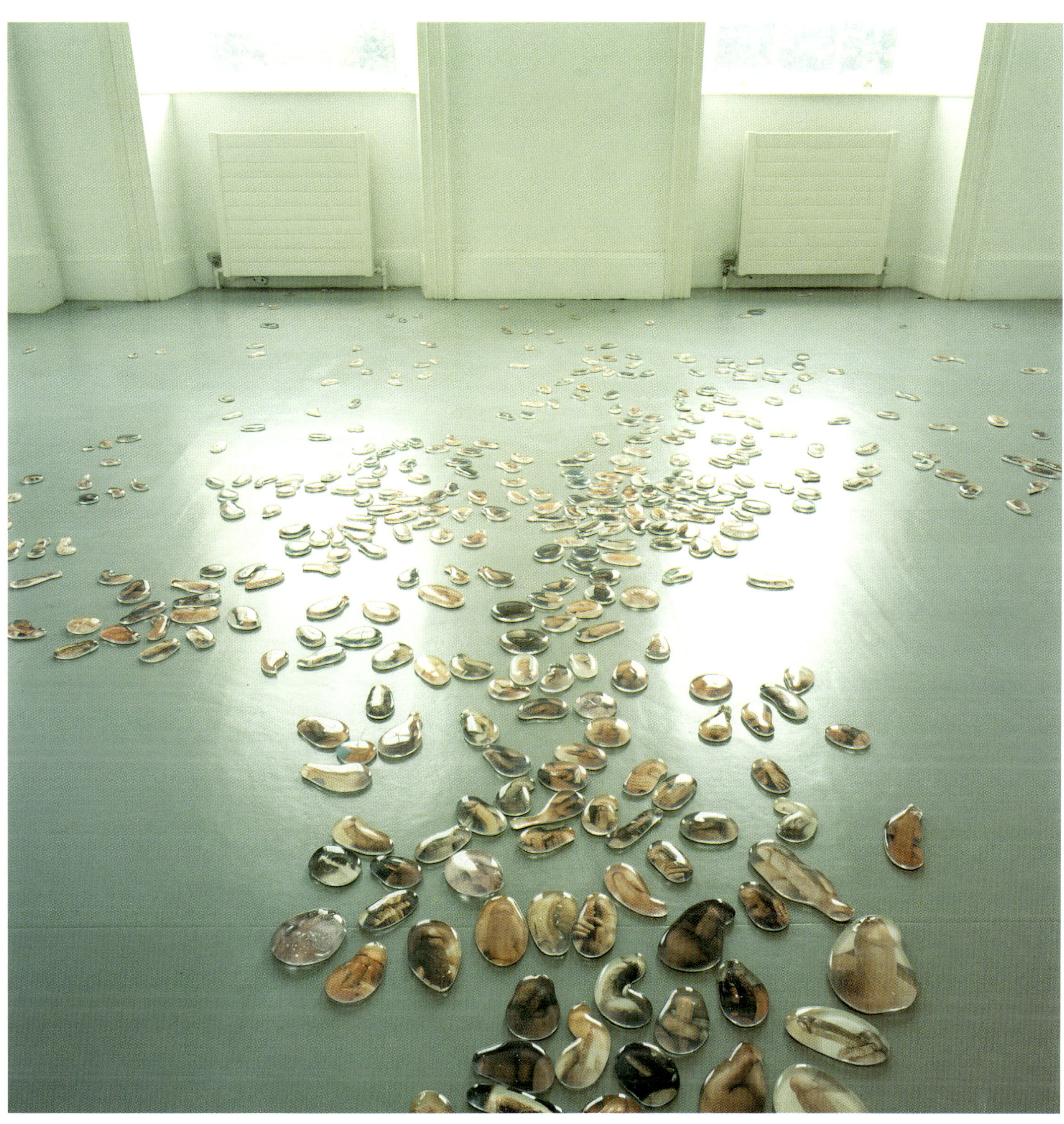

Hermione Wiltshire
My touch
1993
Cibachrome photographs,
glass, silicone glue and
aluminium
Installation: 200 x 100 cm
Unit size: 30-40 cm (diameter)

My touch consists of ten photographs, each 30-40 cm in
diameter, which are enlargements of the artist's own
fingerprints, printed in a saturated red tone. Over each
photograph is a globule of clear glass from which projects a
delicate but very sharp spike, pulled from the glass while
still in a semi-molten state. The ten 'fingerprints' are
mounted on the wall in a configuration resembling an
enormous span of the hand, with the fingers touching
the surface of the wall.

The technique of displaying a photograph beneath a
shiny globule of glass is a device already seen in Wiltshire's
earlier work, *Seamen 1* (1992). Both depend for their impact
on the gradual recognition, on the part of the viewer, of the
imagery contained in the work. The viewer sees from a
distance ten bright red dots on the wall. On moving closer,
the viewer reaches a critical point where the recognition of
the dots as images of fingerprints coincides with the point
at which the viewer risks being stabbed by the protruding
glass spikes. This is the literal and metaphorical point of
communication between the artist and the viewer. On the
artist's part this is a moment that is filled with fear, 'as well
as a kind of desire, a desire to connect'. The work provides
a vivid visual metaphor for these conflicting feelings by
drawing in, and at the same time nearly attacking the
viewer.

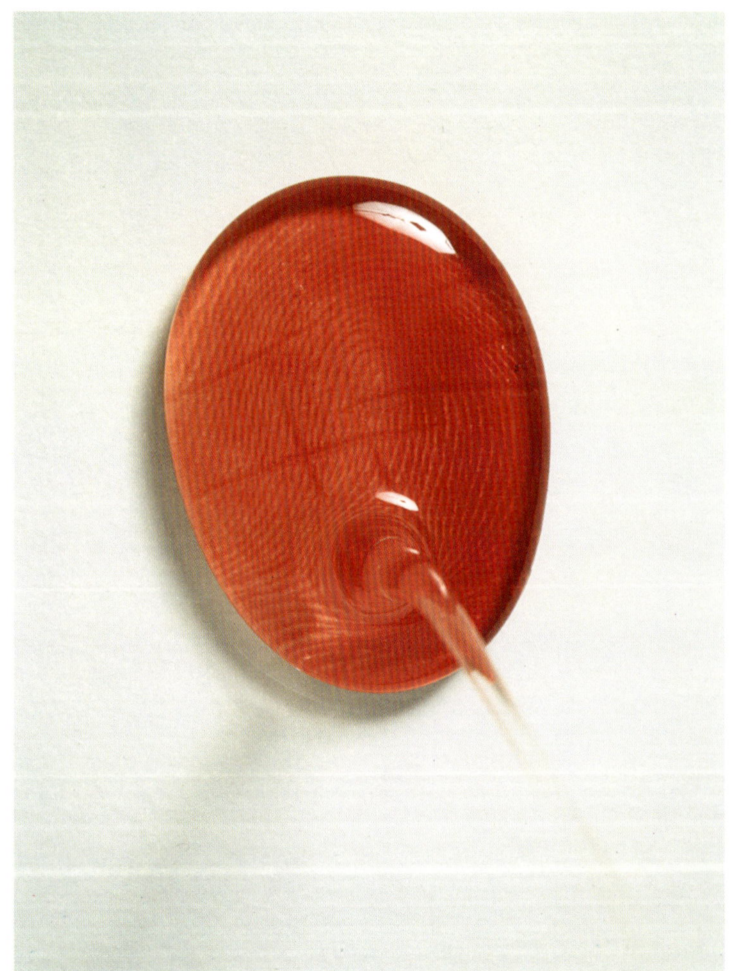

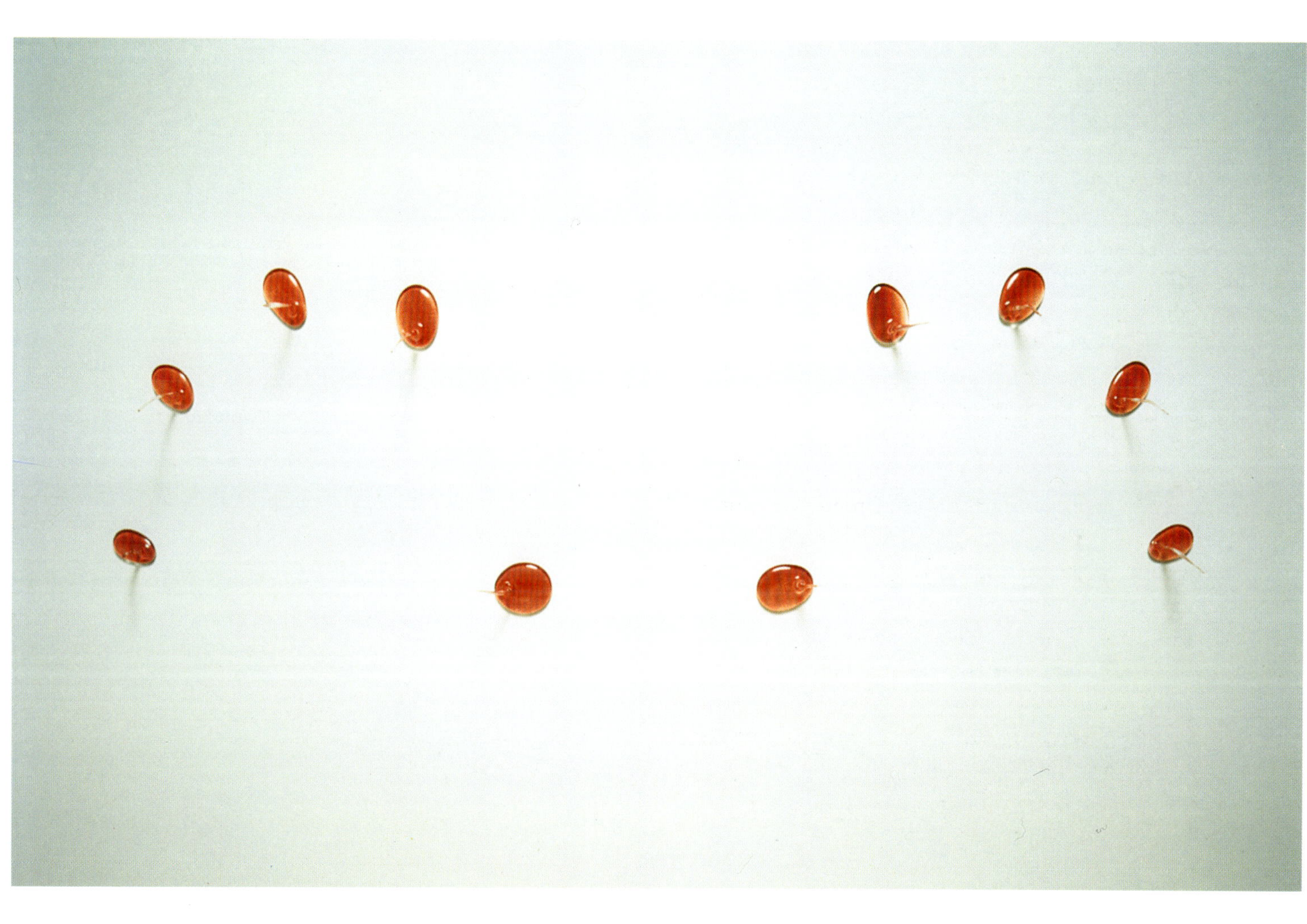

Hermione Wiltshire
Casanova
1994-6
Animated video installation
Screen: 60 x 40 cm
Duration: 2 minutes

Casanova is a digitally generated animation on a
continuous loop. The sequence lasts approximately two
minutes. The piece is seen back-projected on to a 60 × 40
cm screen recessed into the surrounding wall. The work
contains the digitally generated image of a soufflé in a bowl
which gradually rises to fantastic proportions. It bubbles
and browns as it cooks. It hovers at the top, or rather at its
full height, then makes a spectacular collapse, deflating in
an unruly manner until it has fallen back into the bowl.

This witty piece represents a play on gender definitions
and symbols which are not simply masculine. The artist's
choice of a soufflé lay in her desire to conflate both male
and female genders in the one image: the activity of
cooking being generally a female activity and the rising and
falling of the soufflé clearly mimicking a phallic erection.
The movement, tension and ultimate fragility of the soufflé
has parallels in the arena of human desire which Wiltshire
suggests 'is not exclusive to either male or female. . . . The
whole point about them (soufflés) is to get them to rise.
That's how you measure your success.'

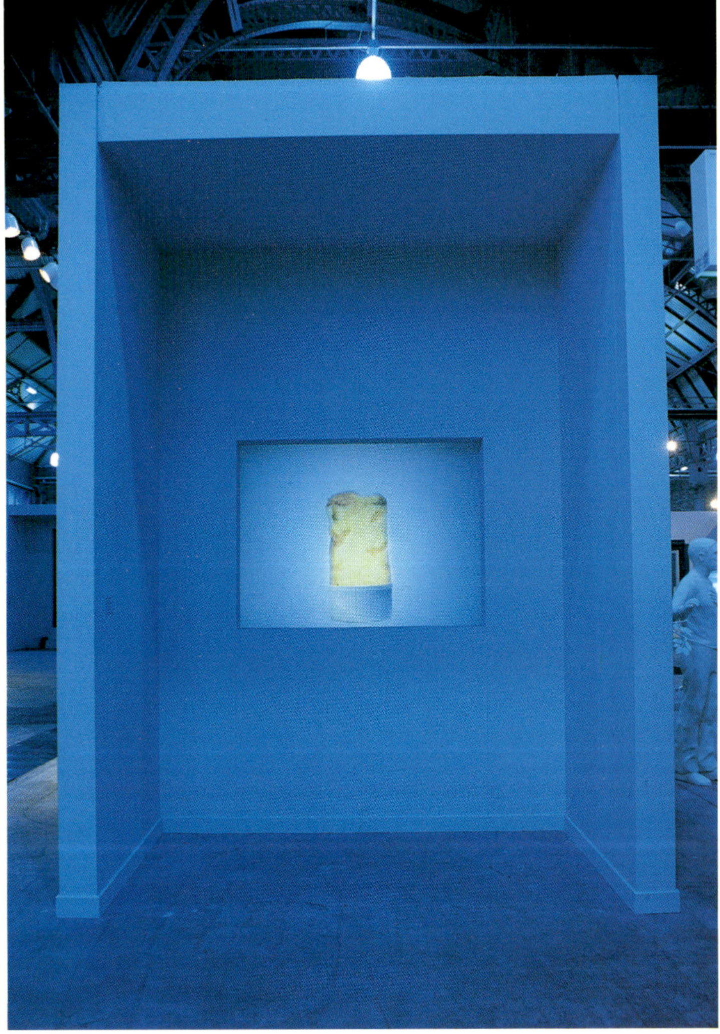

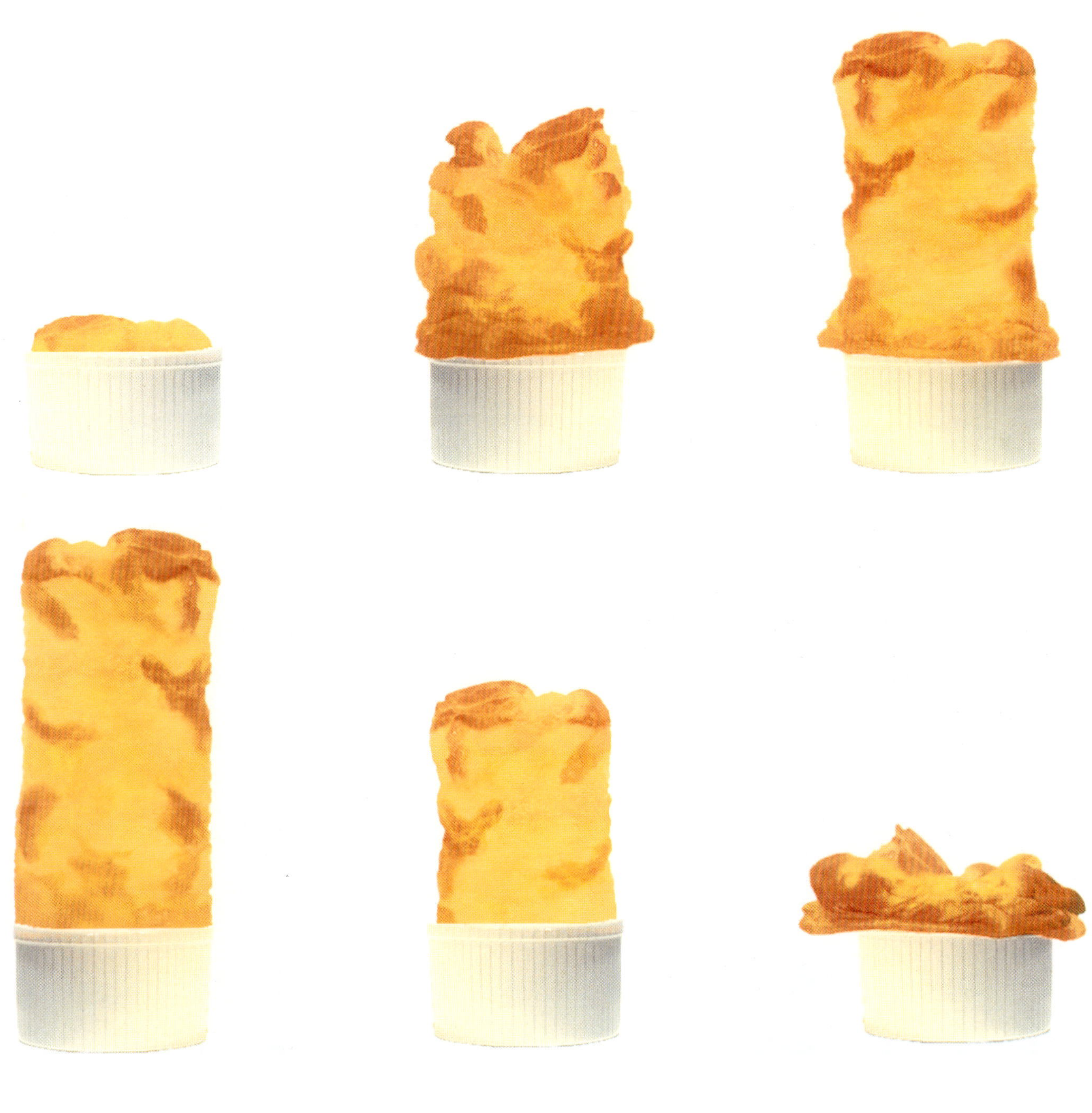

Damien Hirst

**Acquired inability
to escape**
1991
Glass, steel, table, chair,
ashtray, cigarettes, lighter
214 x 305 x 214 cm

Acquired inability to escape presents the viewer with a large vitrine divided into two unequal spaces, into the larger of which fit tightly a table and office chair. The glass panels are held by heavy steel frames bolted together. A packet of cigarettes, a lighter and an ashtray complete with cigarette butts rest on the table. The smaller compartment is empty. There is a narrow slot in the glass panel dividing the two compartments.

The glass case in Hirst's work is both an austere sculptural object and an echo of display mechanisms for precious objects in museums. This device has been a constant presence in Hirst's art, at once containing and sealing off tableaux of life, death and things of the *real world*, and re-presenting them framed by the geometry of the glass cases, which Hirst says makes 'people think about things they don't want to'.

Hirst explains that the title for the work comes from a conversation with curator Ulrich Loock, in which Loock mistranslated the title of a work by Bruce Nauman.

The tableau of *Acquired inability to escape* suggests that a person, now absent, has spent some time inside the glass case smoking cigarettes. Ironically, it is the paraphernalia of the smoker that suggests to us the presence of human life, however inexplicably he or she entered and exited the sealed vitrine. The viewer's imaginative identification with the supposed occupant of *Acquired inability to escape* may evoke a feeling of claustrophobia, and the work plays on the viewer's narrative instinct towards the implied drama of that absent individual.

In interview with Sophie Calle, Hirst says:

'Art seems to me to be about life. If art wasn't around we'd still have life but if life wasn't here you could forget about art so I find it difficult to believe in art. On one hand I want to be an artist and on the other I want to be realistic. There's a clash somewhere and a feeling in me that I can't override; the more I try to escape it the more deviously it evades me; it's an inescapable situation.'[1]

Hirst has also produced two related works to *Acquired inability to escape*. *Acquired inability to escape inverted* (1993) consists of a similar vitrine and contents to the first work, but here the table (complete with ashtray, cigarettes and lighter) and chair are inverted and fixed to the glass ceiling of the vitrine as if it were the floor. *Acquired inability to escape divided* (1993) features the glass, chair and table neatly cut through in the centre of the long side of the vitrine and pulled apart a few inches.

---

[1] Damien Hirst, ICA Exhibition Catalogue, 1991

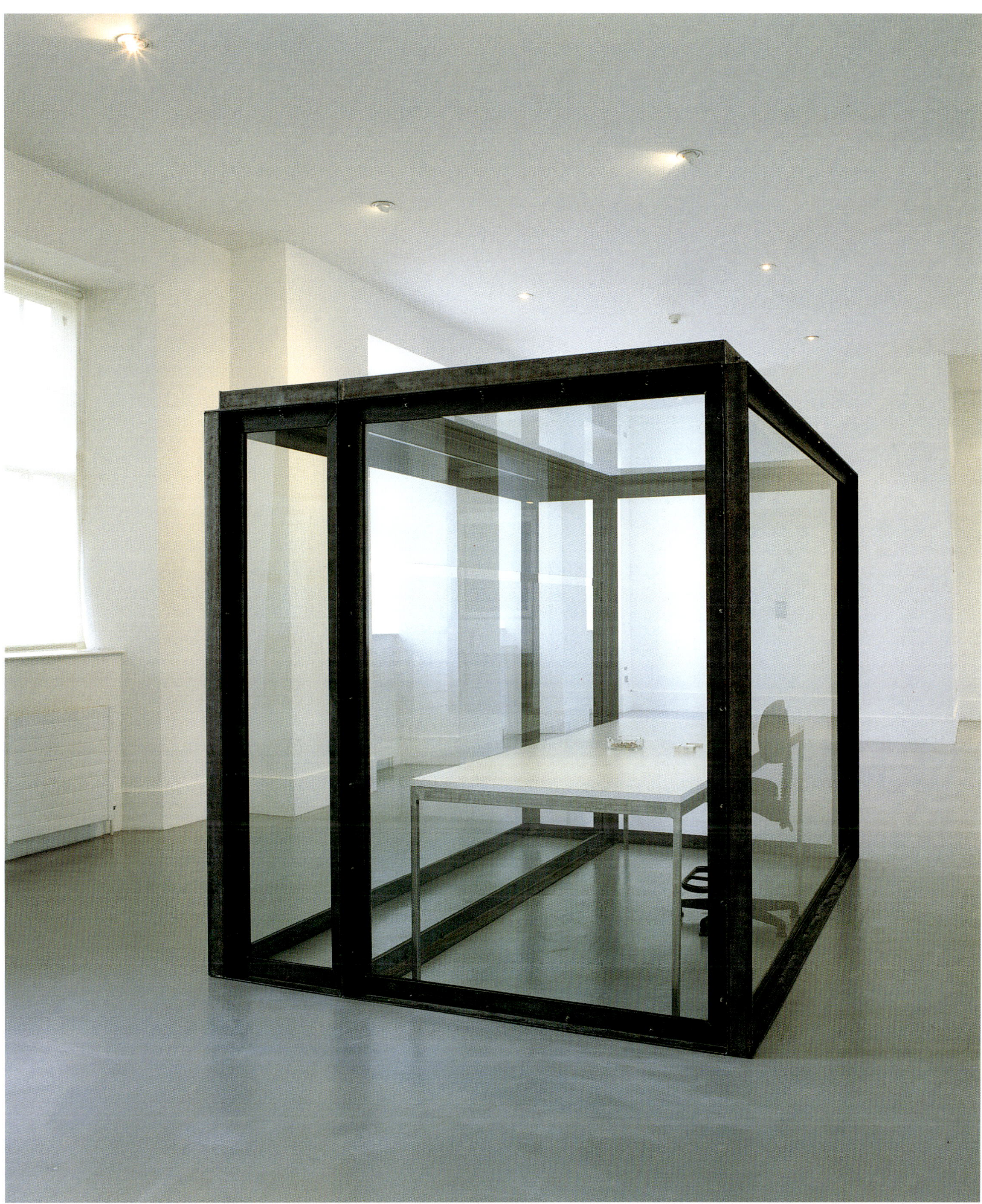

Vong Phaophanit

Neon rice field
1993
rice, clear red neon tubes
35 x 393 x 1460 cm

Neon rice field works directly and effectively on the senses. The sheer material presence of seven tons of white long-grain rice, formed into perfect furrows, is counterpointed by the delicate translucence of the rice where it rests on the long red strips of neon light. Six lines of neon run along the six troughs of the fourteen and a half metre furrowed 'field'. In addition to the work's visual impact, the rice also generates its own particular smell, which pervades the space beyond the material edge of the piece. Its form does not remain static in the viewer's gaze. As the intensity of the red light changes with the changing levels of daylight, the shadows of the window frames across the 'field' pick up the undulation of the rice.

Phaophanit is reluctant to pin down predetermined meanings to his work, preferring to allow for the viewer 'possibilities of meanings' through their own experience of the work:

'Once you've named all the meanings, something still remains, something left over. That's how I work. For instance, I use rice not only as a material, a substance, a smell or a symbol of food in the East, but I want to shake things – see what falls down.'[1]

Claire Oboussier also points out that writing about Phaophanit's work is a 'somewhat paradoxical enterprise in so much as the work itself consciously plays at the borders of what is and is not accommodated by language . . . the work does not illustrate a prefixed idea, but ideas emerge from and are embodied in the work.[2]

Interpretation of Phaophanit's practice has, more often then not, attempted to combine the artist's biographical background (born in Laos, educated in France and living in England) with the cultural associations of the materials the artist employs. This discourse on Phaophanit's practice in terms of a meeting of East and West, in a fixed definition of those terms, hides a more complex and problematic understanding than this dualism will permit. For instance, the identification of rice as standing as a unequivocal 'symbol' or 'metaphor' for the 'East' may serve as such at one level but, as the artist points out, the rice comes from America and the presence of neon, often assigned as a 'Western' motif, is ubiquitous with the cityscapes of any number of 'Eastern' cities such as Hong Kong, Tokyo or Bangkok.

Oboussier suggests that 'the metaphor mobilised here turns upon an impulse to regain and render the materiality of the substances he works with. Phaophanit's expanded form [of metaphor] ensures that the material can never entirely be collapsed into the discursive; it rescues the thing from the sign.'

[1] Interview with Adrian Searle, *Frieze*, Issue 1, 1991
[2] Claire Oboussier *'From Light'. Phaophanit and Piper*. Exhibition Catalogue, 1995

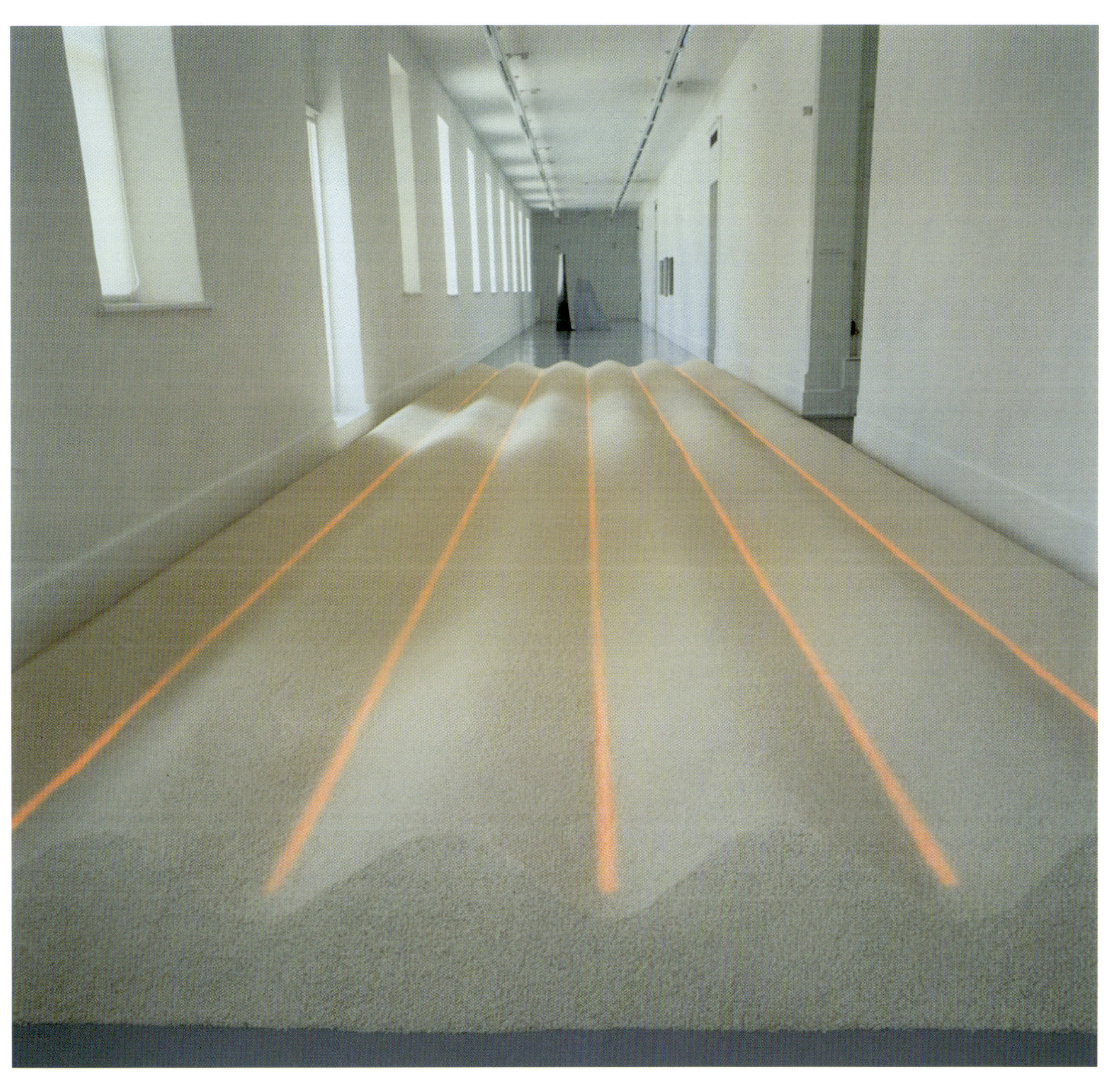

Rachel Whiteread

Untitled (black bed)
1991
Fibreglass and rubber
30 x 213 x 137 cm

Untitled (black bed) is a cast in rubber of the space under a bed. It could be any bed or every bed.

Whiteread turns this space into a discrete object which is imbued with a sense of past human activity in the same way that artefacts in an archaeological museum carry that feeling of past human use and proof of human existence.

At the beginning of her career the artist made casts in plaster. 'Initially I used plaster for its colour, density and inertness . . . its fragility was also important. I began to experiment with rubber as I wanted to use a material that was the complete antithesis of that.'[1]

As with her other casts of rooms, spaces and objects, Whiteread's *Untitled (black bed)* turns the viewer into an outsider to everyday reality. There is a literal displacement of the source object but there is also displacement for the viewer on the border between the familiar and the unfamiliar, between art and life. The work is almost banal – a mark of domesticity that seems transient, like a memento of provisional tenancy in bed-sit land rather than a permanent possession.

The work describes an absence. Beds are where bodies lie and where birth, sex and death take place but here the human body is absent. The sculpture becomes the body/figure on the 'ground' of whatever architectural space it occupies and also the ground of the viewer's imagination and memory. This specific work, and her 'bed' pieces in general, occupy an important position in Whiteread's practice. They combine an acute awareness of the properties of recent significant art like Minimalism, with its formal severity, and of an existential experience and a Freudian displacement of feelings on to objects.

Rachel Whiteread has also said that she 'cast all sorts of objects but one that recurs is the space beneath a bed – a sinister place'. In childhood the space beneath the bed could be attractive as a hiding place, or it could involve fear, a place to be avoided. Since for the artist the latter applies, the sculpture has a funereal feel.

Whereas rubber as a material adds a sensual, even fetishistic, dimension, it also takes on more precisely the characteristics, in reverse, of the source object. An increased emotional range becomes possible and *Untitled (black bed)* never feels simply like a record of a particular space or source object.

It stands at one remove from our everyday reality and it is this which makes it legible as art and allows it to touch the universal.

[1] All quotations from Turner Prize catalogue, Tate Gallery, 1993

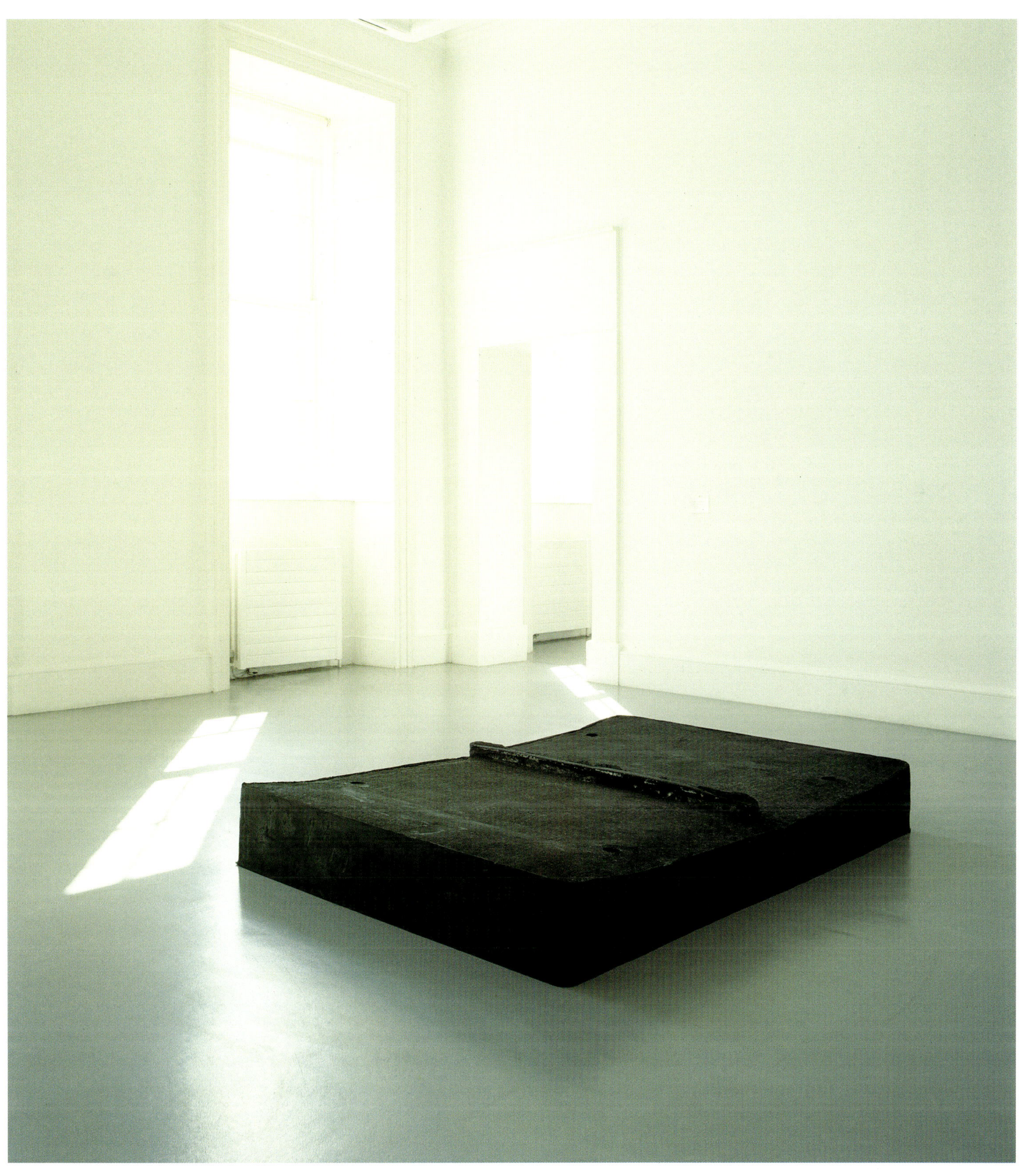

Avis Newman

Compass
1992-3
Four parts:
Diptych, prints and tables
 Acrylic pigment and graphite
on canvas
Boxed lithographic prints
Steel and painted wood
tables

Canvas: 254 x 254 cm each
Tables: 69 x 75 x 75 cm each
Two sets of boxed
lithographic prints:
32 x 31 x 17 cm
and 33 x 31 x 12 cm

Compass by Avis Newman belongs to a body of work begun in 1990 which breaks with her earlier reliance on natural forms. It is a four-part installation which comprises a canvas diptych, two sets of boxed and numbered lithographs, and two tables which rest on pairs of compasses – like steel legs.

The canvases are covered in graphite which has been overlaid with semi-opaque washes of zinc-white. This process involves time, a 'before' and 'after' or 'then' and 'now' state, and also a progression from darkness to light.

The two identical graphited tables are placed symmetrically in front of these canvases but here the symmetry is subtly disturbed. Four sets of prints are laid open on the table on the left while that on the right has six. The four books correspond to the four elements of the *Book of Creation* from the Jewish Kabbalah while the remaining six refer to the six dimensions of space. All ten are a metaphor for the structure of all things in the universe. The apex of the isosceles triangle formed by the elegant compass legs and the printed circle of the books are considered by the artist as generative points or points of renewal.

The 'books' in *Compass* have the numbers 0-||||||||| in letter form printed on them in black, a variation on the similar prints numbered 0-9 in the companion work *Book of number*s, 1991.

The piece encompasses a range of positive and negative, open and closed, light and dark contrasting positions, all held in equilibrium.

The use of letters to represent numbers, which require the mathematical process of counting, draws on literary, mathematical and visual languages. The actual numbers 0-9 represented in letters on the printed pages imply the possibility of infinite permutation, but the boxes which house the prints may represent a need to contain this openness.

Edmund Jabès, who has been acknowledged as an important influence by Newman, declared that true knowledge is the recognition that in the end we know nothing. For him however, the Nothing is also knowledge, 'being the reversal of All, as the air is the reverse of the wing'.[1]

[1]Quoted by Richard Stamelman, 'The Graven Silence of Writing', in *From the Book to the Book: An Edward Jabès Reader*, trans. Rosemarie Waldrop, Wesleyan University Press, 1991, p.14

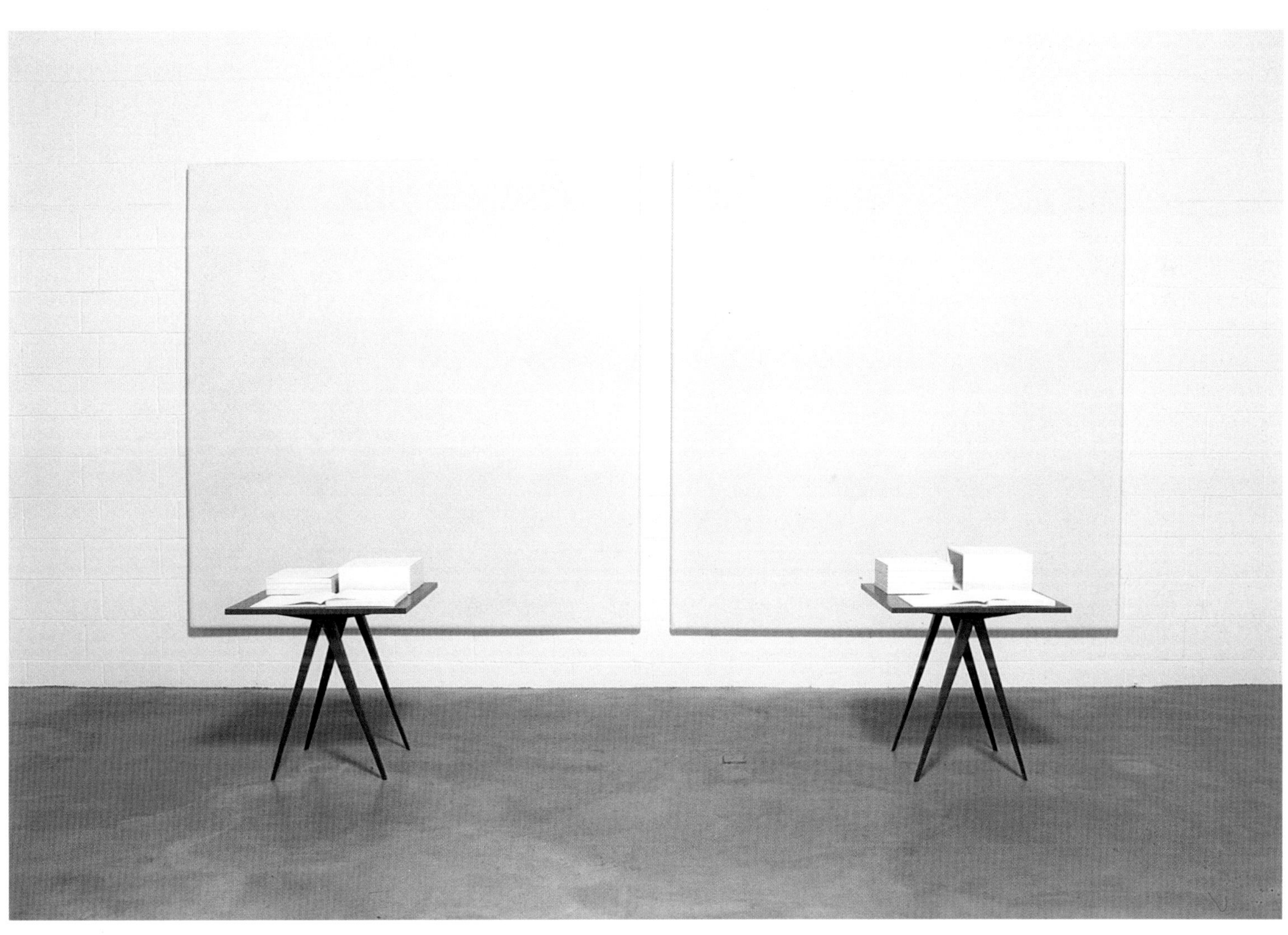

Avis Newman
Nests there are . . .
1986-7
Pigment on muslin, steel,
bird's wing, honeycomb
38 x 38 x 8 cm

The title of this work is taken from Antoine Bourdelle's
lines 'Nests there are where love trembles in soft laughter,
and in the deep, dark forks of the branches are harpies
whose arms end in terrible singers',[1] which he wrote in
response to Rodin's watercolour drawing of *The embrace*
(Metropolitan Museum of Art, New York). The work, with
its complex combination of natural objects (bird's feathers
and honeycomb), industrial material (steel) and painting
refers at once, to nature, craft and art, reflecting the same
layering of meaning and experience as Bourdelle's lines. It
also focuses on the intangibility of the imagination, as real
objects fuse with the artist's drawn image, and symbols of
freedom and nature are tightly contained in its glazed and
boxed frame.

[1] *Rodin: Later Drawings with Interpretations by Antoine Bourdelle* by
Elizabeth Chase Geisbuhler, Peter Owen, London, 1963

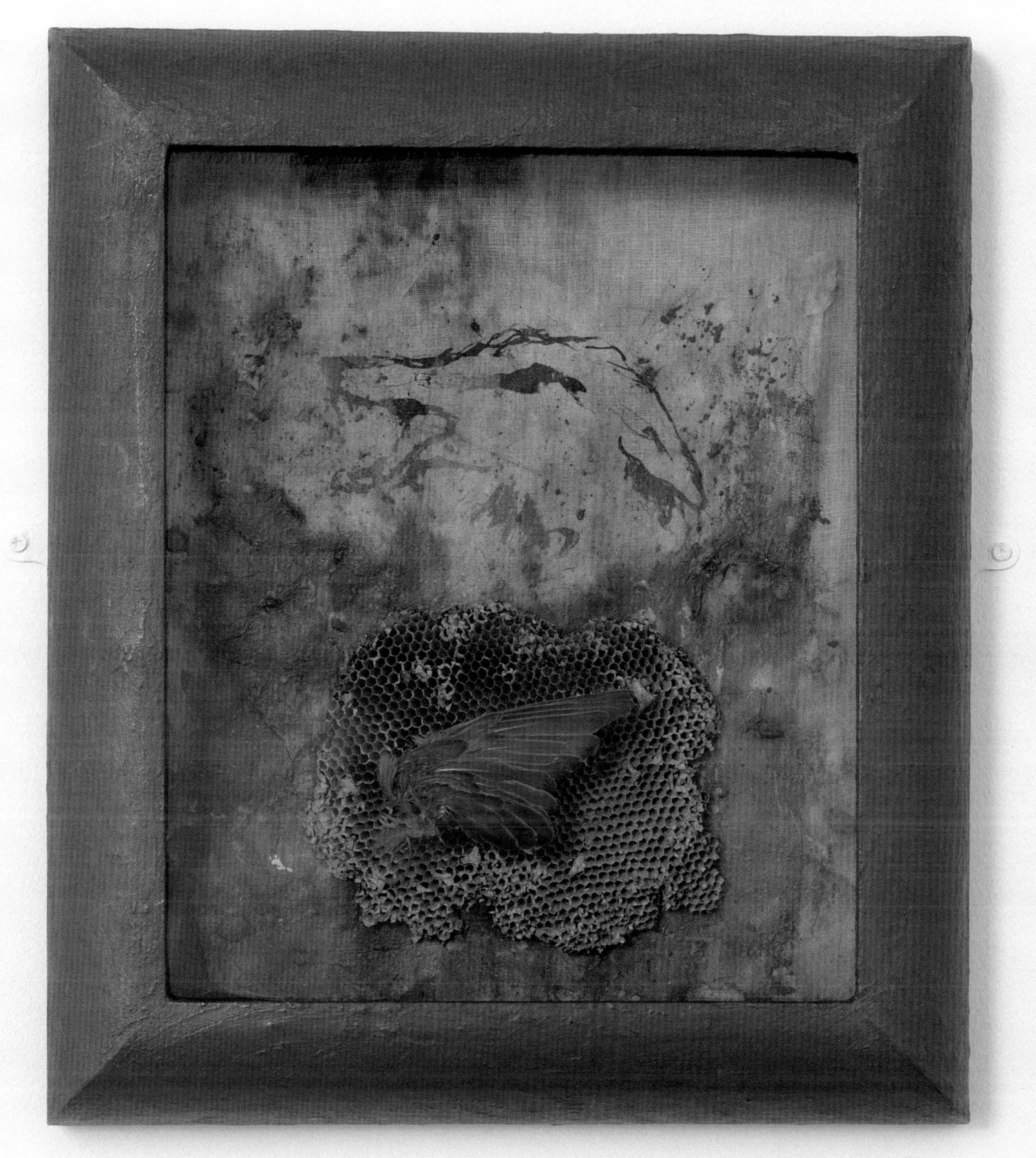

Douglas Gordon

Above all else
1991
Painted directly onto gallery
ceiling
Lettering: 122 cm

Much of Douglas Gordon's artwork prior to 1991 when *Above all else* was installed at the Serpentine Gallery, London, was executed for non-gallery spaces, the context always being central to the meaning of the work. *Above all else*, however, was created very deliberately with the cupola of the Serpentine Gallery in mind. 'I feel that the gallery situation is one where the viewer *expects* (artist's emphasis) to engage with a work rather than experience the surprise of art in public places.' The word 'expects' is important here as Gordon loves to subvert expectations. In the case of *Above all else* he plays on the Baroque convention of *trompe l'oeil* ceiling painting, but instead of cavorting deities, the dome at the Serpentine bore the almost banal message 'We Are Evil' superimposed in four foot high black lettering on a sky-blue background.

The title *Above all else* is at once a reference to the architectural location and the first half of what appears to be a rather negative fundamentalist religious text. Ironically, the source of the words 'we are evil' was a football supporters' chant which Gordon overheard on the train from Glasgow to London.

The use of text – usually composed of single sentences of no more than three or four words – was typical of Douglas Gordon's work in the early 1990s. Unlike the text-based work of such pioneers of Conceptualism as Laurence Weiner, Joseph Kosuth and On Kawara, Gordon is more concerned with psychological space and memory than with the delineation of architectural space. The source of the text used here reflects Gordon's commitment to mass communicability and is fully in keeping with an art practice that makes use of everyday channels of contact such as the letter and the telephone as his media, and who has, since *Above all else,* used popular films as a basis for his art.

Above all else was created for 'The Barclay's Young Artist Award' at the Serpentine Gallery, London, in 1991.

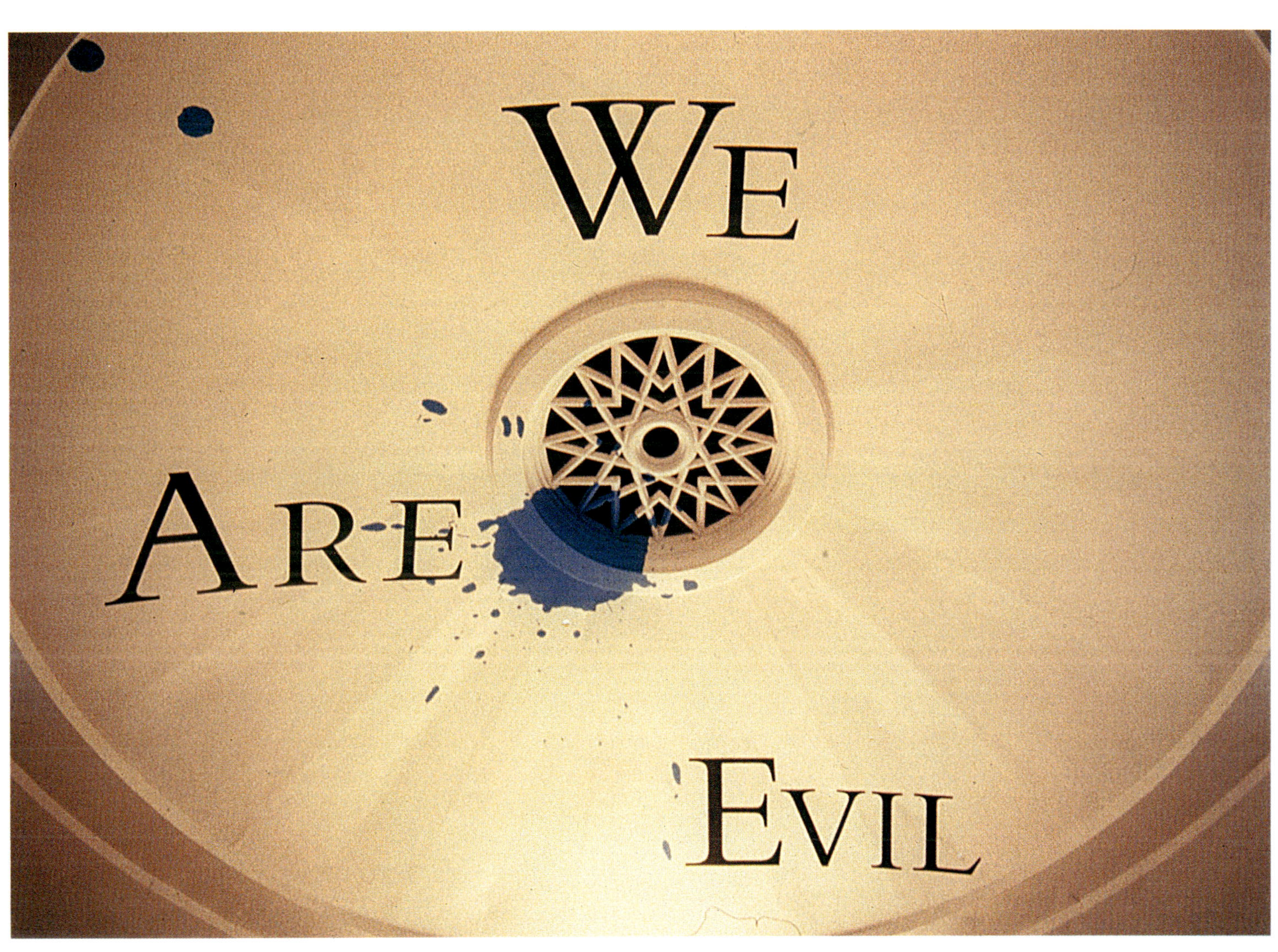

WE
ARE
EVIL

Julian Opie

D/889-E
1990
Paint on wood, glass
98 x 289.5 x 208 cm

D/889-E is a wooden construction consisting of painted white walls at right angles to each other, punctured by various rectangular windows. Julian Opie's sculptures since 1987 resemble and evoke the features of corporate and public interior space and the fittings and accessories associated with large modern buildings such as offices or airports. *D/889-E* is a later work in this period which does not reference the furnishings of these spaces so much as the architecture itself.

D/889-E has three points of reference: sculpture, architecture and painting. Although it is a sculptural object insofar as it inhabits the gallery environment, in form and scale it can be said to have architectural aspirations. The self containment and physical inaccessibility of the work means that the viewer's perception of the space that *D/889-E* occupies can only be experienced imaginatively, apprehended as a pictorial or represented space.

Ulrich Loock sees Opie's work 'as serving to underline and reveal the connection between transparency and denial – granting a view and withholding access'. This can be seen as a deconstruction or critique of the rhetoric of utopian Modernist architecture where the notion of transparency represented a claim to rationality and clarity. Although the work is viewed through the windows, certain parts of the interior are hidden. And whereas from a particular viewpoint each and every corner of the interior can be seen, this does not supply any new visual experience or reveal any significant information about the work's internal structure. Loock states:

'For everything that is on view, it might still be said that there is nothing to be seen – despite the visual access granted by transparency. In Opie's *Houses* transparency itself becomes the subject – but transparency is, in a sense, only a form of opacity. . . . The Houses seem to provide images that lack the object they are hiding or referring to.´. . . This is a characteristic of the new digital electronic imaging in which views, perspectives and projections can be created and manipulated in a plausible way but with no basis in reality.'[1]

[1] *Beyond the Architectural,* in the Julian Opie Exhibition Catalogue at The Hayward Gallery, 1993–4

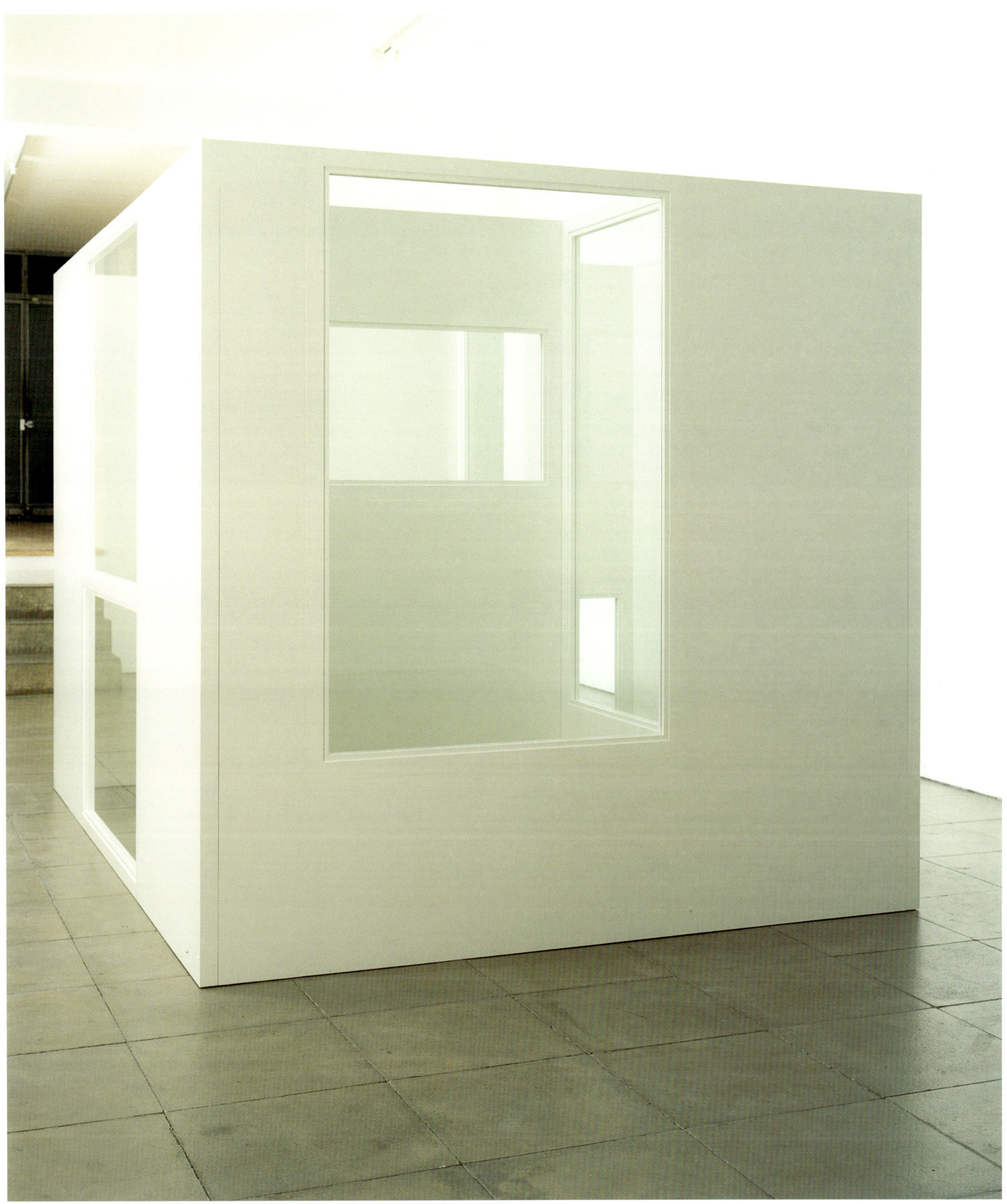

Willie Doherty

**The only good one is a
dead one**
1993
Double screen video
projection with sound
Variable dimensions

Willie Doherty's work is concerned with the way images disseminated through mass media manipulate our interpretations of events and people, particularly in the construction of notions of ethnic or national identity. Doherty's themes and subjects are drawn from his own local experience of Derry, and his practice does not so much seek to present a more authentic representation of the political landscape as to examine and comment upon the 'question of authenticity'.

Jean Fisher describes *The only good one is a dead one* in the following way:

'The work presents a double screen video projection installed in such a way that the two constantly repeated sequences cannot be seen simultaneously. Both sequences, shot at night, draw on documentary and cinematic clichés. One is a shot from the driver's perspective of a journey down a winding country road on the edge of the city; the other is from inside a stationary car observing the pedestrian and traffic movements at a street corner. These are accompanied by a male voice-over narrating an interior monologue that switches between the speculations of a man stalking a target whose life he has intimately observed, and those of one who fears himself to be the same object of another's scrutiny. As the work progresses, we become acutely conscious that killer and target not only share a common cultural space and everyday experiences, but also that these are interchangeable, self-engendering positions trapped in an endless cycle of paranoid fear and hatred that their very commonality renders irrational and ultimately banal. More unnerving is the narrator imagining his own assassination as if he were in a film ("I see the same shot from different angles. I see a sequence of fast edits . . . I could write the script . . ."), as if life were a replay of established fiction.'[1]

Interviewed on Channel 4 during the 1995 Turner Prize, Doherty commented on *The only good one is a dead one*:

'It was very much about trying to visualise a certain kind of fear or paranoia . . . one of the most important things that I could contribute with this work to the whole discussion about sectarian violence, the nature of sectarian violence and how it victimises the population, was to propose that it was possible to imagine oneself in both the role of victim and the role of perpetrator and, I suppose, to look at their mutual dependency. The physical set-up of the piece is crucial in that it directly mirrors that relationship and forces the viewer in the space to bridge that gap and move around and move between those polarities (of victim and perpetrator).'

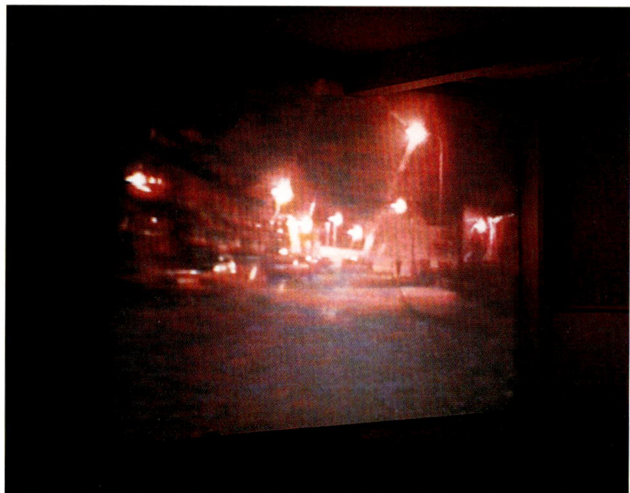

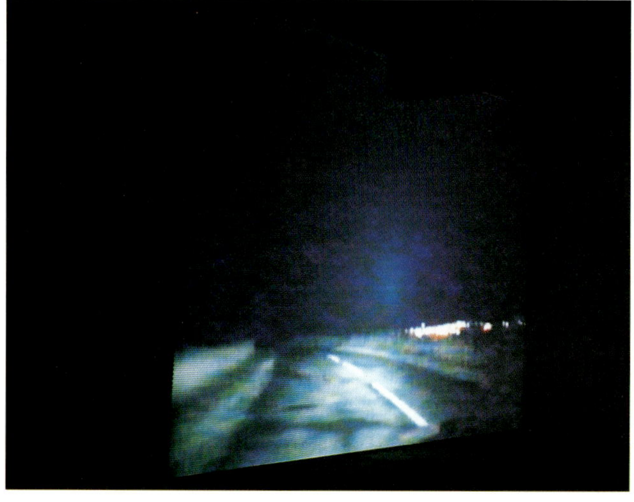

---

[1] Jean Fisher, *The only good one is a dead one*, Exhibition Catalogue at Edmonton and Mendel Art Gallery, Saskatoon, Canada, 1996

Transcript of the soundtrack

I worry about driving the same route everyday . . . . Maybe I should try out different roads . . . alternate my journey. That way I could keep them guessing. I don't remember now when I started feeling conspicuous. . . . A legitimate target.

I've been watching him for weeks now. He does the same things everyday. . . . Sadly predictable, I suppose.

The fucker deserves it.

We've known about him for a long time but we've been waiting for the right moment. Waiting for him to make a move.

I keep thinking about this guy who was shot. . . . I remember his brother said, 'We were sitting having a cup of tea watching the TV when I heard this loud bang at the front door. . . . We both jumped up to see what it was, he was nearer the door than me and got into the hall first. . . . But by that time the gunman was also in the hall and fired three or four shots directly at him . . . point blank range. . . . I'm a lucky man because then he panicked and ran out to the street where a car was waiting for him.'

Sometimes I feel like I'm wearing a big sign, 'SHOOT ME'.

As far as I'm concerned he's a legitimate target.

The only good one is a dead one.

If I'd had the shooter earlier I could have had him a dozen times. Dead easy! . . . I walked right up behind him, looked straight at the back of his head. He was wearing a checked shirt and faded jeans. He didn't even notice me and I walked straight past him.

I'm certain that my phone's bugged and that someone is listening to my conversations. Everytime I lift the receiver to answer a call I hear a loud click as if someone else is lifting the phone at the same time. I'm not imagining it because some of my friends also hear this strange noise when they call me. My anxiety increases when my phone rings occasionally in the middle of the night. This is totally inexplicable as no-one would want to ring me at three or four in the morning. It scares the hell out of me. I think that my killer is ringing to check if I'm at home.

He reminds me of someone, maybe someone I went to school with.

I feel like I know this fucker. I know where he lives, his neighbours, his car . . . I'm sick of looking at him.

I saw a funeral on TV last night. Some man who was shot in Belfast. A young woman and three children standing crying at the side of a grave. . . . Heartbreaking.

One morning, just before I left home at half six, I heard a news report about a particularly savage and random murder. That's how I imagine I will be shot . . . as I drive alone in the dark I visualise myself falling into an ambush or being stopped by a group of masked gunmen . . . I see these horrific events unfold like a scene from a movie. . . . I was very relieved when dawn broke and the sky brightened to reveal a beautiful clear winter morning.

He drives the same road every day, buys petrol at the same garages. . . . It'd be easy. No sweat! I can't stop thinking about the awful fear and terror he must have felt. Maybe it was so quick he didn't know a thing.

I can almost see myself waiting for him along the road. It's fairly quiet so it should be safe to hide the car and wait for him as he slows down at the corner. A couple of good clean shots should do the job.

This particular part of the road is very shaded. Tall oak trees form a luxuriant canopy of cool green foliage. The road twists gently and disappears at every leafy bend.

As my assassin jumps out in front of me everything starts to happen in slow motion. I can see him raise his gun and I can't do a thing. I see the same scene shot from different angles. I see a sequence of fast edits as the car swerves to avoid him and he starts shooting. The windscreen explodes around me. I see a clump of dark green bushes in front of me, illuminated by the car headlights. The car crashed out of control and I feel a deep burning sensation in my chest.

In the early morning the roads are really quiet . . . you can drive for ages without passing another car . . . the landscape is completely undisturbed and passes by like some strange detached movie.

It might be just as easy on the street. . . . I could wait until he's coming out of the house or I could just walk up to the door, ring the bell and when he answers . . . BANG BANG! . . . Let the fucker have it.

It should be an easy job with a car waiting at the end of the street . . . I've seen it so many times I could write the script.

In the past year I've had some really irrational panic attacks. . . . There is no reason for this but I think that I'm a victim.

I worry about driving the same route everyday . . . . Maybe I should try out different roads . . . alternate my journey. That way I could keep them guessing.

I don't remember now when I started feeling conspicuous. . . . A legitimate target.

I've been watching him for weeks now. He does the same things everyday. . . . Sadly predictable, I suppose.

Shirazeh Houshiary

¹ **Defence of light**
1989
Brass, copper, crystal, coal
157.2 x 223.5 x 122 cm

² **The dividing blade is love**
1994
Lead, platinum leaf
99 x 33 x 33 cm

³ **Undoing the knot**
1994
Lead and gold leaf
85 x 150 x 150 cm,
15 x 150 x 150 cm

Defence of light (1989) was the beginning of a series of works that investigate light and its effect on different materials. Concepts of transformation, and 'perhaps a kind of alchemy' lie at the root of Houshiary's work. Her later sculptures, which she regards as a reflection of her paintings, are more austere and ethereal in quality.

For Houshiary her sculptures 'are like a reflection of the paintings now. The paintings are the most intimate experience I have and the sculptures are like the crystallisation of these thoughts.'

While paintings such as *Resonance* result from a physically labour-intensive activity, Houshiary no longer directly makes her sculptures herself, working more like an architect in the design of the objects. The manufacture of the work is done by professional fabricators from detailed drawings by the artist.

The two elements that make up *Undoing the knot* symbolise the concept of Divinity present in Sufi spirituality. In this philosophy the Divine One is a unity, but the Divinity is manifest in the universe through multiplicity.

The duality of the Divine as represented in light and dark is a central feature of Houshiary's work. The materials of gold and lead, in their reflection or absorption of light, symbolise this duality. The use of metals as vehicles of light also refer to planetary systems in *The dividing blade is love*. The light is present in the platinum material. As Houshiary states:

'The colour of light is like the sun or the moon and the work very often has a relationship with the planetary systems. . . . In *The dividing blade is love*, it's very simple; it's almost like the paradox or duality of what is there and what is not there.'[1]

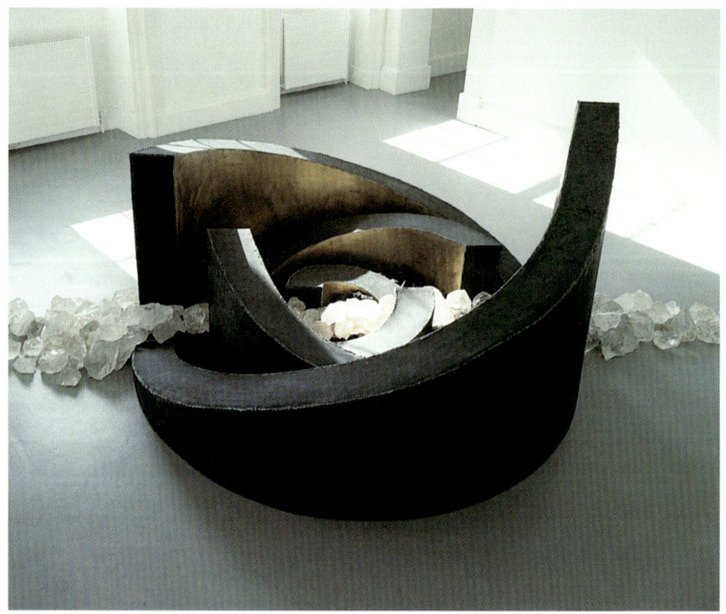

1

---

[1]This and subsequent unattributed quotations by Shirazeh Houshiary in conversation with Ronan McCrea, The Irish Museum of Modern Art, 1997

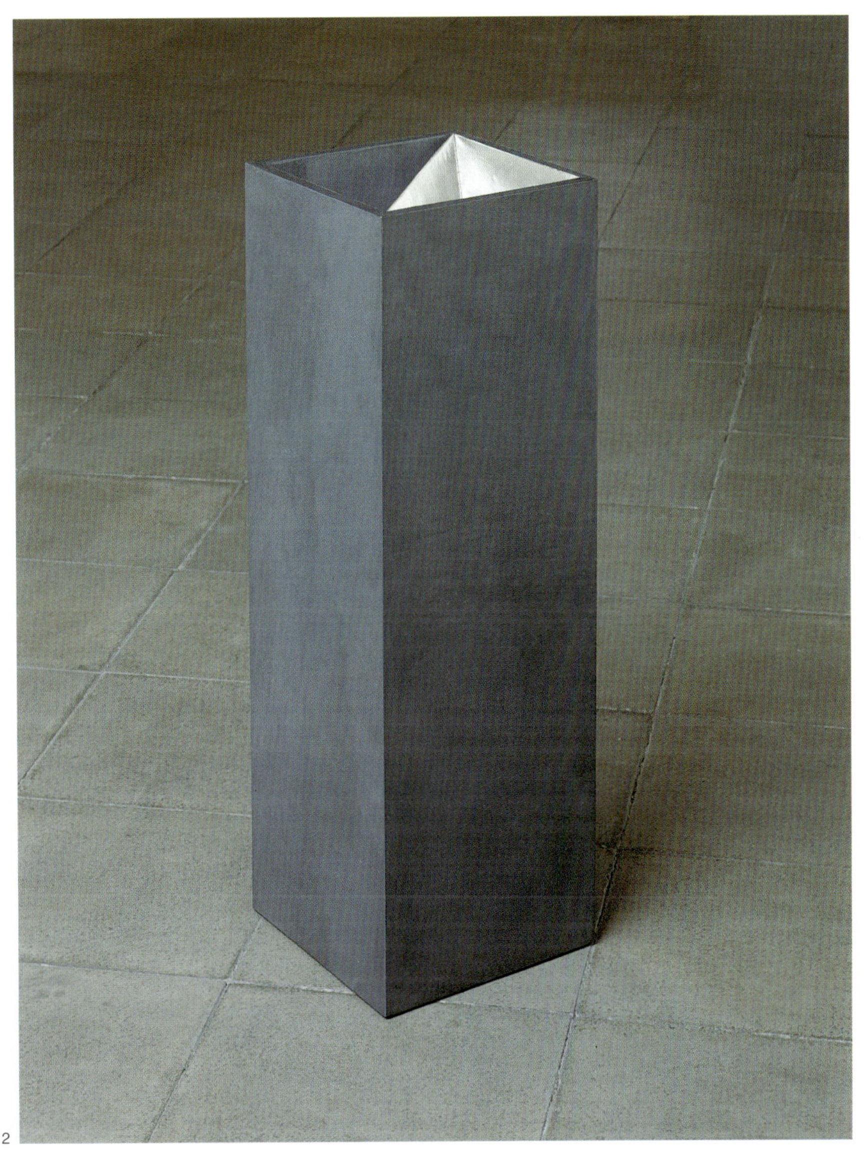

2

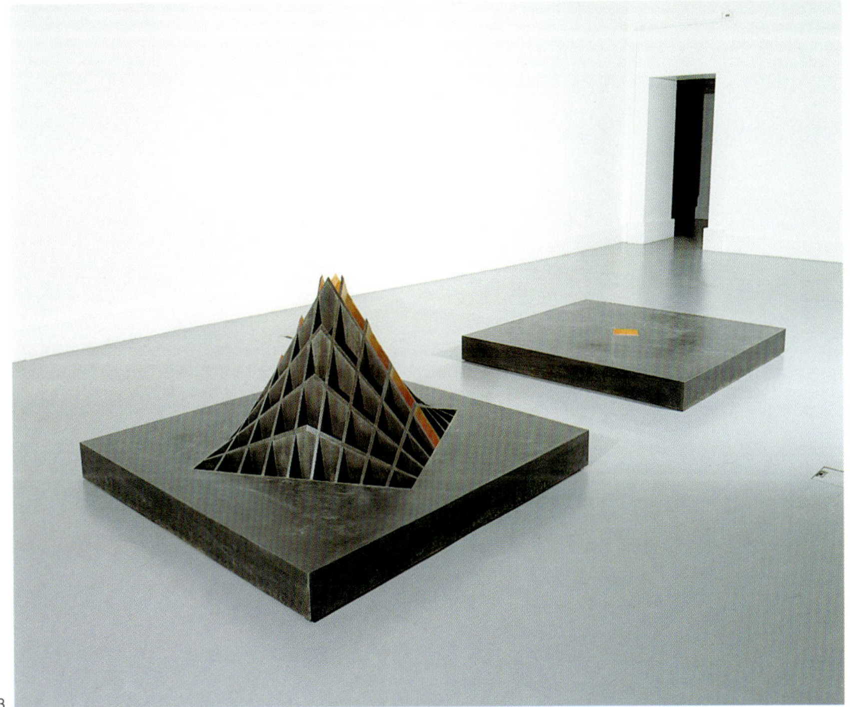

3

Shirazeh Houshiary
Resonance
1994
Graphite and acrylic on
canvas
Five parts: each 134 x 134 cm

The idea that behind the outward appearance of things
lies an inner reality that can be expressed in an abstract
language is central to Houshiary's artistic practice. The
series of forms with which she works are determined by
logical rules and the numerical and geometrical symbolism
drawn from the cosmology of Sufism, the esoteric and
mystical tradition of the Islamic faith. Dating from the
beginning of the eighth century, Sufism seeks the inner
way or spiritual path to mystical union with God.
Houshiary does not celebrate national or individual
identity in her art; rather she seeks to employ forms and
symbols that are universal. The artist also sees such
symbolism in other traditions such as those of ancient
Greece, Judaism and Christianity.

'In my work there is a continual use of already existing forms and
symbols precisely because the problem is not to be original, nor
indeed to establish a distinction between forms of knowledge or
between East and West.'[1]

The use of intricate pattern, geometry and calligraphy in
Islamic sacred art, which symbolise religious doctrines and
universal laws, also reflects the aniconic nature of Islamic
art tradition which forbids the depiction of God or the
Divine in a concrete image. One basis of Islamic art is the
belief that the Divine One is a unity but that his divinity is
manifest in the universe through multiplicity. This duality
of Oneness and Multiplicity, as well as the unity of light
and dark, can be seen in both Houshiary's paintings and
sculptures.

Resonance consists of five square canvases each the
same size. Four are flat black grounds and one is white.
Using graphite, each canvas is painstakingly inscribed
with dense minute Arabic script, the words repeated
many times, spinning out into geometric shapes and woven
so closely together that they become illegible. Houshiary
notes:

'What the word says is irrelevant. Somebody who understood
the language could not read it any more due to the intensity
of writing, and somehow the word loses its meaning, which
creates another meaning, which is the form, which is the activity.'

The poetry of the thirteenth-century Sufi mystic Jalal-
Din Rumi has inspired Houshiary and often provides the
starting point for such work as *Resonance*. In common
with Rumi's poems, the activity of making the paintings
is akin to a chant. As Houshiary points out:

'Rumi wrote thousands and thousands of couplets all about One.
It's like a chant. So for me that is where the relationship comes;
I'm creating forms too, but he does it with words, and we are both
praising life. The activity of the paintings is about *now* –
capturing the moment. Because it is incredibly physical to realise
these paintings, it is like a kind of dance. I have to turn inside the
painting itself to create these works and this act of turning and
movement happens in the body itself . . . my activities have
become more involved with music and dance and my
involvement with poetry has made me conscious that words are
sound and form.'

[1]Interview with Stella Santacatterina, *Third Text* No. 27, 1994

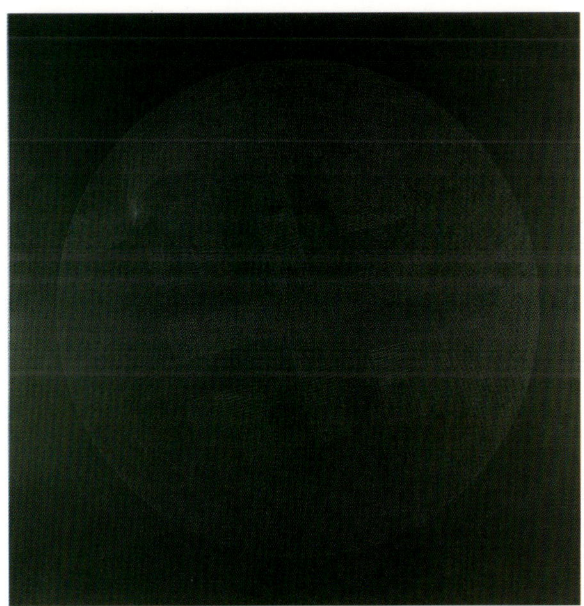

Michael Landy

Costermonger stall no.3
1991
Costermonger stall, flowers,
lights
239 x 183 x 122 cm

Costermonger stall no.3 consists of a brightly painted renovated second-hand costermonger stall filled with a display of fresh flowers and festoon lighting. The stall was acquired by the artist from Tapie Brothers, Lambeth High Street, London, a company engaged in renovating and renting out costermonger stalls to street traders. The company's name and address are inscribed on to the wheels and body of the stall. The term 'costermonger' is derived from nineteenth-century apple sellers (coster being a type of apple), but more generally such stalls are found in London markets used for the sale of fruit, vegetables or flowers.

Landy was asked how an audience might respond to this work:

'The recognition of the object as art is contingent on the context in which it is shown; the institution gives it some credence (as art) so obviously if I wheeled my *Costermonger stall no.3* in and amongst other costermonger stalls at a flower market you wouldn't be able to differentiate between them. My *Costermonger stall no.3* is big and generous and is saying to people: "like me, please", and at the same time it's putting it up to people as well. It gives them (the audience) what they want and then sort of takes it away. People may think it's quaint but that is not what particularly interests me. I like the thing because it's big and yellow and red and so decorative.'[1]

Costermonger stall no.3 was preceded by *Costermonger stall no.1* (a two-wheel model, rather like a wheelbarrow), and *Costermonger stall no.2* consisted of a full costermonger's stall, a similar model to *no.3* but empty and without festoon lighting. Both these works were destroyed by the artist. Asked why, unlike the previous two works, he chose to fill *Costermonger stall no.3* with flowers Landy replied:

'When I showed them (*nos 1* and *2*) with nothing on them they were just themselves, but I wanted it (*no.3*) to look as ridiculous as possible, but also because (in markets) costermonger stalls do have flowers on them. Anyway I just wanted to camp it up a bit.'

Costermonger stall no.4, the last in this series, conceived in 1991 but only executed in 1997 was included in the *Sensation* exhibition as part of the Saatchi collection at the Royal Academy from September to December 1997. It is smaller with slightly different colour combinations but is otherwise identical. The illustration in the *Sensation* catalogue is of *Costermonger stall no.3* when it was exhibited in the Royal Academy's summer exhibition in 1993.

---

[1] This and following quotation in conversation with Ronan McCrea, The Irish Museum of Modern Art, 1996

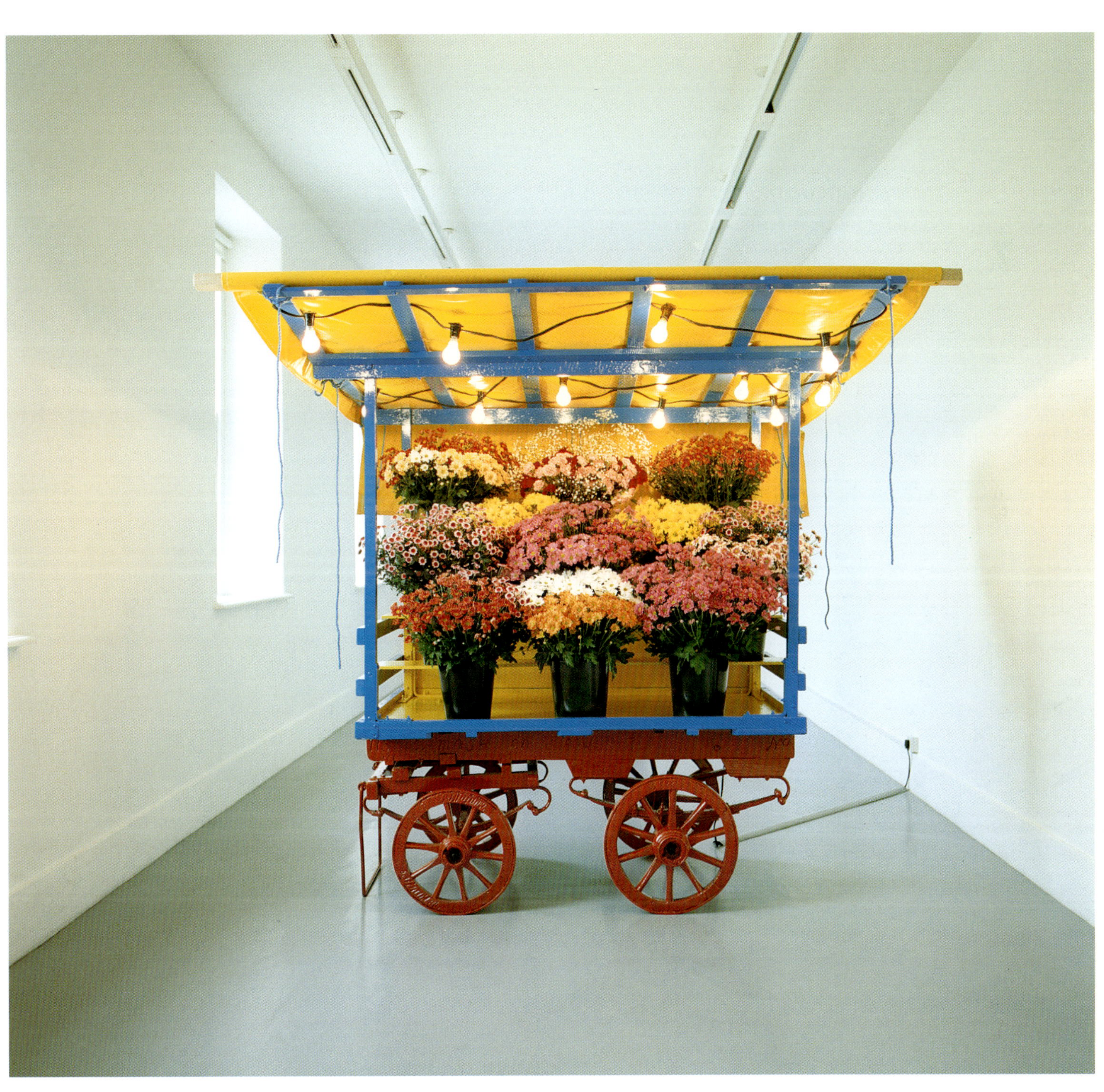

Works on Paper in the Weltkunst Collection

Drawings and Sketchbooks

Edward Allington

After Piranesi 1987
6 drawings
Sepia ink on used ledger paper
(1) 26.5 × 42 cm
(2) 27 × 41.5 cm
(3) 35 × 45 cm
(4-6) 21 × 27 cm

Grenville Davey

Group of 58 sketches 1986-93
Varying dimensions, pencil and coloured
inks on plain, lined or coloured paper, which
includes working drawings for *Butt* 1990,
Vinyl (pair) 1988, *Fat edge* 1989, *Trommel*
1989, *By air* 1989, *Labil* 1988, *Cover* 1987,
Purl 1988, *Button* 1988, *Blass* 1988.

Group of 112 sketches 1987-90
Various dimensions, pencil and coloured inks
on paper, which include working sketches
relating to *Grey seal* 1987, *Fat edge* 1989,
Plain 1989, *Vent* 1987, *By air* 1989, *Over* 1989,
Quad 1988, *Button* 1988, *Right 3rd and 6th*
1989, *Vinyl* (pair) 1988, *Blesa* 1989.

Group of 10 sketches 1988-9
Ink on paper, includes 9 sketches for the
works *Plain* 1989 and *Red giant* 1988.

Group of 40 sketches 1992-3
38 sketches which relate to Chisenhale
invitation card, *Eye, Q*, 1993.

Group of 11 sketches (undated)
Varying dimensions, pencil and coloured inks
on paper which include sketches relating to
the works *Cover* 1987, *Labil* 1988 and *Quad*
1988.

Sketchbook 2 1988-9
56 sketches, 54 ink on paper, 2 pencil on
paper, which include sketches related to
Right 3rd and 6th 1989, *Fat edge* 1989, *Plain*
1989, *Quad* 1988, *Labil* 1988, *Button* 1988.

Sketchbook 3 1988-9
55 sketches on Letraset A4, pencil and ink on
paper including sketches relating to *Fat edge*
1989, *Quad* 1988, *Button* 1988, *Purl* 1988, *By
air* 1989, installation plan for the Lisson
Gallery 1989 exhibition, *Vinyl* (pair) 1988,
Runner 1989.

Sketchbook 4 1985-9
12 miscellaneous studies, various
dimensions, pencil/ink on paper.

Sketchbook 5 1986-94
48 Sketches on Letraset A4, pencil and ink on
paper, which include sketches relating to
Manubrium 1994, *Labil* 1988, *By air* 1989,
Over 1989, *Err* (complete) 1989, *Drum* 1989,
Button 1988, *Quad* 1988, *Grey seal* 1987, *Dry
table* 1991, *Butt* 1990.

Richard Deacon

Untitled, 1986
Pencil on paper
21 × 29.5 cm

Study for *The back of my hand No. 2* 1986
Pencil on paper with tape
32.5 × 19 cm

3 studies for *The back of my hand No. 4* 1986
Pencil on paper
(1) 21 × 23.5 cm
(2) 24 × 20.5 cm
(3) 19 × 23.5 cm

2 preparatory sketches for *Krefeld sculpture*
1987
Pencil on paper
21 × 29.5 cm

Preparatory sketches for *First Newcastle
project* 1987
Pencil on paper
20 × 25 cm

10 preliminary drawings for *Body of thought*
1988
Pencil on tracing paper
(1-7) 21 × 29.5 cm
(8-10) 59 × 84 cm

2 working drawings for *Body of thought No. 1*
1988
Pencil, crayon and ink on squared paper
59 × 84 cm

Drawings for Toronto Commission, *Between
the Eyes* 1990
Mild Steel (painted), stainless steel, cement
and granite base
800 × 1900 × 700 cm

Forty-five drawings marked T1-T45 1987-89
Pencil and/or ink on poster board or tracing
paper
Varying dimensions

Antony Gormley

Space 1980
Oil and pigment
38 × 38 cm

Return 1988
Oil and pigment
28 × 38 cm

Present Time 1988
Oil and pigment
28 × 38 cm

Hold 1988
Oil and pigment
137.5 × 101 cm

Suspension 1989
Oil and pigment
28 × 39 cm

Moment 1991
Blood and semen
28 × 39 cm

Shirazeh Houshiary

Untitled 1987
Drawing/mixed media on paper
57 × 76.5 cm

Untitled 1988
Mixed media on paper
57 × 76 cm

Untitled 1988
Mixed media on paper
57 × 76 cm

Untitled 1990
Drawing/watercolour
136 × 163 cm

Study for *Between earth and sky I* 1987
Drawing/mixed media on paper
56 × 76.5 cm

Study for *Between earth and sky II* 1987
Drawing/mixed media on paper
56 × 76.5 cm

Study for *From great above to great below*
1987
Drawing/mixed media on paper
56 × 76 cm

Anish Kapoor

Untitled No. *103* 1987-8
Papier mâché and pigment on paper
37 × 5 × 54.5 cm

Untitled No. *124* 1987-8
Gouache on paper
56 × 46 cm

Untitled No. *140* 1987-8
Gouache on paper
31 × 45 cm

Untitled (undated)
Graphite and gouache on paper
39 × 52 cm

Avis Newman

9 studies for *Webs*
(Backlight Series) 1994 FIG. I
Ink pigment acrylic on paper
Varying dimensions
1. 32.5 × 32.5 cm
2. 32.5 × 28 cm
3. 42.5 × 50 cm
4. 48 × 56 cm
5. 78.8 × 51.3 cm
6. 50.5 × 75.5 cm
7. 39 × 47 cm
8. 51 × 76 cm
9. 51 × 77 cm

FIG. I (NO.2)

Lucia Nogueira

Untitled 1992
Watercolour
38 × 28 cm

Untitled 1995
Watercolour
28 × 38 cm

Untitled 1995
Watercolour and pencil
28 × 38 cm

Untitled (undated)
Graphite and watercolour
28 × 38.5 cm

Untitled (undated)
Watercolour
28 × 38 cm

Rachel Whiteread

Untitled (Doorknob) 1993
Correction fluid and ink on tracing paper,
mounted on graph paper
46 × 61 cm

Untitled (Doorknob) 1993
Correction fluid, ink and watercolour on
graph paper
45.5 × 30.5 cm

Study for *Floor ceiling piece* 1993
Correction fluid, watercolour and ink on
graph paper
45.5 × 30.5 cm

Study for *Floor ceiling piece* 1993
Correction fluid and ink on graph paper
50 × 72 cm

Untitled (Floor) 1993
Correction fluid on white paper
59 × 42 cm

Floor 1993
Correction fluid and ink on graph paper
122 × 45.5 cm

Study for *Room* 1993
Varnish and ink on graph paper
72 × 50 cm

Study for *Room* 1993
Correction fluid and ink on graph paper
59 × 42 cm

Study for *Room* 1993
Correction fluid and ink on graph paper
42 × 59.5 cm

Study for *Ceiling piece* 1993
Ink and correction fluid on graph paper
50 × 72 cm

Alison Wilding

Untitled (Angry drawing 6) 1988
Charcoal and oil crayon on paper
41 × 59 cm

Untitled 1988
Charcoal and oil crayon and wash on paper
42 × 59 cm

Untitled 1990
Charcoal, gouache and crayon on paper
37 × 56 cm

Hermione Wiltshire

Drawings
2 sketchbooks (undated)
19.2 × 25.3 cm (red hardback)
26 × 21.5 cm (turquoise hardback)
Miscellaneous artist's notes and sketches

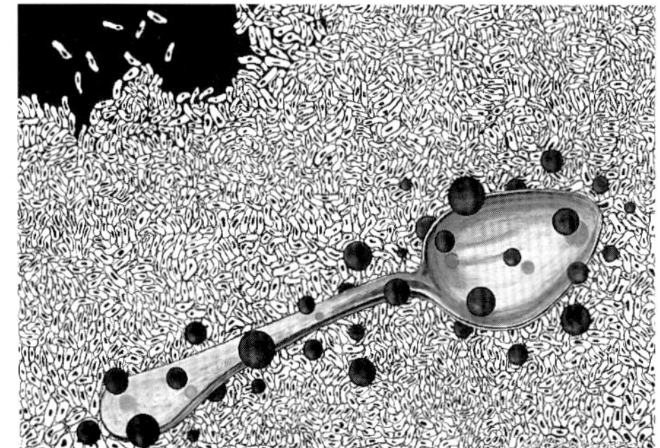

FIG. 2

Bill Woodrow

Untitled 1993 (FIG. 2)
Oilstick on paper
161.5 × 233 cm

Prints

Tony Cragg

Laboratory Still Life 1 (**State 1**) 1988
Aquatint etching
29.7 × 48.5 cm (image size)
58 × 60 cm (paper size)
Edition of 30

Laboratory Still Life 1 (**State 2**) 1988
Aquatint etching
29.7 × 48.5 cm (image size)
58 × 60 cm (paper size)
Edition of 30

Laboratory Still Life 2 (**State 1**) 1988
Aquatint etching
29.3 × 90 cm (image size)
53.5 × 111.5 cm (paper size)
Edition of 30

Laboratory Still Life 2 (**State 2**) 1988
Aquatint etching
29.3 × 90 cm (image size)
53.5 × 111.5 cm (paper size)
Edition of 30

Laboratory Still Life 3 1988
Aquatint etching
29.7 × 35 cm (image size)
58.5 × 60.5 cm (paper size)
Edition of 20

Laboratory Still Life 4 1988
Aquatint etching
46 × 48.5 cm (image size)
76 × 77 cm (paper size)
Edition of 40

Six bottles (**State 1**) 1988
Aquatint etching
18.5 × 32.4 cm (image size)
44 × 56 cm (paper size)
Edition of 25

Six bottles (**State 2**) 1988
Aquatint etching
18.5 × 32.5 cm (image size)
44 × 56 cm (paper size)
Edition of 25

Two bottles (**State 1**) 1988
Aquatint etching
23.6 × 18.8 cm (image size)
44 × 37 cm (paper size)
Edition of 25

Two bottles (**State 2**) 1988
Aquatint etching
23.6 × 18.8 cm (image size)
44 × 37 cm (paper size)
Edition of 25

Anish Kapoor

Untitled 1988
Etching
44.3 × 34.8 cm (image size)
66 × 50 cm (paper size)
Edition of 20

Untitled 1988
Etching
43.6 × 34.3 cm (image size)
64 × 50 cm (paper size)
Edition of 20

Untitled 1988
Colour aquatint etching
45 × 34.3 cm (image size)
58.4 × 45.7 cm (paper size)
Edition of 20

Untitled 1988
Etching
44.7 × 34.7 cm (image size)
65.5 × 50 cm (paper size)
Edition of 20

Untitled II 1988
Colour spitbite etching and aquatint
89 .5 × 112.5 cm (image size)
135 × 107 cm (paper size)
Edition of 20

Individual Portfolios

Grenville Davey

Eye 1993 (FIG. 3)
6 computer generated screenprints (3 pairs A,
B and C)
(A-B) 72 × 83.5 cm
(C) 86.5 × 72 cm
Edition of 40
Publisher: Paragon Press

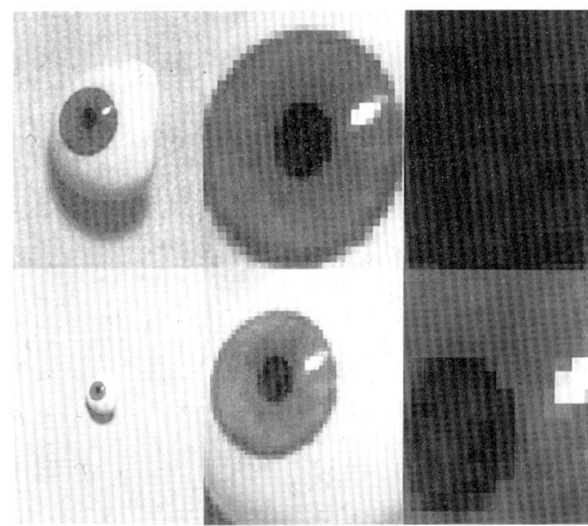

FIG. 3 Pair A (left side)

Hamish Fulton

Ten toes towards the rainbow (FIG. 4)
Ten seven-day walks, Cairngorm Mountains,
Scotland – March 1985, January 1993
A portfolio of 9 screenprints with certificate
and statement in portfolio case bound in grey
buckram
1985-93
Edition of 35
Publisher: Paragon Press

Individual titles, dates and sizes

1. *Night life*
(one walk, March 1991)
62.7 × 95.7 cm

2. *No talking for seven days*
(one walk, February 1988)
44.3 × 95.3 cm

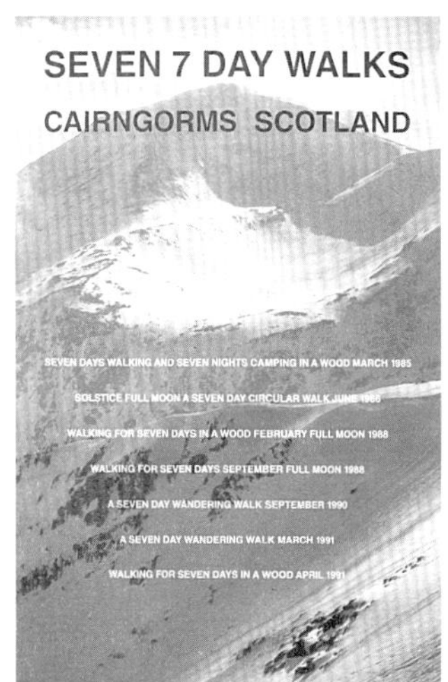

FIG. 4 (NO.4)

3. *The crow speaks*
(two walks, summer 1991 and June 1986)
63.1 × 93.2 cm

4. *Seven 7 day walks*
(March 1985, June 1986, February 1988,
September 1988, September 1990, March
1991, April 1991)
95.5 × 63 cm

5. *Seven days walking and seven nights
camping in a wood, Scotland*
(one walk, March 1985)
61.3 × 94.8 cm

6. *Eroded rock outline, Beinn Mheadhoin*
(two walks, summer 1991 and September
1988)
62.2 × 91.2 cm

7. *Geese flying south*
(one walk, September 1990)
63 × 96.6 cm

8. *Wind through the pines*
(two walks, March 1985 and April 1991)
58.6 × 93 cm

9. *Song path*
(two walks, January 1992 and June 1993)
62.7 × 93.3 cm

Hamish Fulton

Fourteen works 1982-9
Print version of works listed in full in Plate
Section entry, page 46
14 offset lithographs in portfolio case bound
in black buckram
Edition of 35
Publisher: Paragon Press

Shirazeh Houshiary

Round dance 1992
5 colour etchings and 5 poems by Jalal al-Din
Rumi (printed on separate sheets) and
colophon in portfolio case bound in grey
buckram and lead with hand-embossed title
60 × 60 cm (plate size)
77 × 76 cm (paper size)
71 × 71 cm (poems printed on paper)
Edition of 20
Publisher: Paragon Press

Antony Gormley

Body and soul 1990 (FIG. 5)
9 untitled etchings with title-page and
colophon in portfolio case bound in black
buckram
30 × 40 cm (plate size)
50 × 58.1 cm (paper size)
Edition of 30
Publisher: Paragon Press

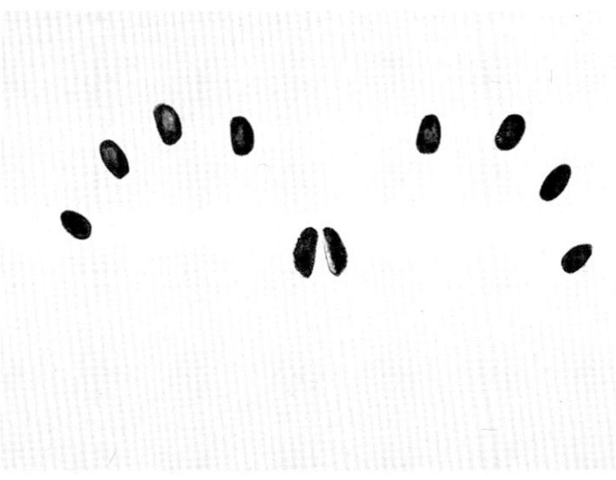

FIG. 5

Anish Kapoor

Untitled 1994-5 (FIG. 6)
15 etchings
35 × 28 cm (plate size)
51 × 58 cm (paper size)
Edition of 30
Publisher: Paragon Press

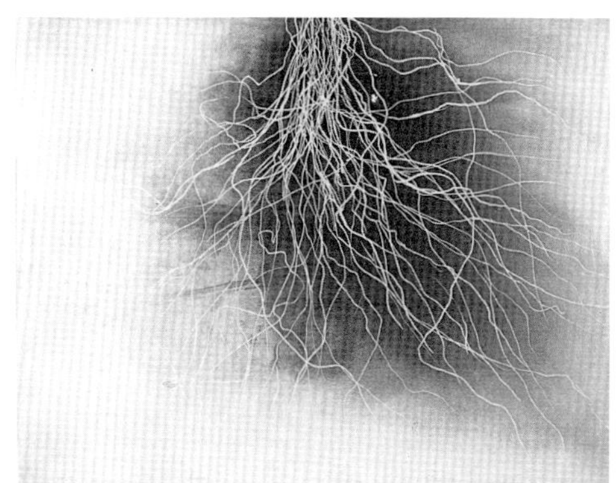

FIG. 6

Richard Long

Rock drawings 1994
*Rock drawings: an eight day walk in
Rimrock area of the Mojave Desert, Southern
California*
13 colour screenprints (12 rock drawings and
one photo-piece and certificate in portfolio
case bound in black buckram)
Rock drawings: 79 × 73.5 cm (paper size)
Photograph: 49 × 73.5 cm
Edition of 35
Publisher: Paragon Press

Rachel Whiteread

Demolished 1996 (FIGS. 7, 8)
Portfolio of 12 duo-tone screenprints, title
page, colophon and bound in black buckram
case
48.5 × 74 cm
Edition of 35
Publisher: Paragon Press

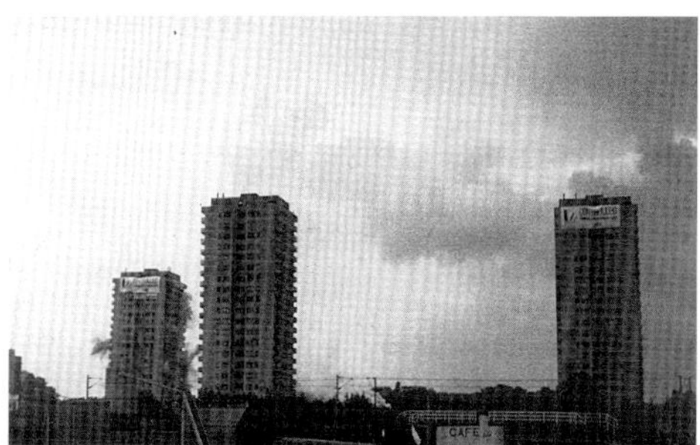

FIG. 7

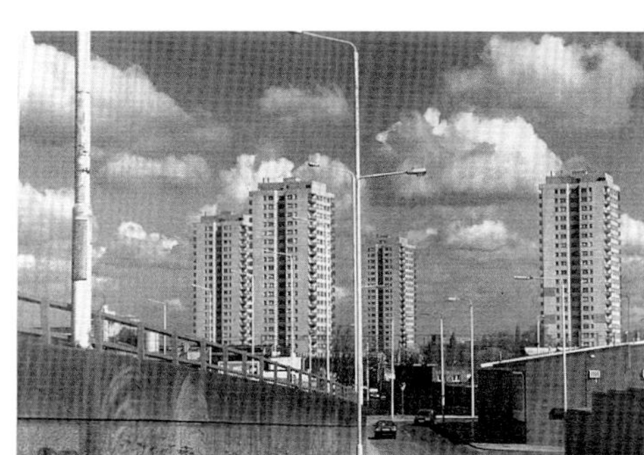

FIG. 8

Bill Woodrow

Greenleaf 1992 (FIG. 9)
5 etchings, title page and colophon in
portfolio case bound in brown-black cloth
with 'hair on' leather insertions
50.3 × 60.3 cm (plate size)
68.7 × 76 cm (paper size)
Edition of 35
Publisher: Paragon Press

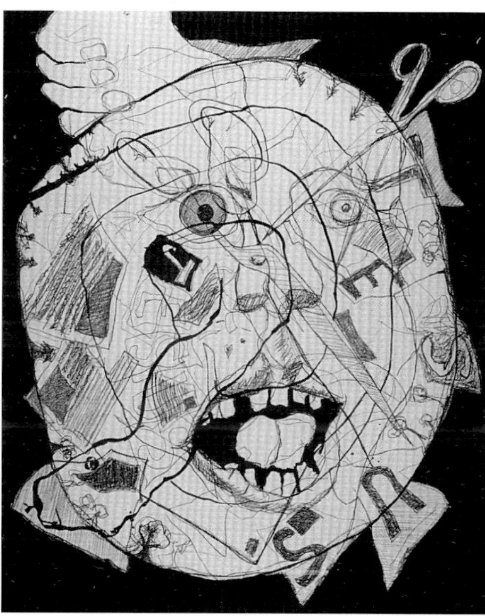

FIG. 9

The periodic table 1994
21 black and white linocuts with title page,
index and colophon in solander box bound in
black buckram
38.3 × 35.8 cm (approximate image size)
50 × 43 cm (paper size)
Edition of 30
Publisher: Paragon Press

Group Portfolios

Other men's flowers 1994
A publication of 15 text-pieces by 15 London-based artists, curated by Joshua Compston. The artists are: Henry Bond, Stuart Brisley, Don Brown, Helen Chadwick, Mat Collishaw, Itai Doron, Tracey Emin, Angus Fairhurst, Liam Gillick, Andrew Herman, Gary Hume, Sarah Staton, Sam Taylor-Wood, Gavin Turk, Max Wigram.
A book edition of 100 copies with 20 artist proofs consisting of 15 prints, title page, colophon
47 × 61 cm (all prints)
Edition of 100
Publisher: Paragon Press

*London Group
Portfolio* 1992
11 Prints, title page and colophon, in portfolio case bound in black buckram
Edition of 65
Publisher: Paragon Press

Artists and prints:

Dominic Denis
Untitled
Eight-colour screenprint
75 × 47 cm (image size)
76 × 82.5 cm (paper size)

Angus Fairhurst
*When I woke up this morning,
the feeling was still there*
Three-colour screenprint with varnish
86.5 × 65.8 cm

Damien Hirst
Untitled
Eight-colour screenprint with varnish
86 × 62.4 cm

Michael Landy
Cor! what a bargain
One-colour screenprint, laminated in plastic with black marker-pen
68.5 × 85.7 cm

Langlands & Bell
UNO city
Blind embossed print
71 × 74 cm

Nicholas May
Anabatic print
Ten-colour screenprint with high-gloss varnish
75 × 47 cm (image size)
88.5 × 60 cm (paper size)

Marc Quinn
Template for my future plastic surgery
Four-colour screenprint with varnish
86 × 68 cm

Marcus Taylor
Untitled
Six-colour screenprint with varnish
86 × 70.5 cm

Gavin Turk (FIG. 10)
Gavin Turk right hand and forearm
Thirteen-colour screenprint with varnish
86 × 68 cm

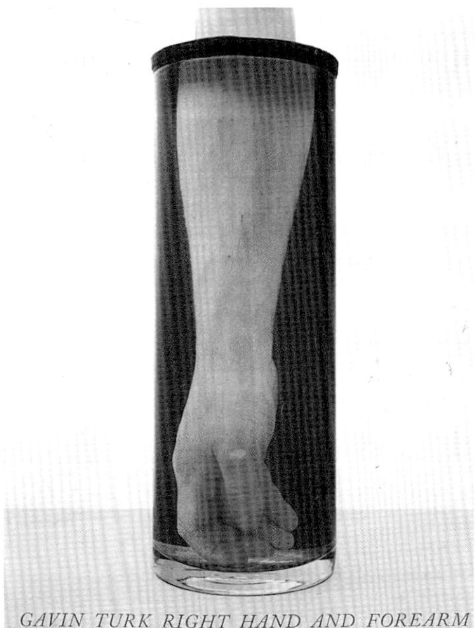

FIG. 10

Rachel Whiteread (FIG. 11)
Mausoleum under construction
Four-colour screenprint with mezzotint screens
55.6 × 79 cm (image size)
71 × 88 cm (paper size)

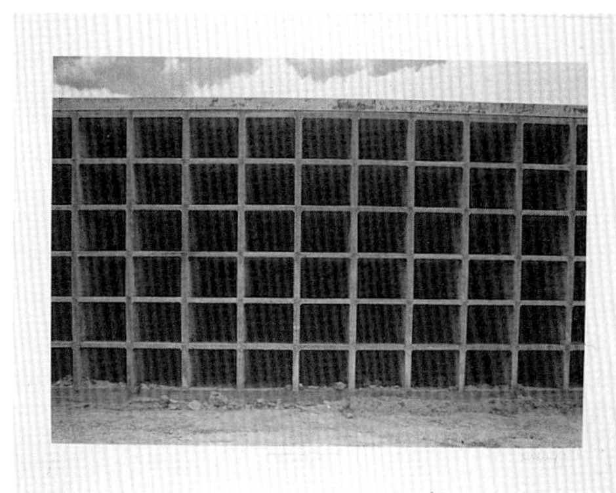

FIG. 11

Craig Wood
Safeway gel air freshener, alpine garden
(detail)
One-colour screenprint with mould-cut sections and varnish
66 × 86 cm

Artists' Biographies

Allington, Edward
Born: 1951 Westmoreland, England
Studied: Lancaster College of Art, 1968-71
Central School of Art and Design, 1971-4
Royal College of Art, 1983-4
Selected Solo Exhibitions: 1b, Kensington
Church Walk, London, 1977
Exe Gallery, Exeter, 1982
Spectro Gallery, Newcastle-upon-Tyne
and ICA, London, 1983
Lisson Gallery, London and Gallery Schmela,
Düsseldorf, 1984
Riverside Studios, London and Lisson
Gallery, London, 1984
Kohji Ogura Gallery, Nagoya, Japan, 1991
Le Théâtre le Rex, Paris, 1993
Prizewinner: John Moore's Liverpool
Exhibition, 1989
Gregory Fellow in Sculpture at Leeds
University, 1989
Lives in London

Art & Language
Born: Mel Ramsden 1944 Derbyshire,
England
Michael Baldwin 1945 Oxfordshire, England
Studied: Victoria College of Art, Melbourne
Coventry College of Art
Selected Solo Exhibitions: *Hardware Show*,
Architectural Association, London, 1967
Galerie Daniel Templon, Paris, 1971
Art & Language 1966-1975, Museum of
Modern Art, Oxford, 1975
Hostage Paintings 1987-1991, ICA London
(touring), 1991
Galeria Juana de Aizpuru, Madrid, 1995
Live in Northamptonshire

Bainbridge, Eric
Born: 1955 County Durham, England
Studied: Newcastle Polytechnic, 1974-7
Royal College of Art, London, 1978-91
Solo Exhibitions: Ayton Basement,
Newcastle, 1978
Currents, ICA, Boston, 1985
Karsten Schubert Gallery, London, 1987
Salvatore Ala Gallery, New York, 1988
Stedelijk Museum, Amsterdam, 1989-90
Lives in London

Bond, Henry
Born: 1966 London
Studied: Goldsmiths' College,
University of London
Selected Solo Exhibitions: Ars Futura, 1992
Die Appel, Amsterdam, 1994
Schipper and Krome Gallery, Cologne, 1996

Brisley, Stuart
Born: 1933 Haslemere, Surrey, England
Studied: Guildford School of Art, 1949-54
Royal College of Art, London, 1956-9
Florida State University, 1960-2
Solo Exhibitions: Documenta 1977, Kassel
São Paulo Bienal, 1985
Black, South London Art Gallery, 1996
Artist-in-Residence: Imperial War Museum,
1987
Lives in London

Brown, Don
Born: 1982 Norfolk
Studied: Central School of Art, London, 1983-5
Royal College of Art, London, 1985-8
Solo Exhibitions: *Bavaria* (with Stephen
Murphy), Hayward Gallery, London, 1996
Missiles (with Stephen Murphy) Lisson
Gallery, London, 1996
Don Brown, Sadie Coles HQ, London, 1997
Lives in London

Chadwick, Helen
Born: 1953 Croydon, London
Studied: Brighton Polytechnic, 1973-6
Chelsea School of Art, 1976-7
Selected Solo Exhibitions: Art Net,
London, 1978
Spectro Gallery, Newcastle-upon-Tyne and
National Portrait Gallery, London, 1983
Museum of Modern Art, Oxford, 1989
Serpentine Gallery, London and Fundacio,
'La Caixa', Barcelona, 1994
Shortlisted: Turner Prize, 1987
Died 1996

Collins, Hannah
Born: 1956 London
Studied: Slade School of Fine Art, 1974-8
University College, London, 1974-8
Solo Exhibitions: *Film Stills* , Matt's Gallery,
London, 1986
Heart and Soul, Ikon Gallery,
Birmingham, 1987
Large Scale Photoworks, 't Venster Gallery,
Rotterdam, 1988
Leo Castelli Gallery, 1996
Award: Fulbright-Hays Scholarship, 1978-9
Shortlisted: Turner Prize, 1993
Lives in Barcelona, Spain

Collishaw, Mat
Born: 1966 Nottingham
Studied: Goldsmiths' College,
University of London
Solo Exhibitions: Cohen Gallery,
New York, 1992
CAC Marigny, 1993
The Eclipse of Venus, Regency Palace Hotel,
London, 1994
Lives in London

Compston, Joshua
Born: 1970 London
Studied: Courtauld Institute, London
Died 1996

Cragg, Tony
Born: 1949 Liverpool, England
Studied: Gloucestershire College of Art and
Design, Cheltenham, 1968
Wimbledon School of Art, 1969-72
Royal College of Art, London, 1973-7
Selected Solo Exhibitions: Lisson Gallery,
London, 1979
Arnolfini Gallery, Bristol and Franco Toselli,
Milan, 1980
Marian Goodman and Art and Project,
Amsterdam, 1983
Hayward Gallery, London, 1987

Venice Biennale, British Pavilion, 1988
Lisson Gallery, London, 1992-3
Galleria Civica di Arte Contemporanea,
Trento, 1994
Won: Turner Prize, 1988
Lives in Germany

Davey, Grenville
Born: 1961 Launceston, Cornwall
Studied: Exeter College of Art and
Design, 1981
Goldsmiths' College, University of
London, 1982-5
Solo Exhibitions: Lisson Gallery,
London, 1987, 1989
Kunsthalle, Bern, 1989
Württembergischer Kunstverein,
Stuttgart, 1993
Won: Turner Prize, 1992
Lives in London

Deacon, Richard
Born: 1949 Bangor, Wales
Studied: Somerset College of Art,
Taunton, 1968
St Martin's School of Art, London, 1970-3
Royal College of Art, 1974-7
Selected Solo Exhibitions: British Oxygen
Corporation, 1986
Victoria Park, Plymouth, 1990
Marian Goodman Gallery, New York, 1997
Won: Turner Prize, 1987
Lives in London

Denis, Dominic
Born: 1963 London
Studied: Chelsea School of Art, 1984-6
Goldsmiths' College, University of
London, 1986-9
Solo Exhibitions: Galerie Harry Zellweger,
Basel, 1991
Anthony Wilkinson Fine Art, London, 1996
Group Exhibitions: *Freeze*, London
Docklands, 1988
Take Five, Anthony Wilkinson Fine Art,
London, 1995
Lives in London

Doherty, Willie
Born: 1959 Derry, Northern Ireland
Studied: Ulster Polytechnic, Belfast, 1977-81
Solo Exhibitions: Orchard Gallery, Derry,
1980, 1982
Oliver Dowling Gallery, Dublin, 1986
Two Photoworks, Third Eye, Glasgow, 1988
Matt's Gallery, London, 1990
Lives in Derry

Doron, Itai
Born: 1967 Tel Aviv
Studied: Goldsmiths' College,
University of London
Solo Exhibitions: *The Immaculate
Stereoscopic Conception of Mr D.*, *Jay
Jopling*, London, 1993
Mr D's Journey to the Heart of Lightness,
Tanya Bonaldar, New York, 1995
75 Matador, Galerie Tanja Grunert,
Cologne, 1996
The Secret Life and Archaic Times of Mr D.
White Cube Gallery, London
Lives in Israel

Emin, Tracey
Born: 1963 London
Studied: Maidstone College of Art, Kent and
Royal College of Art, London
Solo Exhibitions: *My Major Retrospective*,
White Cube Gallery/Jay Jopling, London,
1994
Tracey Emin Museum, 221 Waterloo Road,
London, SE1, 1995
I Need Art Like I Need God, South London
Gallery, London, 1997
Lives in London

Fairhurst, Angus
Born: 1966 Kent, England
Studied: Canterbury College of Art, 1985-6
Goldsmiths' College, University of
London, 1986-9
Solo Exhibitions: Karsten Schubert Ltd.,
London, 1990-4
Group Exhibitions: *Some Went Mad, Some
Ran Away*, Serpentine Gallery, London, 1994
Brilliant! New Art from London, Walker Art
Center, Minneapolis, 1995
Lives in London

Finn-Kelcey, Rose
Born: Northampton, England
Studied: Northampton School of Art
Ravensbourne College of Art
Chelsea School of Art
Solo Exhibitions: *Projects UK*, Laing Gallery,
Newcastle, 1987, touring to Cartwright Hall,
Bradford and Cornerhouse, Manchester
Ikon Gallery, Birmingham, 1993
The Rhetorical Image (group), New Museum
of Contemporary Art, New York, 1990
Documenta (group), Kassel, 1992
Young British Artists (group), Saatchi
Collection, 1993
Lives in London

Fulton, Hamish
Born: 1946 London
Studied: Hammersmith School of Art,
London, 1964-5
St Martin's School of Art, London, 1966-8
Royal College of Art, London, 1968-9

Solo Exhibitions: Galerie Konrad Fischer,
Düsseldorf, 1969
Kunstmuseum, Basel, 1975
Touring exhibition organised by the Stedelijk
van Abbemuseum, Eindhoven, 1985
Albright-Knox Art Gallery, Buffalo and the
National Gallery of Canada, Ottawa, 1990
Lives in Canterbury, Kent

Gillick, Liam
Born: 1964 Aylesbury, England
Studied: Hertfordshire College of Art, 1983-4
Goldsmiths' College, University of
London, 1984-7
Solo Exhibitions: *McNamara Papers,
Erasmus and Ibuks! Realisations*, *The What
If? Scenarios*, Le Consortium, Dijon,
Kunstverein, Hamburg, 1997
Lives in London

Gordon, Douglas
Born: 1966 Glasgow, Scotland
Studied: Glasgow School of Art, 1984-8
Slade School of Art, London, 1988-90
Solo Exhibitions: *24 Psycho*, Tramway,
Glasgow and Kunst-Werke, Berlin, 1993
Lisson Gallery, London, 1994
The End, Jack Tilton Gallery,
New York, 1995
24 Hour Psycho, Kunstakademie,
Vienna, 1995
Lives in Glasgow

Gormley, Antony
Born: 1950 London
Studied: Archaeology, Anthropology and Art
History, Trinity College, Cambridge, 1968-70
Central School of Art and Design, London,
1973-4
Goldsmiths' College, University of
London, 1974-7
Slade School of Art, London 1977-9
Solo Exhibitions: Whitechapel Art Gallery,
London, 1981
Kunstverein, Frankfurt, 1985
Louisiana Museum of Modern Art,
Humblebaek, 1989
Malmö Kunsthall, 1993
Tate Gallery Liverpool and Irish Museum
of Modern Art, 1993-4
Won: Turner Prize, 1994
Lives in London

Herman, Andrew
Born: 1961 London
Studied: Bath Academy of Art and
Goldsmiths' College, University of London
Group Exhibitions: *Superstore*,
Middlesborough Art Gallery, 1995
Underwood Street and ICA, London, 1996
Transmission Gallery, Glasgow, 1996
Lives in London

Hirst, Damien
Born: 1965 Bristol, England
Studied: Goldsmiths' College, University of London, 1986-9
Solo Exhibitions: ICA, London, 1991
Mattress Factory, Pittsburgh, 1994
DAAD Gallery, Berlin, 1994
Dallas Museum, Texas, 1994
Won: Turner Prize, 1995
Lives in London and Berlin

Houshiary, Shirazeh
Born: 1955 Iran, moved to London, 1973
Studied: Graduated Chelsea School of Art, 1973
Solo Exhibitions: Lisson Gallery, London, 1992, 1994
Camden Arts Centre, London, 1993
Touring exhibition in USA, 1993
Touring exhibition in Le Magasin, Grenoble, 1995
Showed at Venice Biennale, 1993
Lives in London

Hume, Gary
Born: 1962 Kent
Studied: Liverpool Polytechnic and Goldsmiths' College, University of London
Solo Exhibitions: *Gary Hume*, Karsten Schubert Gallery, London, 1989
Gary Hume, Galerie Tanja Grunert, Cologne, 1993
Gary Hume, Matthew Marks Gallery, New York, 1994
Gary Hume, São Paulo Bienal, São Paulo, 1996
Lives in London

Kapoor, Anish
Born: 1954 Bombay, India
Studied: Hornsey College of Art, London, 1973-7
Chelsea School of Art, 1977-8
Solo Exhibitions: Kunsthalle, Basel, 1985
British Pavilion, XLIV Venice Biennale, 1990 (awarded *Premio Duemila*)
Tate Gallery, London, 1991 (drawings only)
Kunstverein, Hanover, 1991
Lisson Gallery, London, since 1982
Artist-in-Residence: Walker Art Gallery, Liverpool, 1982
Won: Turner Prize, 1991
Lives in London

Landy, Michael
Born: 1963 London
Studied: Goldsmiths' College, University of London, 1985-8
Solo Exhibitions: Gray Art Gallery, New York, 1989
Studio Marconi, Milan, 1990
Karsten Schubert Ltd., London, 1989-93
Lives in London

Langlands & Bell
Born: Ben Langlands 1955 London
Nikki Bell 1959 London
Studied: Middlesex Polytechnic, London, 1977-80
Exhibitions: London, Frankfurt, Rome, Paris and elsewhere since 1986
Live in London

Long, Richard
Born: 1945 Bristol, England
Studied: St Martin's School of Art, London, 1966-8
Solo Exhibitions: Galerie Konrad Fischer, Düsseldorf, 1968
Scottish National Gallery of Modern Art, Edinburgh, 1974
Solomon R. Guggenheim Museum, New York, 1986
Hayward Gallery, London, 1991
Kunstsammlung Nordrhein-Westfalen, Düsseldorf, 1994
Palazzo Delle Esposizioni, Rome, 1994
Lives near Bristol

May, Nicholas
Born: 1962 Limavady, County Derry, Northern Ireland
Studied: Bath Academy of Art, 1981-4
Goldsmiths' College, University of London, 1988-90
Solo Exhibitions: John Hansard Gallery, University of Southampton, 1990
Frith Street Gallery, London, 1991
Victoria Miro, London, 1994
Touring Show at South London Gallery, Cornerhouse, Manchester and Leeds Metropolitan University, 1994
Lives in London

Newman, Avis
Born: 1946 London
Studied: Central School of Art, London and Goldsmiths' College, University of London
Solo Exhibitions: Matt's Gallery, London, 1982
Galerie Akumaltory 2, Poznan, 1985
Lisson Gallery, London, 1987
Arnolfini Gallery, Bristol, 1990
Douglas Hyde Gallery, Dublin, 1993
Lives in London

Nogueira, Lucia
Born: 1950 Brazil
Studied: Chelsea School of Art, 1976-9
Central School of Art, 1979-80
Residency: Fondation Cartier, Paris
Solo Exhibitions: Carlile Gallery, London, 1988
Chisendale Gallery, London, 1990
Antony Reynolds Gallery and Artère Sud, Brussels, 1992
Camden Arts Centre, London, 1994
Lives in London

Opie, Julian
Born: 1958 London
Studied: Goldsmiths' College, University of London
Solo Exhibitions: Lisson Gallery, London, 1983
Lisson Gallery and ICA, London, 1985
Galeria Montenegro, Madrid, 1988
Kohji Ogura Gallery, Nagoya, Japan, 1991
Hayward Gallery, London, 1993
Lives in London

Phaophanit, Vong
Born: 1961 Laos
Studied: Ecole des Beaux Arts, Aix-en-Provence, France, 1980-2
BA Fine Art, Aix-en-Provence, 1982-5
Solo Exhibitions: Chisenhale Gallery, London, 1991
Stephen Friedman Gallery, London, 1996
Atopia, DAAD, Berlin, 1997
Shortlisted: Turner Prize, 1993
Lives in London

Poncelet, Jacqueline
Born: 1947 Liège, Belgium
Studied: Wolverhampton College of Art, 1965-9
Royal College of Art, London, 1969-72
Solo Exhibitions: British Crafts Council Gallery, London, 1977
Miharudo Gallery, Tokyo, Japan, 1984
Third Eye Centre, Glasgow, 1989
The Decorative Sublime, Museum of Modern Art, Oxford, 1995
Awards: British Council Bicentennial Arts fellowship, 1978-9
British Council exhibition and travel grant to Japan, 1984
Lives in London

Quinn, Marc
Born: 1964 London
Studied: History and History of Art, Cambridge University, 1982-5
Worked as assistant to sculptor Barry Flanagan
Solo Exhibitions: *Out of Time*, Jay Jopling/ Grob Gallery, London, 1991
Marc Quinn, Jean Bernier, Athens, 1993
The Blind Leading the Blind, The White Cube, London, 1995
Lives in London

Ryan, Veronica
Born: 1956 Plymouth, Montserrat
Studied: St Albans College of Art and Design, 1974-5
Bath Academy of Art, 1975-8
Slade School of Art, London, 1978-80
School of Oriental and African Studies, 1981-90

Solo Exhibitions: *Drawings and Sculpture,*
Tom Allen Centre, London, 1980
Arnolfini Gallery, Bristol (touring), 1987
Kettle's Yard, Cambridge and Riverside
Studios, London, 1988
Awards: Boise Travelling Scholarship, 1980
GLA Awards Second Prize Winner, Cleveland
(UK), International Drawing Biennale, 1983
GLA Award, 1985
Henry Moore Foundation Award, 1987
Lives in London

Staton, Sarah
Born: 1961 London
Studied: St Martin's School of Art, London
Solo Exhibitions: Hales Gallery,
London, 1995
Duncan Cargill Gallery, London, 1997
Lives in London

Taylor, Marcus
Born: 1964 Belfast
Studied: Ulster Polytechnic and Camberwell
School of Art, London, 1982-6
Slade School of Art, London, 1986-8
Solo Exhibitions: White Cube Gallery,
London, 1993
Group Exhibitions: *The British Art Show 4,*
Cardiff and Edinburgh, 1995-6
Lives in London

Taylor-Wood, Sam
Born: 1967 London
Studied: Goldsmiths' College,
University of London
Solo Exhibitions: *Pent-Up*, Chisenhale
Gallery, London, 1996-7
Travesty of a Mockery, White Cube
Gallery/Jay Jopling, London, 1995-6
*Sam Taylor-Wood; Five Revolutionary
Seconds*, Sala Montcada de la Fundacio 'La
Caixa', Barcelona, 1997
Lives in London

Turk, Gavin
Born: 1967 Guildford, England
Studied: Royal College of Art, London,
1988-91
Solo Exhibitions: White Cube Gallery/
Jay Jopling, London, 1993-4
Lives in London

Wentworth, Richard
Born: 1947 Samoa
Studied: Hornsey College of Art,
London, 1965
Royal College of Art, London, 1970

Solo Exhibitions: Greenwich Theatre Gallery,
London, 1972
Lisson Gallery, London, 1984
Quint Krichman Projects, San Diego, 1990
Serpentine Gallery, London, 1993
Arnolfini Gallery, Bristol, 1994
Lives in London

Whiteread, Rachel
Born: 1963 London
Studied: Brighton Polytechnic, 1982-5
Slade School of Fine Art, London, 1985-7
Solo Exhibitions: Chisenhale Gallery,
London, 1990
Stedelijk Van Abbemuseum, Eindhoven, 1993
Touring Show beginning at Kunsthalle, Basel,
1994
Won: Turner Prize, 1993
Represented Britain Venice Biennale, 1997
Lives in London

Wigram, Max
Born: 1966 London
Studied: Courtauld Institute, London
Group Exhibitions: *Gang Warfare*, McKinney
Contemporary, Texas, 1995
The Meaning of Life, Centre for
Contemporary Arts, Glasgow, 1996
Fool's Rain, ICA London, 1996
Runs Independent Art Space, London
Lives in London

Wilding, Alison
Born: 1948 Lancashire, England
Studied: Ravensbourne College of Art and
Design, Kent, 1967-70
Royal College of Art, London, 1970-3
Selected Solo Exhibitions: Young Friends of
the Tate Gallery, London, 1970
Kettle's Yard Gallery, Cambridge, 1982
Museum of Modern Art, New York, 1987-8
Douglas Hyde Gallery, Dublin, 1996
Lives in London

Wilson, Richard
Born: 1953 London
Studied: London College of Printing, 1970-1
Hornsey College of Art, 1971-4
Reading University, 1974-6
Selected Solo Exhibitions: *11 Pieces*,
Coracle Press Gallery, London, 1976
20:50 Matt's Gallery, London, 1987
Jamming Gears, Serpentine Gallery,
London, 1996
Château de Sacy, Picardy, France, 1997
Lives in London

Wiltshire, Hermione
Born: 1963 London
Studied: Central School of Art, London, 1982-5
Chelsea School of Art, London, 1986-7
Selected Solo Exhibitions: *Lost at Sea and
Found on the Ground*, Eugen Lendl Gallerie,
Graz, 1994
Lisson Gallery, London, 1992
Riverside Studios, London, 1991
Lives in London

Wood, Craig
Born: 1960 Leith, Edinburgh
Studied: Goldsmiths' College,
University of London, 1986-8
Solo Exhibitions: Laure Genillard Gallery,
1990, 1992
Städtisches Museum Abteiberg,
Mönchengladbach, 1992
Kunsthalle, Nuremberg, 1993
Lives in Wales

Woodrow, Bill
Born: 1948 Oxfordshire, England
Studied: Winchester School of Art, 1967-8
St Martin's School of Art, London, 1968-71
Chelsea School of Art, 1971-2
Solo Exhibitions: Kunsthalle, Basel, 1985
Fruitmarket Gallery, Edinburgh, 1986
Kunstverein Munich, 1987
Imperial War Museum, London, 1989
21st São Paolo Bienal, 1991
Lives in London

Photographic Credits

Edward Allington 17 (bottom)
Annely Juda Fine Art, London 14 (top)
Anthony d'Offay Ltd, London 14 (bottom)
Arts Council of Great Britain/Hayward Gallery, London
16 (bottom), 22 (top)
Chisenhale Gallery, London 24 (bottom)
The Douglas Hyde Gallery, Dublin 101
Karsten Schubert Ltd, London 19
Konstantinos Ignatiadis 87
Irish Museum of Modern Art 14 (centre), 24 (top), 43, 45, 49, 51,
59, 61 (both), 75 (both), 89, 95, 97, 107, 110, 111 (bottom), 113 (all),
115, 117, 118, 120 (Fig.5)
John Kellet 43, 45, 49, 51, 53, 59, 61 (both), 63, 65, 69, 75 (both),
81, 85, 89, 95, 97, 107, 110, 111 (bottom), 113 (all), 115
R. King Lassman 105
Lisson Gallery, London 15, 16 (top), 22 (bottom), 23, 26, 49, 53, 55,
58, 63, 65 (both), 66, 67 (all), 71, 73 (both), 74, 75, 81, 85, 87, 99,
103, 105, 111 (top)
Matt's Gallery, London 41, 57, 108 (both)
Denis Mortell 17 (top), 31, 32, 33, 34 (both), 35, 36, 37 (both), 38,
55, 71, 73 (both), 74, 75, 99, 117, 118, 120 (Fig.4), 121 (all), 122
(both)
Sue Ormerod 41, 49, 58
Paragon Press, London 120 (Figs 3 and 4)
Veronica Ryan 20, 76 (both), 77, 78, 79
Eüchim Sakata 67 (top left)
Salvatore Ala Gallery, New York 83
Peter White 11 (top)
White Cube Gallery/Jay Jopling 27
Hermione Wiltshire 90, 91, 92, 93 (all)
Edward Woodman 57, 67 (top right and bottom left), 101, 108
(both)

Index of Artists